24 August 2016 at 12:16

Look
If you had one shot or one opportunity
To seize everything you ever wanted
In one minute
Would you capture it or just let it slip?

His palms are sweaty, wrists weak, arms
feel heavy, there's sharpie on his fingers
already, hands unsteady,
He's nervous, but on the surface he looks
calm and read to drop OMBs, but he keeps
on forgettin'
What he wrote down, the whole crowd
goes so loud, he puts pen to page, but the
ideas won't come out
He's chokin', how, everybody's jokin' now
The clocks run out, times up, over, blaow!

OMBLive - the tournament.
One rule, one minute, one shot

#OMBLive3   @Dissential

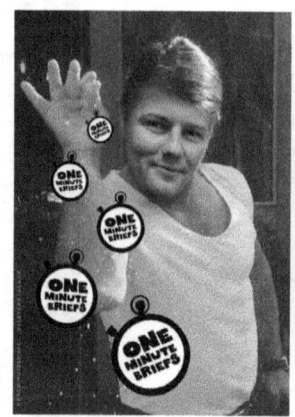
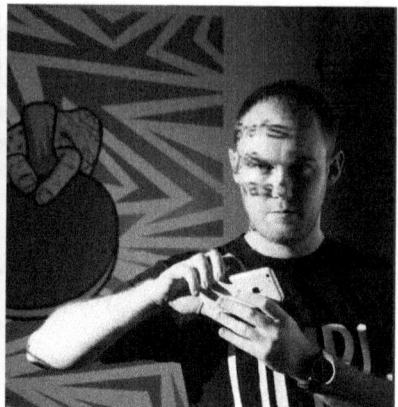

About the creator of OMB

Nick Entwistle

Nick has produced and overseen numerous award-winning campaigns for major brands in his role as a Creative Director in Manchester.
As well as this, he runs popular Twitter feeds @AgencyQuotes, @BOC_ATM and, of course, @OneMinuteBriefs. He also delivers talks/workshops for the likes of D&AD, Glug & BBC and has had projects featured in publications such as the New York Times, The Drum and Campaign.

interest@bankofcreativity.co.uk

Twitter:
@OneMinuteBriefs

Website:
www.oneminutebriefs.co.uk

CONTENTS

THE OMBRIGINAL

Below is the first ever One Minute Brief. It was created as a random break from creative block during a long advertising brief deadline at University. We decided to advertise Rolex in a minute and, although Rolex may not run something like the ad below, there is definitely an idea there that I wouldn't have written if I'd been given an hour, a day, or a week. Discovering my creative instinct began to inspire me to do more and it helped to improve my overall creativity whilst having fun in the process. To this day, I still use this way of thinking to generate ideas and I hope it will help others to do so for many years to come.

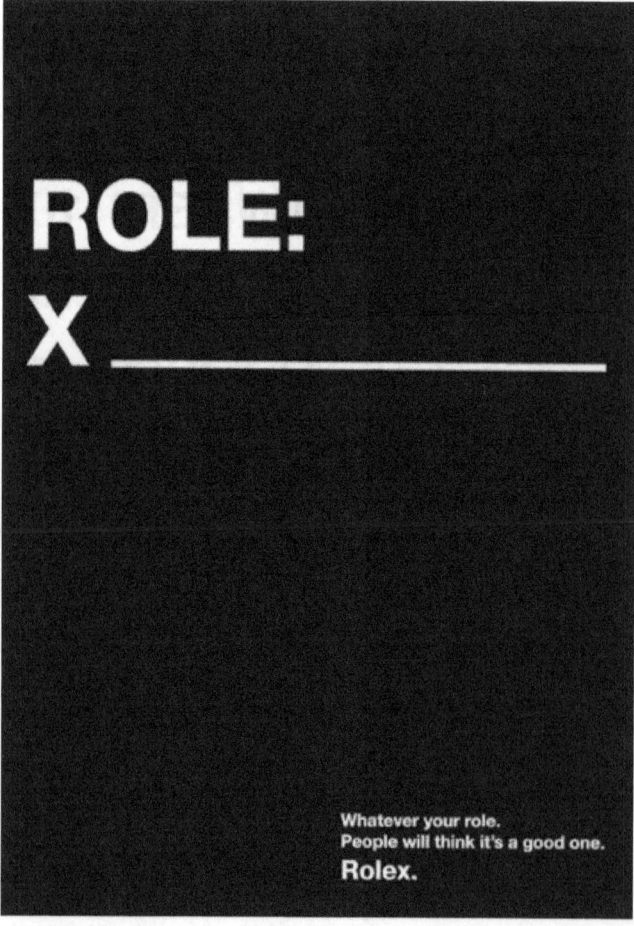

4.

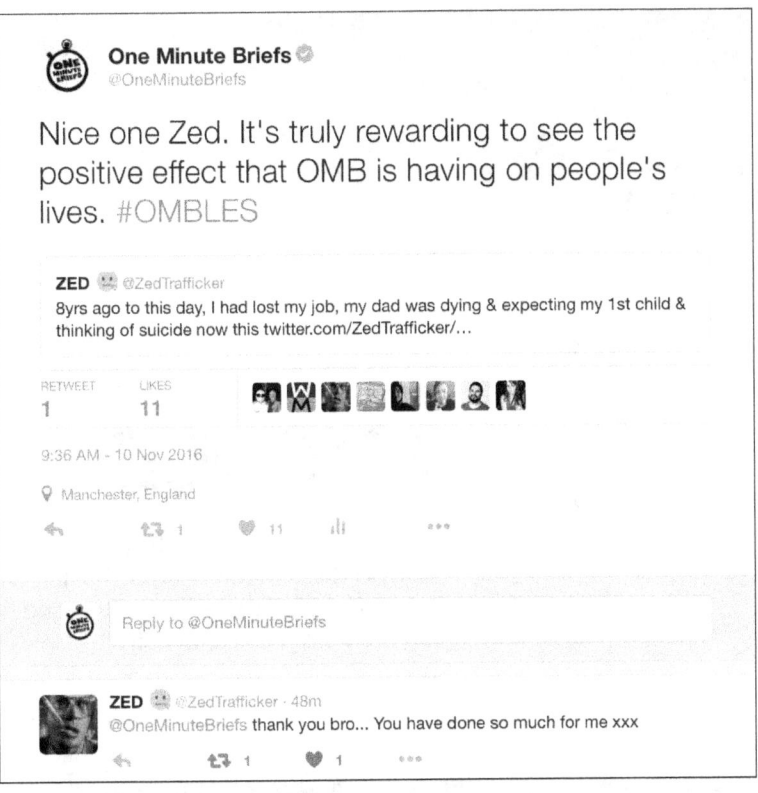

One Minute Briefs ✓
@OneMinuteBriefs

Nice one Zed. It's truly rewarding to see the positive effect that OMB is having on people's lives. #OMBLES

ZED 🙂 @ZedTrafficker
8yrs ago to this day, I had lost my job, my dad was dying & expecting my 1st child & thinking of suicide now this twitter.com/ZedTrafficker/...

RETWEET 1   LIKES 11

9:36 AM - 10 Nov 2016

📍 Manchester, England

↩   🔁 1   ♥ 11   ili   •••

Reply to @OneMinuteBriefs

ZED 🙂 @ZedTrafficker · 48m
@OneMinuteBriefs thank you bro... You have done so much for me xxx
↩   🔁 1   ♥ 1   •••

HOW FAR HAS THAT ONE MINUTE GONE?

Above is a tweet from one of OMB's followers. And, I feel it sums up what One Minute Briefs has become. What started as a silly way of coming up with ideas whilst procrastinating at Uni, has become an online community of people who encourage each other to do better. It's a place where real friendships have been made, where people have found confidence in themselves and their ideas. Some people have even changed their careers and are now doing something that they really have a passion for. To see that One Minute Briefs has become so much more than an advertising platform and is genuinely life-changing is truly rewarding. People like Zed inspire me to keep going with OMB as it can spread positivity, fun and creativity all the way around the world very quickly. With that comes great opportunities for everyone involved and long may that continue.

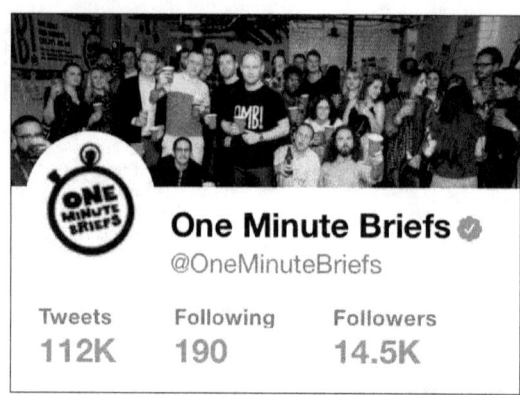

One Minute Briefs ✔
@OneMinuteBriefs

Tweets	Following	Followers
112K	190	14.5K

VERIFIED

As we head towards 15,000 followers, I was delighted OMB was Verified by Twitter. The blue tick is a testament to everyone involved and hopefully everybody will reap the benefits of the extra exposure it brings.

THE OMBUCCINO

A One Minute Brief is the first thing all creatives should have before taking on their creative day.

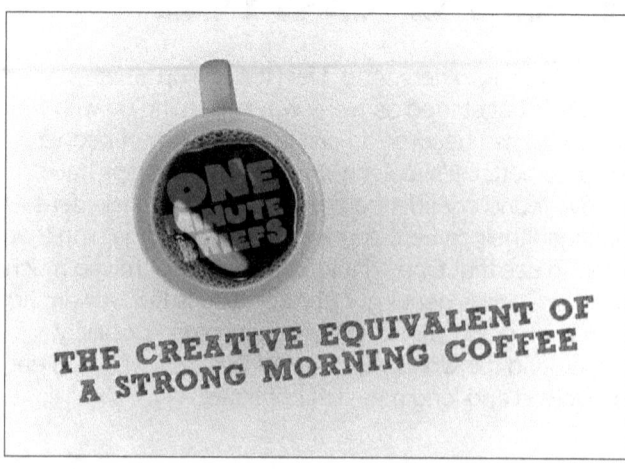

THE CREATIVE EQUIVALENT OF A STRONG MORNING COFFEE

ONE MIN MEMES

A few memes have started to pop up over our Twitter. Here's a selection.
Feel free to tweet us more!!

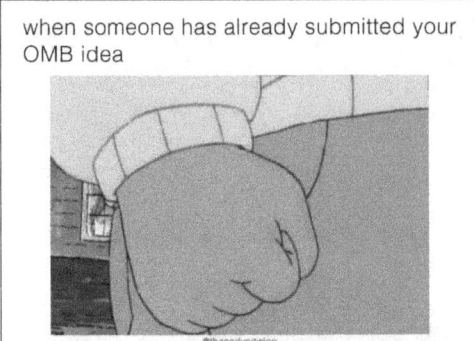

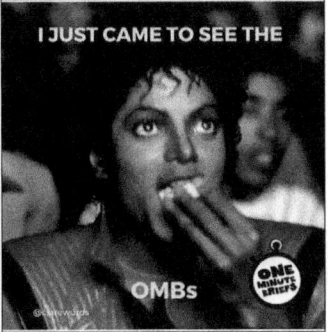

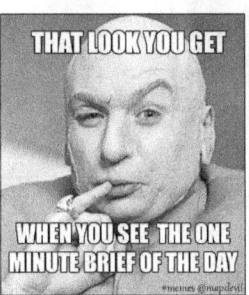

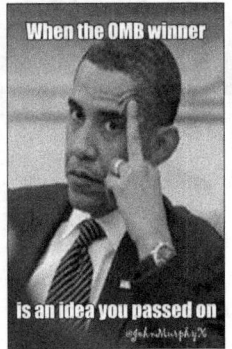

PUN OF THE YEAR

With quick ideas, come puns. None more so than this beauty by Zack Gardner.
Best OMB pun ever.

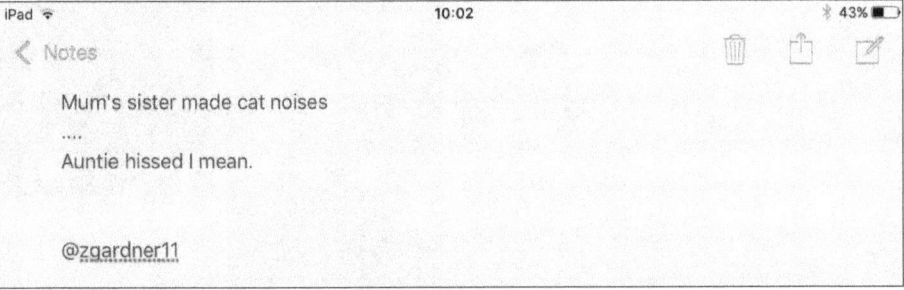

A ONE MINUTE BRIEF TO ADVERTISE ONE MINUTE BRIEFS. OMBVIOUSLY.

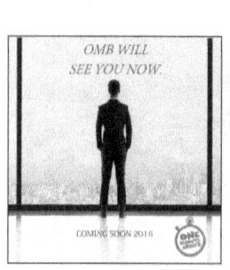

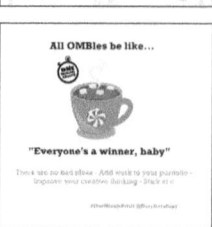

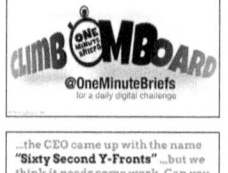

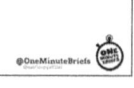

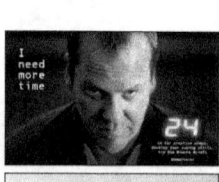

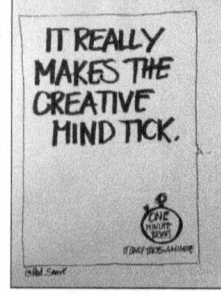

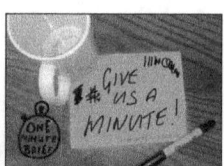

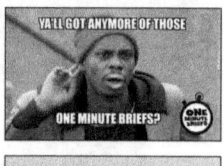

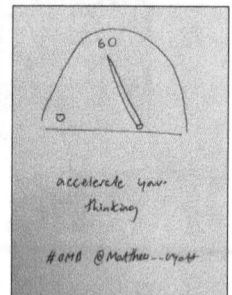

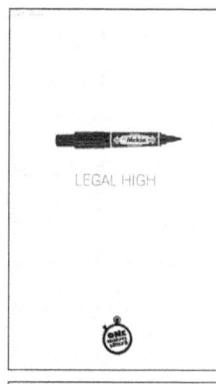

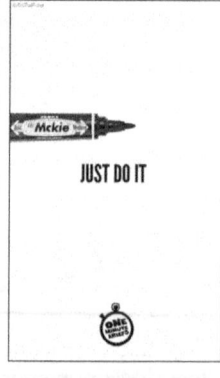

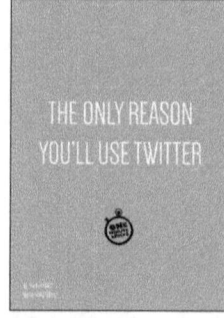

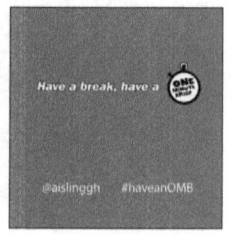

KEEP IT BRIEF

BRIEF
IS THE
BRIEF

@OneMinuteBriefs
@BMMarketer

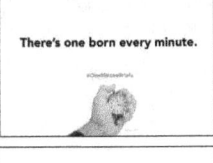

There's one born every minute.

@OneMinuteBriefs

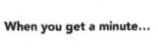

When you get a minute...

@OneMinuteBriefs

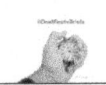

FOR ONCE IT'S GOOD TO FINISH UNDER ONE MINUTE.

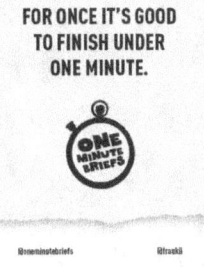

@oneminutebriefs

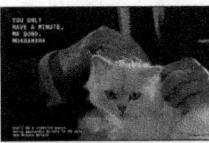

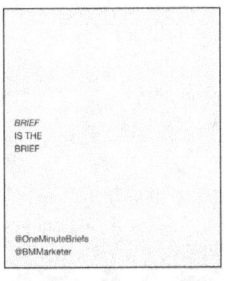

QUICK OFF THE MARK (ER)

#OMB

Hungry to prove yourself? Have seconds.

@OneMinuteBriefs

Most ideas come in the nick of time. These come in the time of Nick... @oneminutebriefs

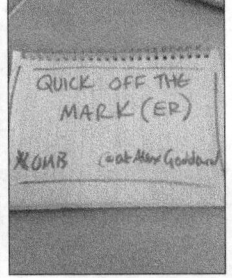

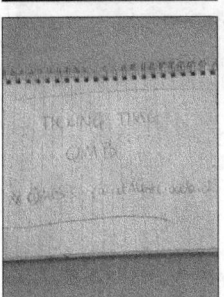

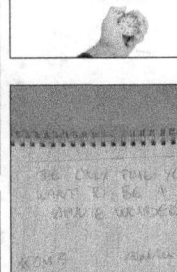

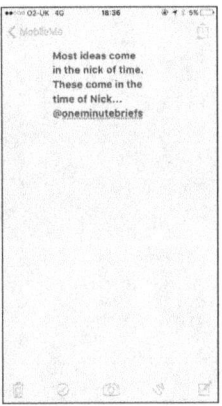

#ONEMINUTEBRIEF MORE EXPOSURE THAN YOU BARGAINED FOR

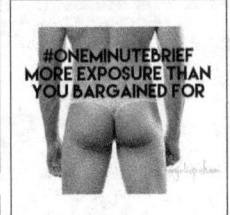

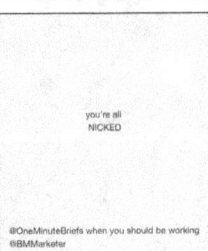

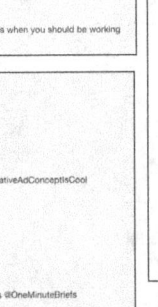

One dream,
One soul,
One prize,
One goal,
One golden glance of what it should be...

@OneMinuteBriefs It's a kinda magic!

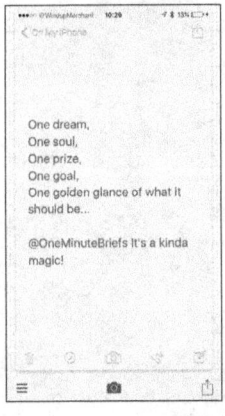

you're all
NICKED

@OneMinuteBriefs when you should be working
@BMMarketer

#FuckMeThatCreativeAdConceptIsCool

Every 60 seconds @OneMinuteBriefs
@BMMarketer

Win it or bin it? Just a...

@OneMinuteBriefs

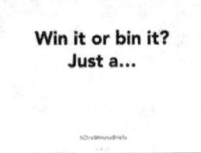

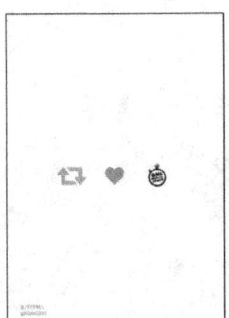

@VERTISING

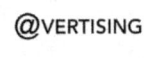

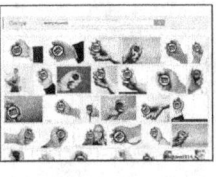
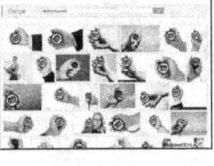

9.

OMB PROJECTS

Where has one minute taken us?

One Minute Briefs added 136 new photos to the album: LIKE YOUR FAVE #SAVEOURNHS ADS HERE.
22 October at 18:35

Today we ran a collaborative brief with The Gate Films to raise awareness of the #SaveOurNHS campaign. The winning idea will be developed and turned into a film. Get 'Liking' to register your votes!!

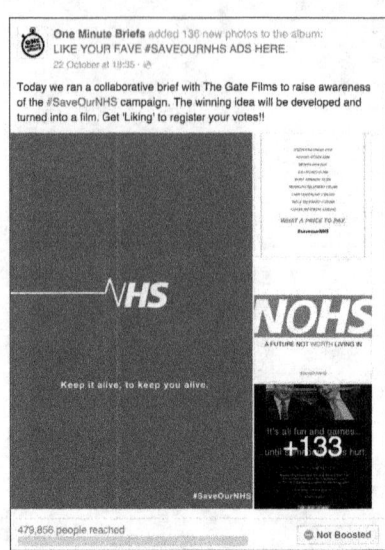

479,856 people reached

Not Boosted

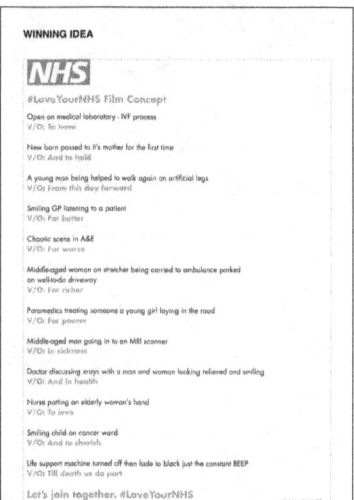

#LoveYourNHS Film Concept

Open on medical laboratory - IVF process
V/O: To love

New born passed to it's mother for the first time
V/O: And to hold

A young man being helped to walk again on artificial legs
V/O: From this day forward

Smiling GP listening to a patient
V/O: For better

Chaotic scene in A&E
V/O: For worse

Middle-aged woman on stretcher being carried to ambulance parked on welll-to-do driveway
V/O: For richer

Paramedics treating someone a young girl laying in the road
V/O: For poorer

Middle-aged man going in to an MRI scanner
V/O: In sickness

Doctor discussing xrays with a man and woman looking relieved and smiling
V/O: And in health

Nurse patting an elderly woman's hand
V/O: To love

Smiling child on cancer ward
V/O: And to cherish

Life support machine turned off then fade to black just the constant BEEP
V/O: Till death us do part

Let's join together. #LoveYourNHS

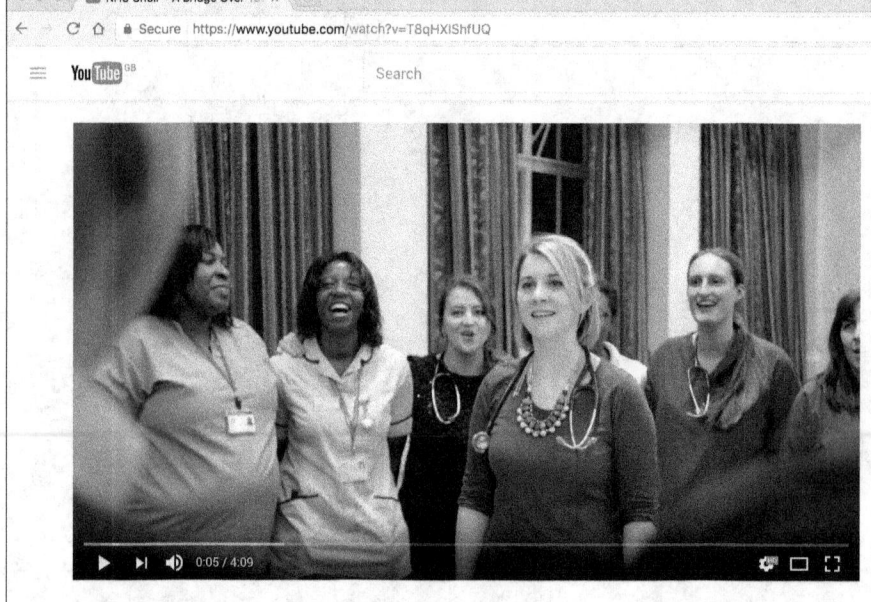

NHS Choir - A Bridge Over You #LoveYourNHS 2015 #XmasNo1

1,418,782 views

7K   155

LoveYourNHS
Published on Dec 15, 2015

Official #XmasNo1 2015 #LoveYourNHS
Concept & Production by @TheGateFilms & @OneMinuteBriefs
Directed by @DingoBill

SUBSCRIBE 1.3K

NHS 4 XMAS NO.1

We ran a One Minute Brief to get ideas for a film to raise morale in the NHS. @StephenHunter21 won with a great idea based on 'vows'. We were then contacted by the NHS Choir to make the idea into their music video for their campaign to get to Xmas No.1. We also created an 'I DO' campaign that asked the public to show that they love their NHS.

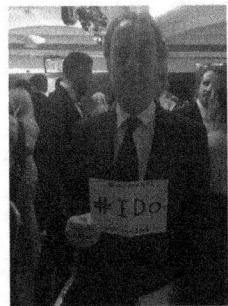
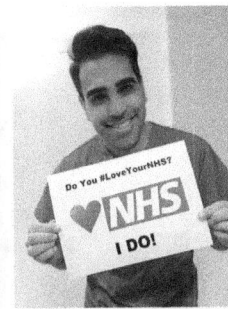
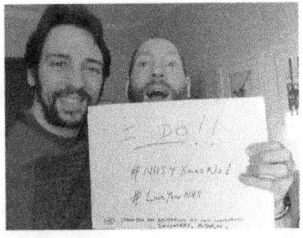
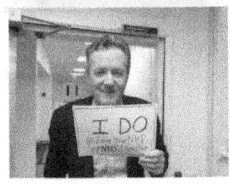
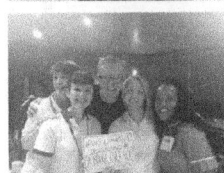
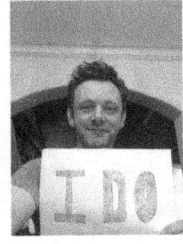
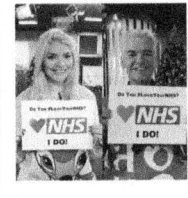
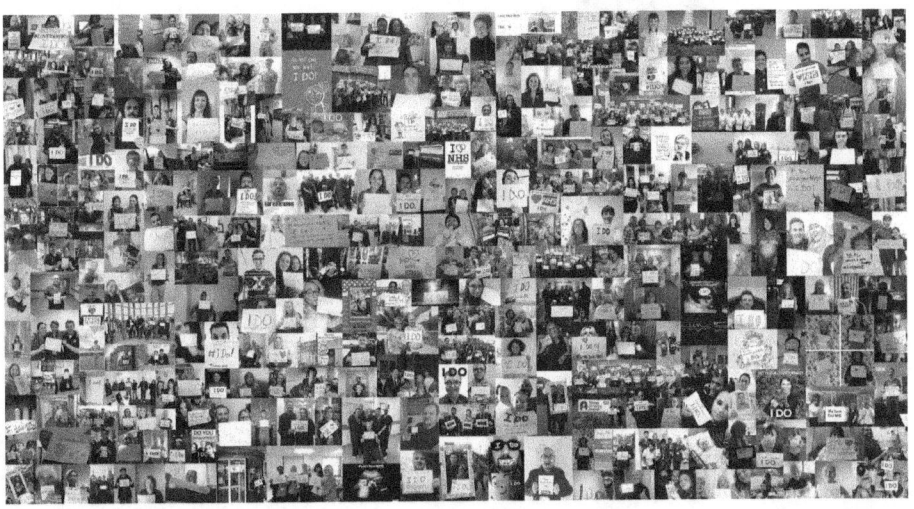

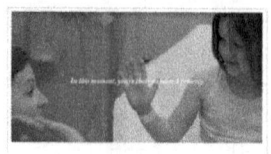
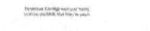
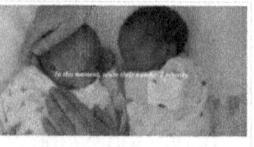

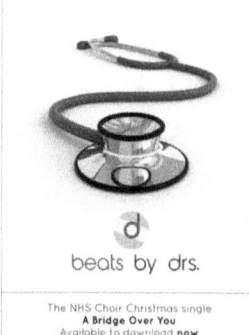

beats by drs.

The NHS Choir Christmas single
A Bridge Over You
Available to download **now**
nhsno1.com/download/

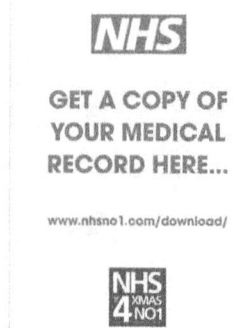

NHS

GET A COPY OF
YOUR MEDICAL
RECORD HERE...

www.nhsno1.com/download/

NHS
XMAS
4 NO1

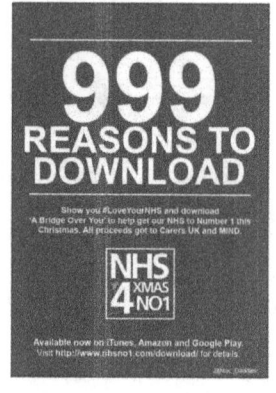

999
REASONS TO
DOWNLOAD

Show you #LoveYourNHS and download
'A Bridge Over You' to help get our NHS to Number 1 this
Christmas. All proceeds got to Carers UK and MIND.

NHS
XMAS
4 NO1

Available now on iTunes, Amazon and Google Play.
Visit http://www.nhsno1.com/download/ for details.

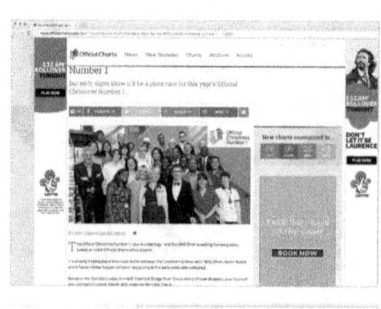

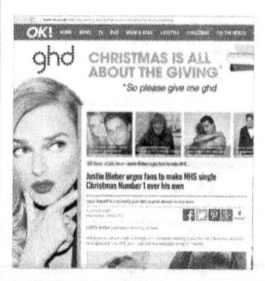

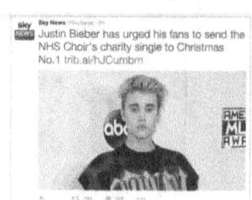

Justin Bieber has urged his fans to send the
NHS Choir's charity single to Christmas
No.1 trib.ai/hJCumbm

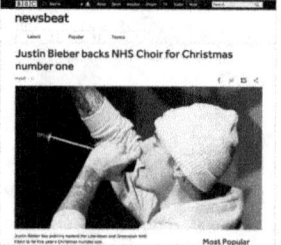

Justin Bieber backs NHS Choir for Christmas
number one

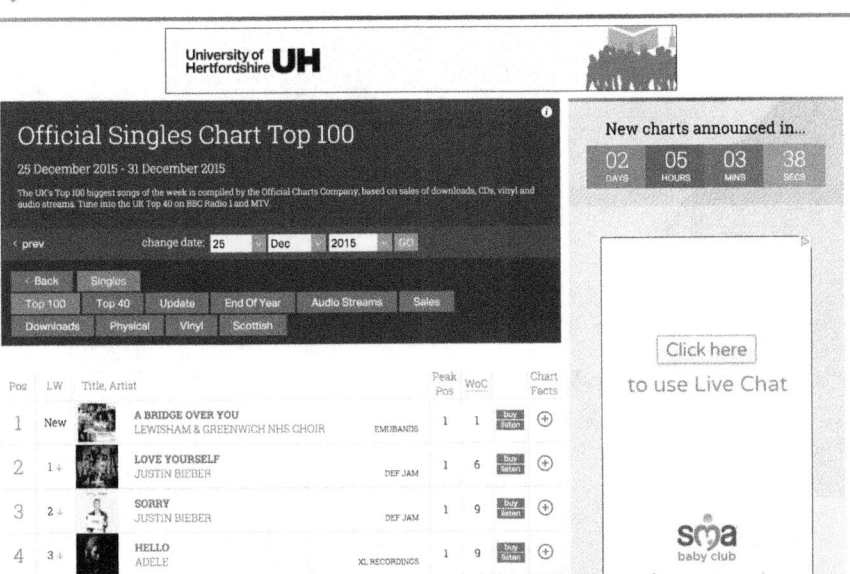

University of Hertfordshire **UH**

Official Singles Chart Top 100

25 December 2015 - 31 December 2015

The UK's Top 100 biggest songs of the week is compiled by the Official Charts Company, based on sales of downloads, CDs, vinyl and audio streams. Tune into the UK Top 40 on BBC Radio 1 and MTV.

New charts announced in...

02	05	03	38
DAYS	HOURS	MINS	SECS

‹ prev   change date: 25 Dec 2015   GO

‹ Back   Singles
Top 100   Top 40   Update   End Of Year   Audio Streams   Sales
Downloads   Physical   Vinyl   Scottish

Pos	LW		Title, Artist		Peak Pos	WoC	Chart Facts
1	New		A BRIDGE OVER YOU LEWISHAM & GREENWICH NHS CHOIR	EMUBANDS	1	1	buy listen ⊕
2	1↓		LOVE YOURSELF JUSTIN BIEBER	DEF JAM	1	6	buy listen ⊕
3	2↓		SORRY JUSTIN BIEBER	DEF JAM	1	9	buy listen ⊕
4	3↓		HELLO ADELE	XL RECORDINGS	1	9	buy listen ⊕
5	5		WHAT DO YOU MEAN JUSTIN BIEBER	DEF JAM	1	17	buy listen ⊕

Click here
to use Live Chat

sma baby club
You're doing great

WE DID IT!!

Following numerous One Minute Briefs to encourage downloads, our odds shortened and we were neck and neck with Justin Bieber in the charts. He himself even tweeted in support of our campaign and on Christmas Day we reached Xmas No.1 with our music video being played before the Queen's speech! Thanks to everybody who made this happen!

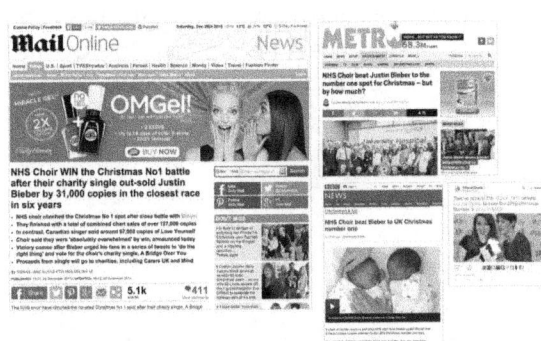

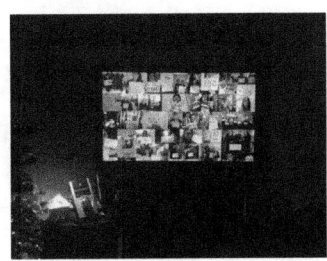

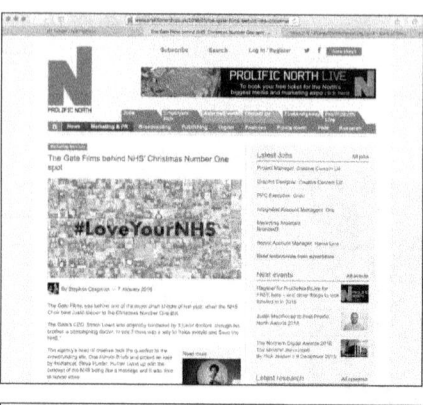

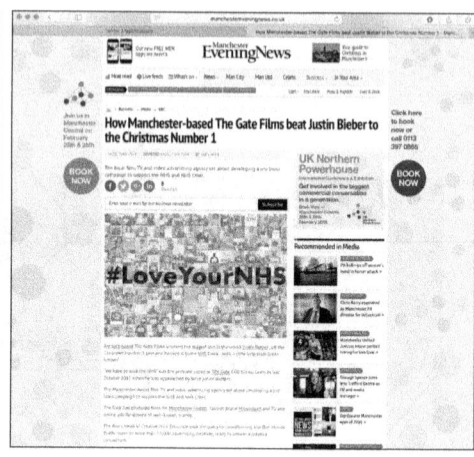

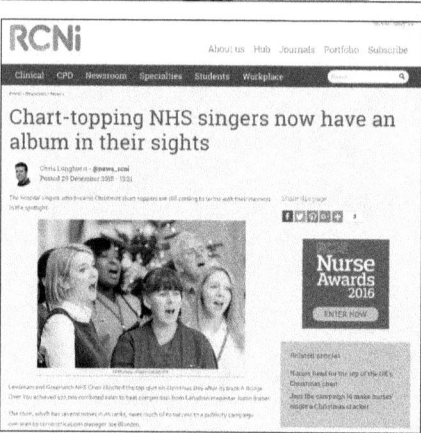

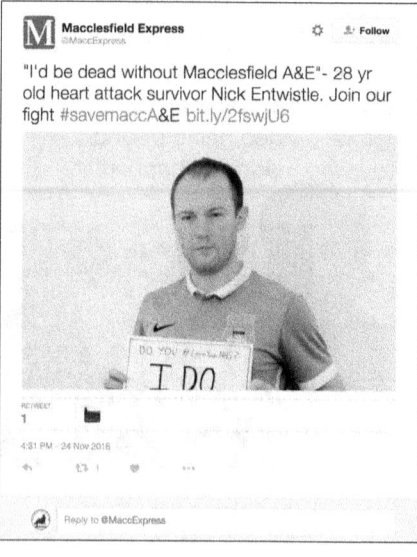

WHAT HAPPENED NEXT?

Our campaign was featured in local and national press and our initial aim of raising awareness and morale within the NHS had been achieved. Since then, the NHS Choir have been working on an album and I have personally been able to continue my support of the NHS and ran a successful campaign to save the A&E department that saved my life.

HW Gan @hwganendodoc · 6h
My mother sent this to me - Choir_NHS you've made international news!
NHS4XmasNo1 NHSIsXmasNo1 LoveYourNHS
freemalaysiatoday.com/category/leisu...

 5   8   •••

LoveYourNHS Retweeted

Ben Munro @benmunro251 · 10h
Just seen the @Choir_NHS video! Absolutely Blown away! Well done guys!
#LoveYourNHS #NHS

 4   3   •••

Jeremy Corbyn MP @jeremycorbyn · 24h
Fantastic news that @Choir_NHS are #ChristmasNo1 - NHS in our hearts all year
round

 1.6K   2.5K   •••

Jo Cox MP @Jo_Cox1 · Dec 26
Congratulations to NHSChoir for making it to Christmas Number One! And nice
work justinbieber for promoting them LoveYourNHS

 650   533   •••

Jonathan Butler @JonButlerUK · 18h
What an achievement to all involved, @BOC_ATM aka Nick, @thegatefilms and
the #OMBLES who have been true legends!

Bank of Creativity @BOC_ATM

Big thanks to @bigbrandideas @JonButlerUK @timbutlerdesign @danbellj for
supporting the @NHS4XmasNo1 @LoveYourNHS campaign. We did it!!

    2   •••

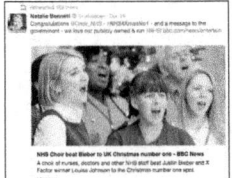
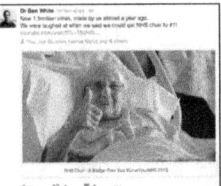
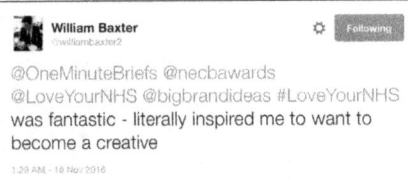

William Baxter   Following
@williambaxter2

@OneMinuteBriefs @necbawards
@LoveYourNHS @bigbrandideas #LoveYourNHS
was fantastic - literally inspired me to want to
become a creative

1:29 AM · 18 Nov 2016

GOING GOLD

We began a campaign to turn Manchester GOLD to welcome home our Olympic and Paralympic heroes. This started with a One Minute Brief that generated loads of amazing ideas that inspired the public to go gold on the day. Johnny Vegas helped spread the word and the sea of gold was recognised on national press and TV channels.

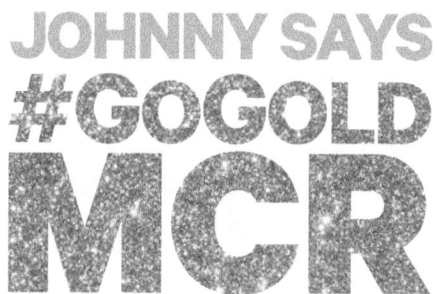

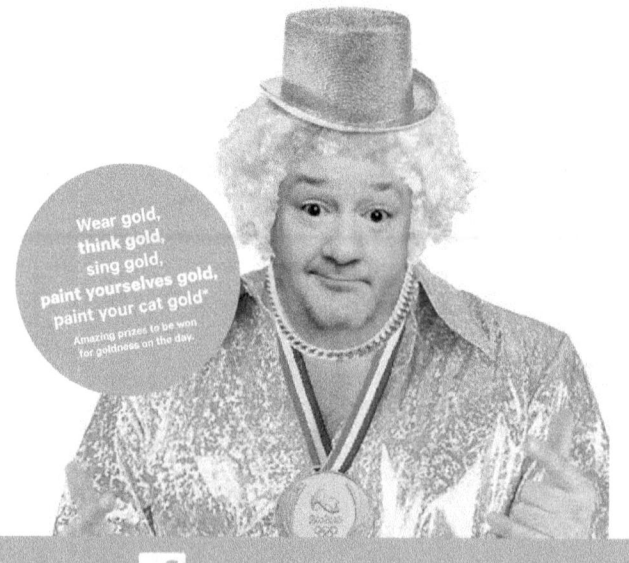

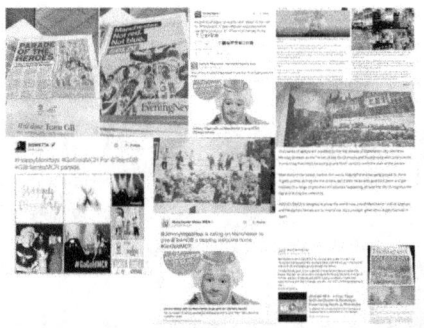

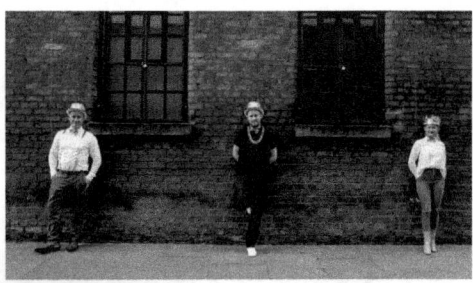

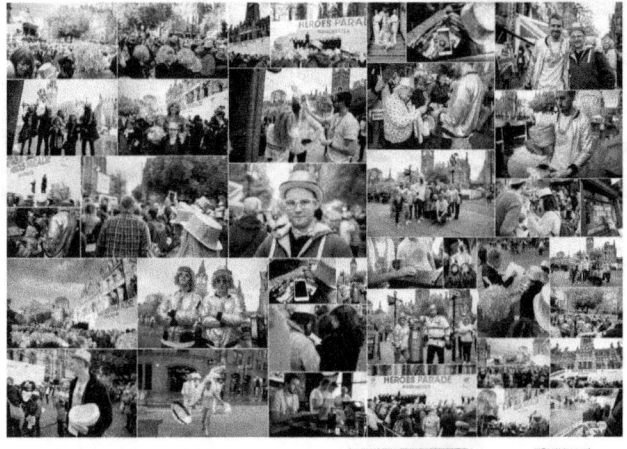

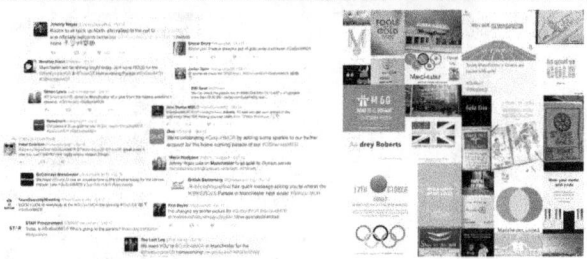

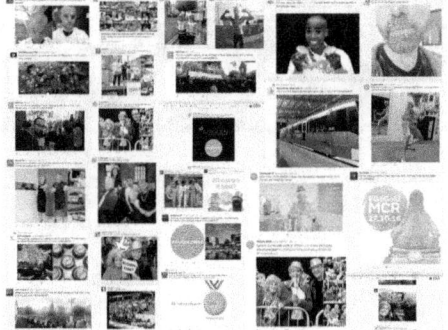

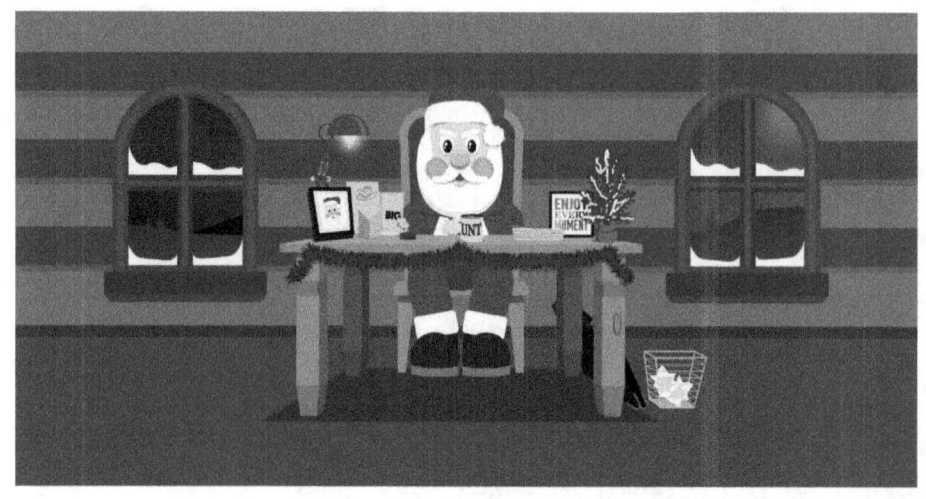

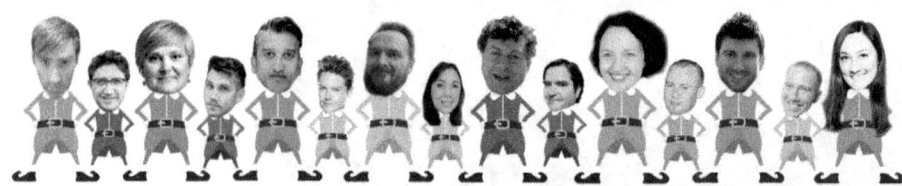

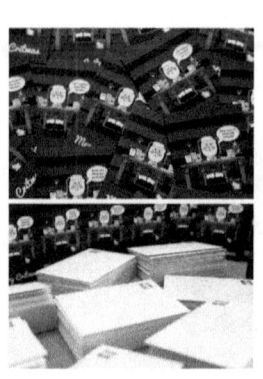

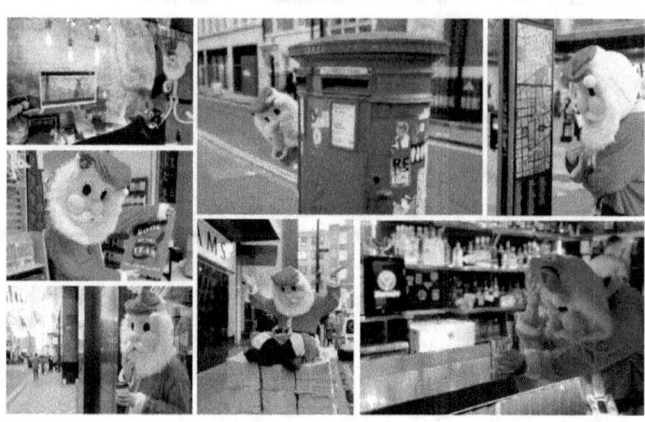

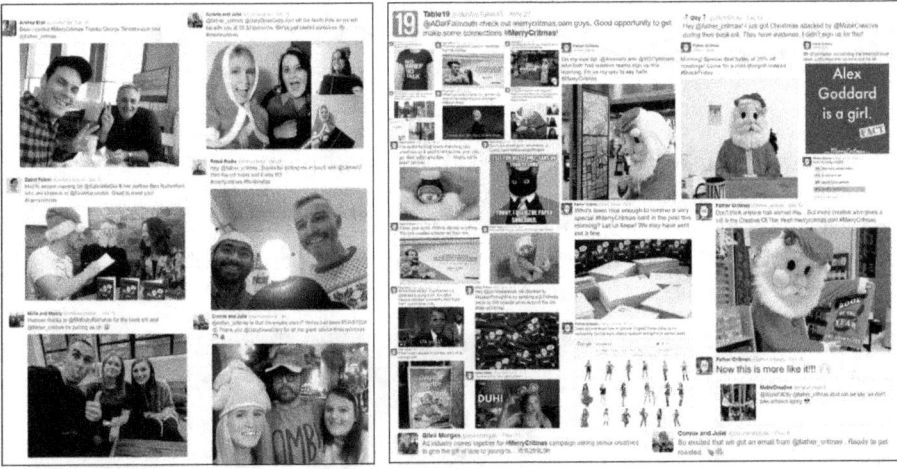

#MerryCritmas

We helped bring an amazing idea by Asa, Alex & David to life. We spread the word via One Minute Briefs after we had created Father Critmas, the best and grumpiest Creative Director in the world. He went on tour and we filmed one if his infamous book crits as we helped match young creatives for portfolio reviews around the world and gained lots of press coverage in the process.

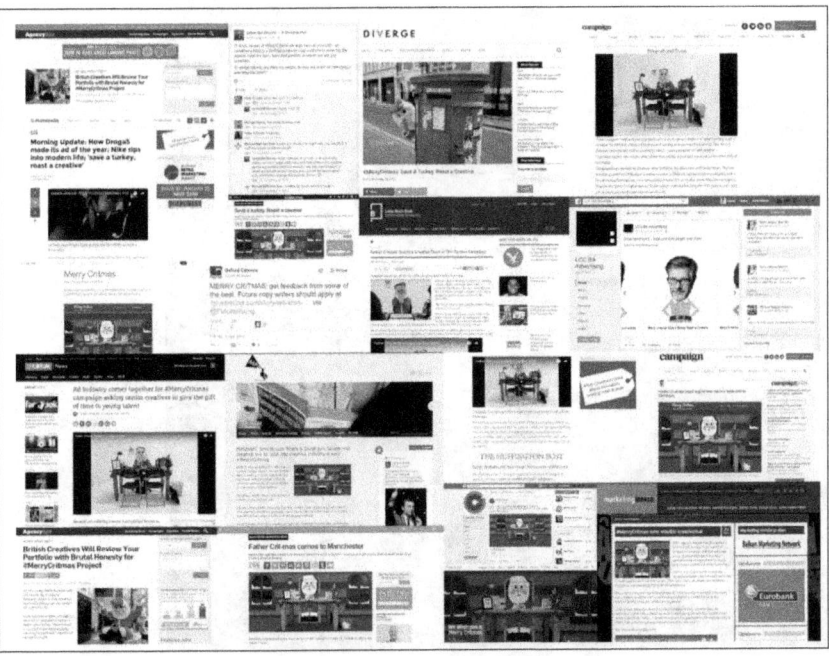

MAGNAFICENT SEVEN

In my previous role at MAGNAFI, I set a special One Minute Brief for our creative placement recruitment campaign. We asked people to create one minute films to advertise themselves and received entries from creatives around the world. Out of the 7 shortlisted, Zack Gardner won and spent 10 weeks with us whilst building up a great portfolio of TV work and is now working freelance in the industry.

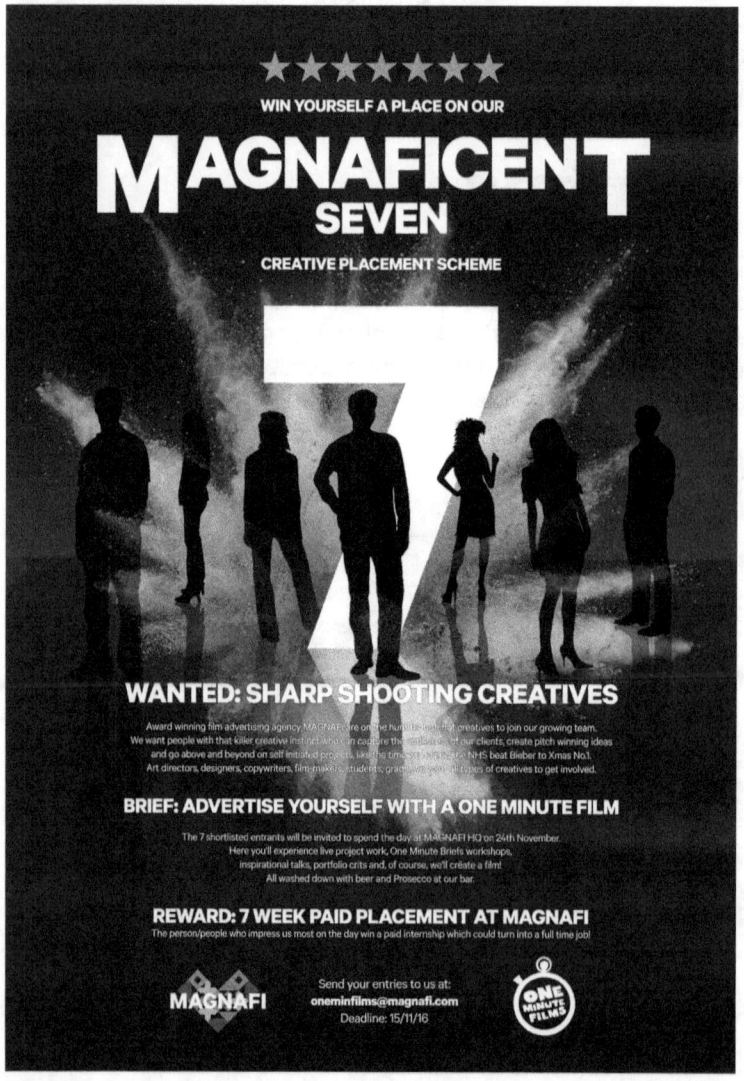

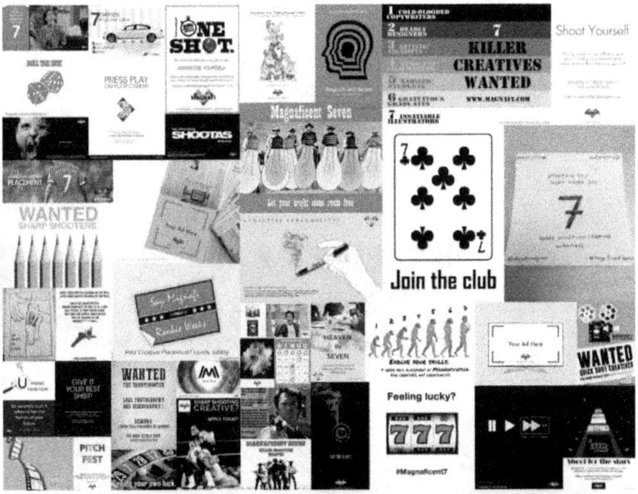

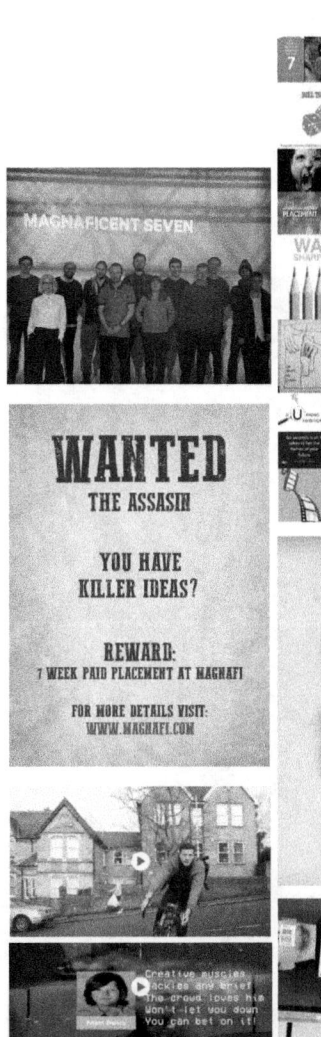

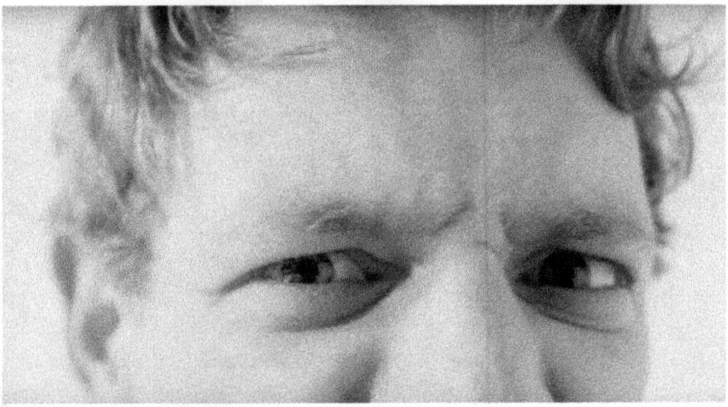

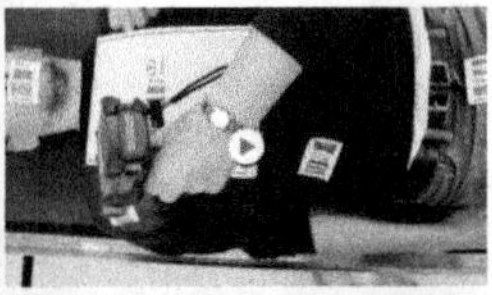

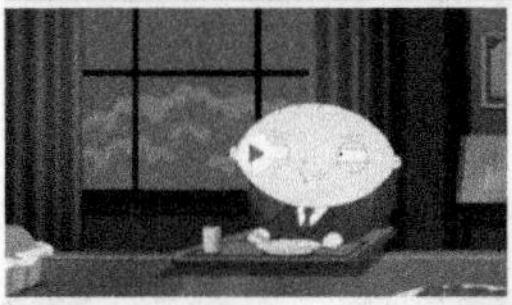

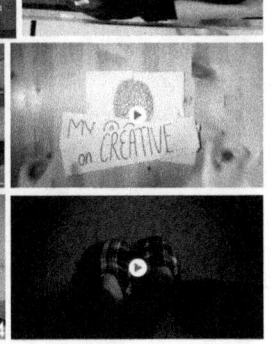

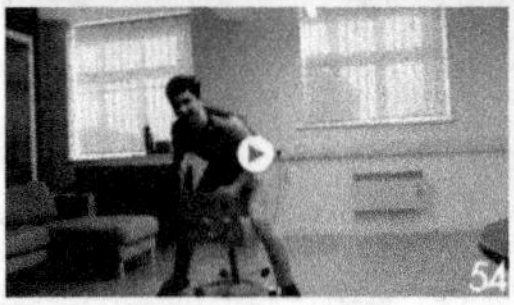

COLLAB WITH THE DRUM

We often team up with The Drum for creative campaigns and this brief was particularly fun as we asked people to send us their ads featuring Donald Trump. We also gave a #Microchips Chip Shop Award to @iaingorman for his Tipp-Ex advert which came out on top of a very strong shortlist which you see here.

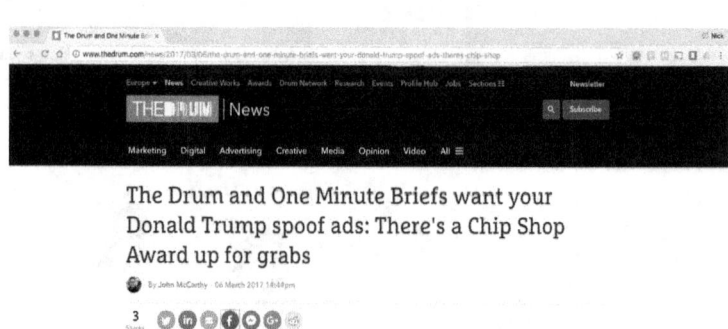

The Drum and One Minute Briefs want your Donald Trump spoof ads: There's a Chip Shop Award up for grabs

By John McCarthy · 06 March 2017 16:48pm

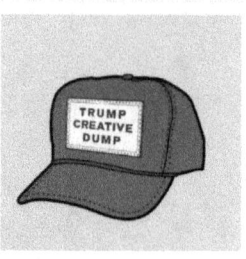

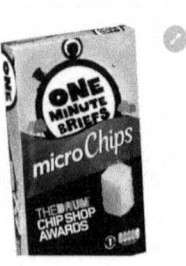

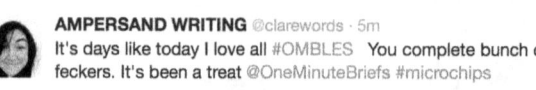

AMPERSAND WRITING @clarewords · 5m
It's days like today I love all #OMBLES You complete bunch of clever and funny feckers. It's been a treat @OneMinuteBriefs #microchips

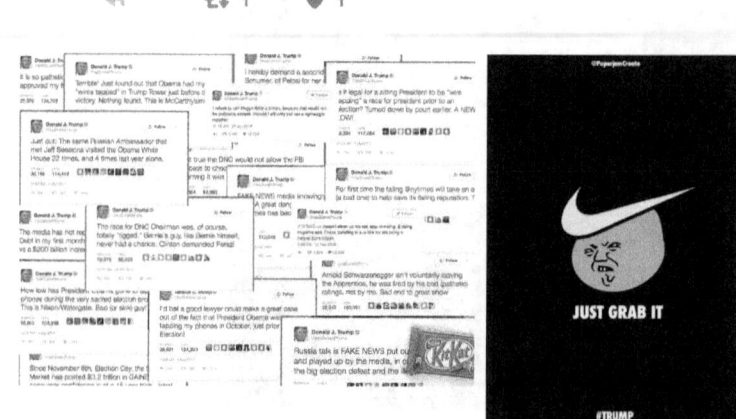

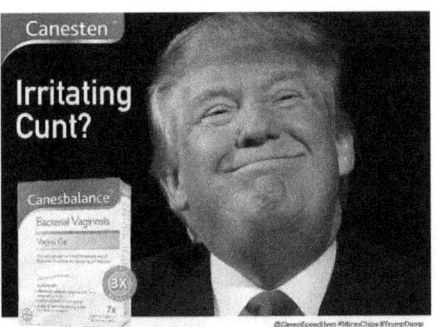

Canesten

Irritating Cunt?

Canesbalance
Bacterial Vaginosis
Vaginal Gel

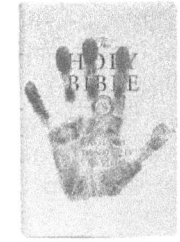

THE PRESIDENT
SWEARS BY IT

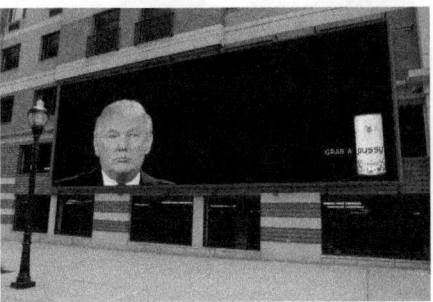

GRAB A PUSSY

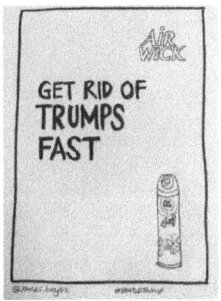

GET RID OF
TRUMPS
FAST

**PEOPLE LAUGHED WHEN I SAID I WOULD RUN.
LOOK AT ME NOW.**

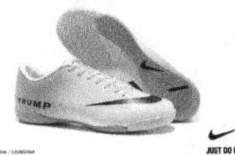

JUST DO IT.

33. Harry S. Truman
34. Dwight David Eisenhower
35. John Fitzgerald Kennedy
36. Lyndon Baines Johnson
37. Richard Milhous Nixon
38. Gerald Rudolph Ford
39. James Earl Carter, Jr.
40. Ronald Wilson Reagan
41. George Herbert Walker Bush
42. William Jefferson Clinton
43. George Walker Bush
44. Barack Hussein Obama
45.

"I will build a great wall –
and nobody builds walls
better than me, believe me"

Donald Trump

it's like it never happened

Tipp-Ex

EARTH HOUR

We collaborated with WWF to raise awareness of Earth Hour, where people are encouraged to turn off their lights to help save the planet. And, @WorldOfOlly came up with this beautifully simple poster idea. It went from a simple sketch, to a live poster, to an international award winner. That's what OMB is all about.

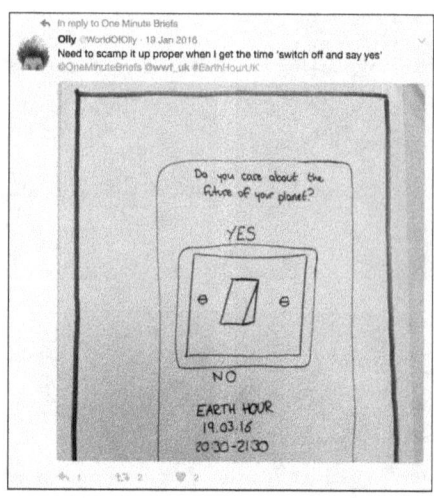

Olly @WorldOfOlly · 4 Mar 2016
I'm honoured and proud to say my work with @wwf_uk and @OneMinuteBriefs is live: po.st/EHOMB16

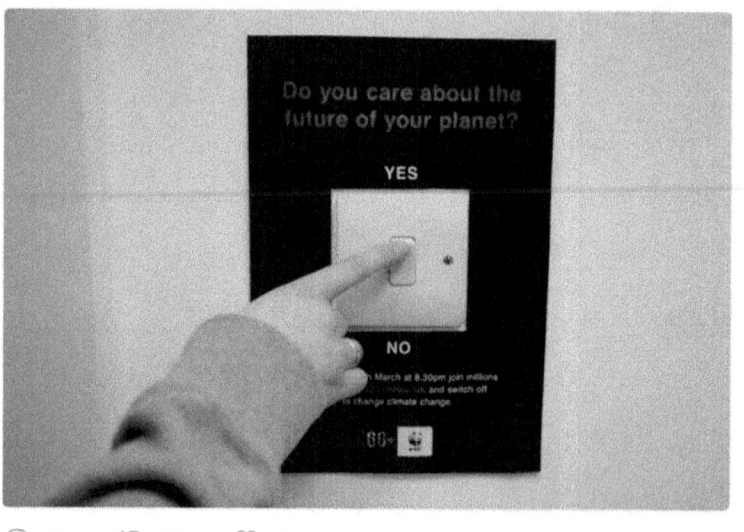

♡ 12 ↻ 20 ♡ 79 ✉

David Dibbs @daviddibbs · 19 Mar 2016

Incredibly inspiring evening at the @wwf_uk #EarthHour evening. Props to @WorldOfOlly for the invite, and props to earth for existing.

 1   3

WindupMerchant and 1 other liked

WWF UK @wwf_uk · 18 Mar 2016

@OgilvyUK @OneMinuteBriefs We love it too. Thanks for all the hard work for #EarthHourUK @WorldOfOlly 🐼

    2   5

In reply to Olly

Ben Jack Thomas @benjackthomas · 14 Mar 2016

@WorldOfOlly @wwf_uk @OneMinuteBriefs this is brilliant. Should be on every light switch 👏 🕯️ 🌍

 1   1   3

WWF UK @wwf_uk · 4 Mar 2016

Show you care about our planet & download a lightswitch poster po.st/EHOMB16 Thanks @WorldOfOlly & @OneMinuteBriefs #EarthHourUK

    15   18

Louise Chorley and 2 others Retweeted

Olly @WorldOfOlly · 17 Apr 2016

Can officially say I am an award-winning creative. @AMCP_Awards @OneMinuteBriefs @wwf_uk

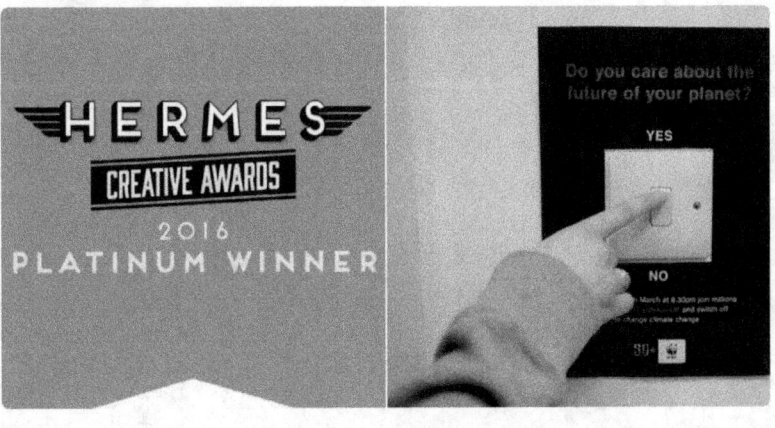

16   6   62

OMB AWARDS

The Pitch – Top 100 Small Businesses – 2015

NECB Awards – Best Social Media – Winner – 2015

NECB Awards – Best Small Business – Winner – 2015

GBEA Awards – Social Enterprise Entrepreneur of the Year & Special Merit Award – 2015

GBEA Awards – Social Enterprise Special Merit Award – 2015

The Drum – Social Buzz Top 50 – 2015

Official Charts – Christmas Number 1 – 2015

Creative Circle – #LoveYourNHS – Silver – Best Social Networking Campaign – 2016

The Drum Marketing Awards -#LoveYourNHS – Winner – Best Social Media Campaign – 2016

Roses Creative Awards -#LoveYourNHS – Gold – Best Online/Viral Film – 2016

Roses Creative Awards -#LoveYourNHS – Gold – Best Integrated Campaign – 2016

Roses Creative Awards - #LoveYourNHS – Grand Prix Award – 2016

MPA Awards – Rising Star – Finalist – 2016

MPA Awards – Collaboration – #LoveYourNHS – Winner – 2016

MPA Awards – Best Agency Campaign -#LoveYourNHS – Winner – 2016

Brand Republic Digital Awards – Best Social Campaign – #LoveYourNHS – Winner – 2016

Campaign Big – Best Social Media – Winner – #LoveYourNHS – 2016

NECB Awards – Best Social Networking – Winner – 2016

MPA Awards – Finalist – Best Collaboration – #MerryCritmas – 2017

MPA Awards – Finalist – Best Social Media Campaign – 2017

Small Biz Awards UK – Shortlisted – 2017

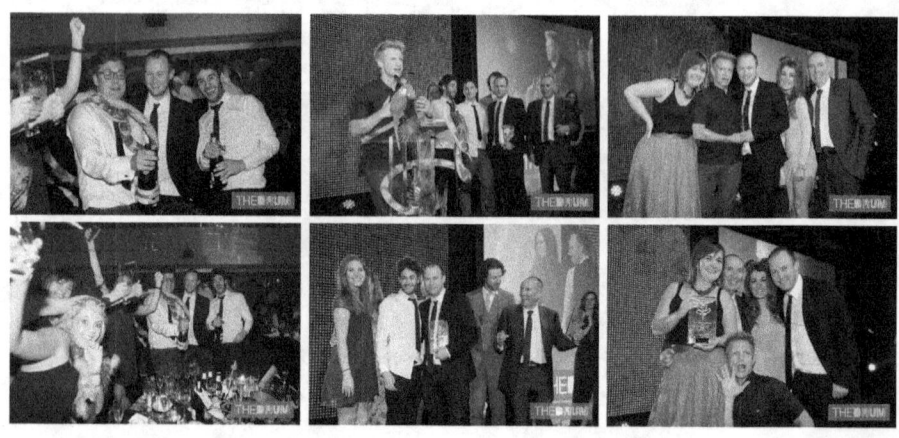

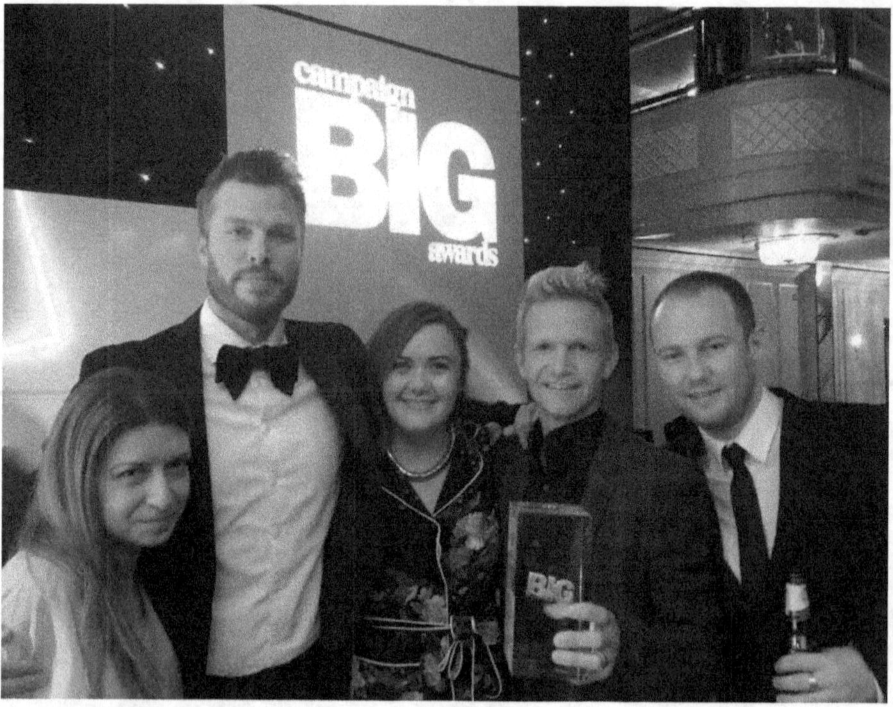

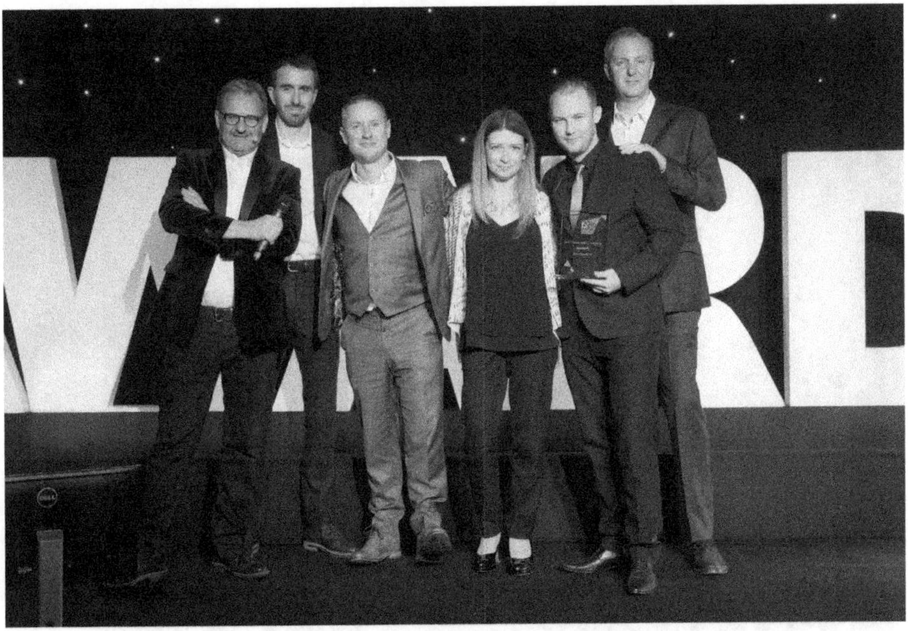

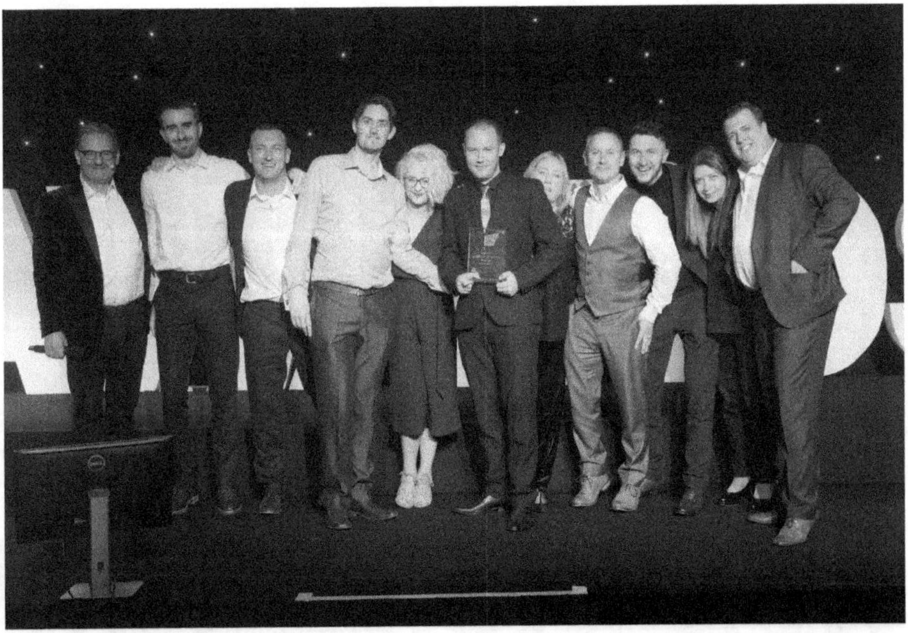

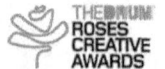 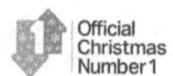 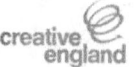 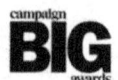

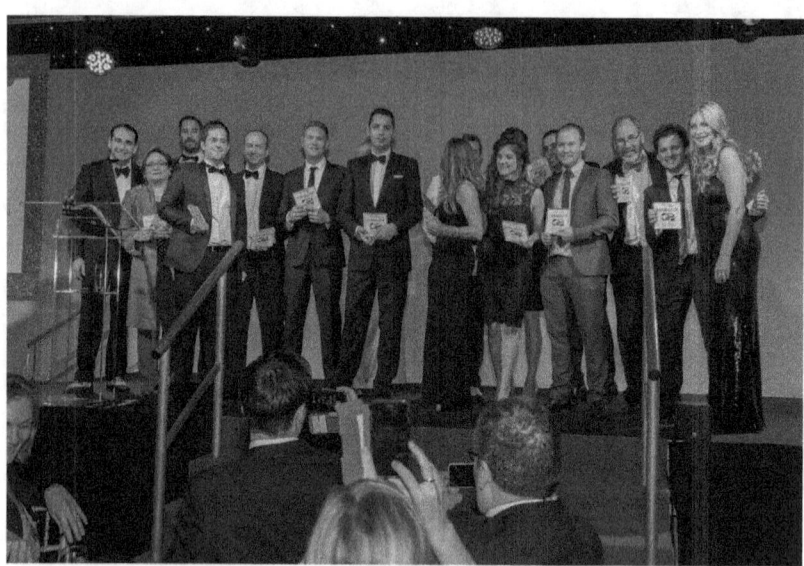

On stage with Carol Smillie and Caprice.
Life goals achieved.

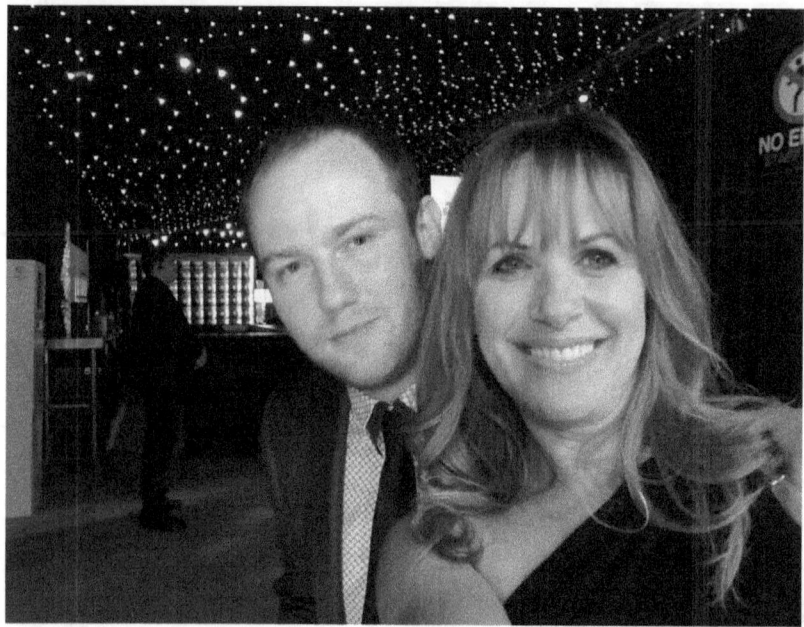

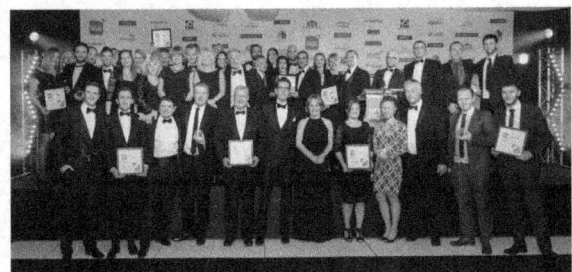
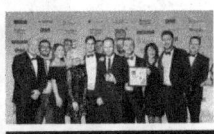
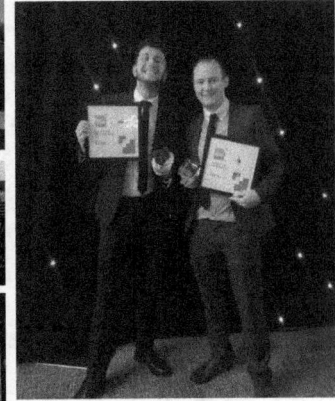
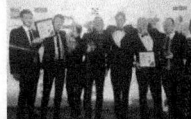
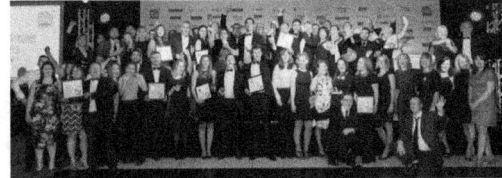
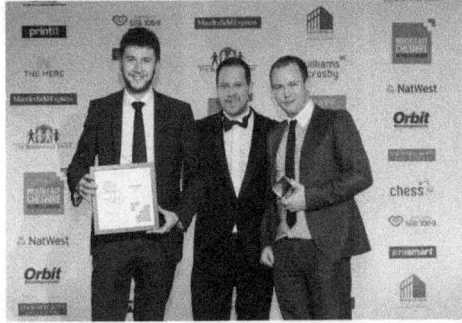
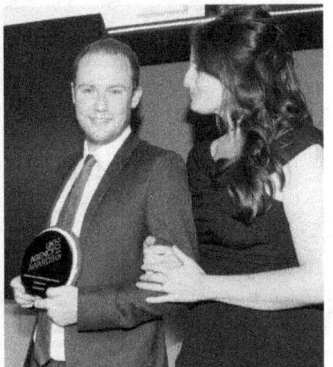
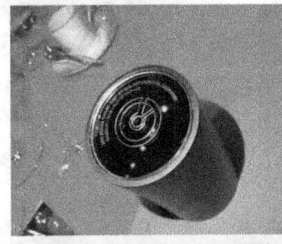
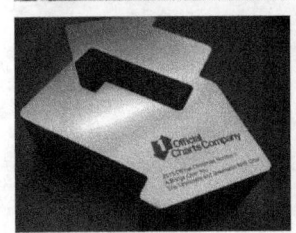
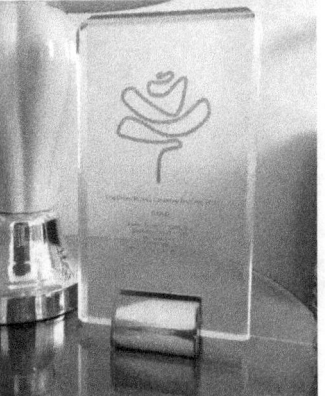

OMBLES

Some pics of the OMBLES and a special brief where we advertised each other!

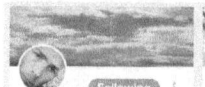

Matt Rogers ✓
@MiracleTraining Follows you

I help a vastly diverse range of Entrepreneurs to learn, integrate & profit from ...

Followed by Connor Dickson...

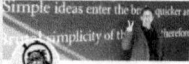

David Felton
@doritosyndrome Follows you

Ad creative, #OMBLE, will walk your dog for free.

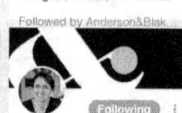

John Vingoe
@ElevenBlackUK Follows you

Design. Food. Coffee. | Creative Director at @hideoutuk | @oneminutebriefs -...

Followed by Jamie Webb an...

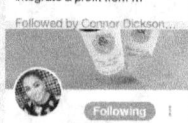

AMPERSAND WRITING
@clarewords Follows you

North West freelance copywriter for hire 📝 |@oneminutebriefs Most...

Followed by Jamie Webb an...

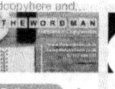

cal
@Skit92cal Follows you

Tribute act. #OMBLE

Followed by Adcopyhere und...

Jason Hutton
@c_m_y_l Follows you

Digital creative in Leeds. Lover of ads and a good story. Designer, thinker, #OMBLE...

Followed by Anderson&Blak...

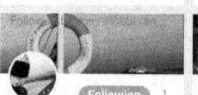

∧∨∨
@Matthew__Wyatt Follows you

Daddy, award winning creative, proud #OMBLE, 173 x @oneminutebriefs winner....

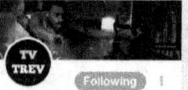

Dave Harland
@wordmancopy Follows you

Anti-bullshit copywriter with massive fingers. Plain English specialist. #OMBLE. Dead...

Followed by Anderson&Blak...

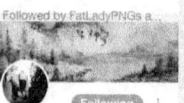

Shireen Dew
@ShireenDew Follows you

Thinking: back to front. Smiling: inside out. Creative: through & through. Co-founder of...

Followed by Ryan Wheeler a...

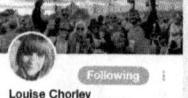

Gareth Horn
@Gazzamatazzzz Follows you

Chef, Copywriter, Cyclist. And other C words. Head rooster @henhouse_uk ...

Followed by Jamie Webb an...

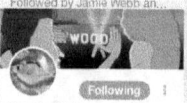

TV Trev
@TrevorAKP Follows you

Blogger, brother, bad ass mother...part time OMBie, aspiring illustrator, award...

Followed by FatLadyPNGs a...

Connor Dickson
@MrConnorDickson Follows you

Graphic Designer & Art Director Follow me on Twitter and Instagram for #Creative ...

Followed by Anderson&Blak...

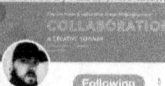

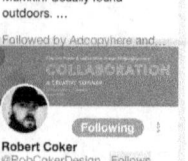

Louise Chorlev
@Chorles Follows you

Freelance creative, and senior designer for @_makemarks. Big passion for clever concept...

Followed by Jamie Webb an...

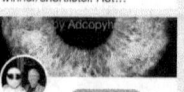

Joe Brooks
@Joe_From_Essex Follows you

Devout #OMBLE and 57 time @OneMinuteBriefs winner/shortlister. Hot...

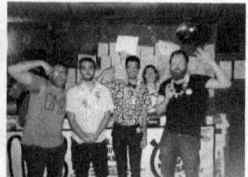

Emma Cook
@cookoocopy Follows you

Freelance Copywriter. Country Mumkin. Usually found outdoors. ...

Followed by Adcopyhere and...

Dan Scott ✐
@CreativeBrummie Follows you

49x @OneMinuteBriefs winner, most prolific #OMBLE 2015, The YES Awards winner...

Brian
@BMMarketer Follows you

Award-winning marketer. Amateur novelist. #OMBLE. I love creativity, great writin...

Followed by Jamie Webb an...

Robert Coker
@RobCokerDesign Follows you

Freelance Graphic Designer. Also a #OMBLE @OneMinuteBriefs

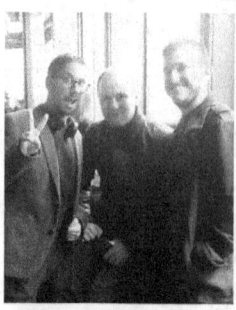

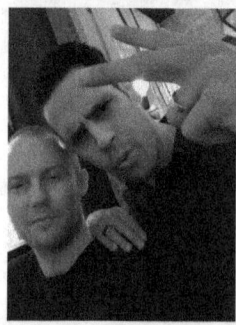

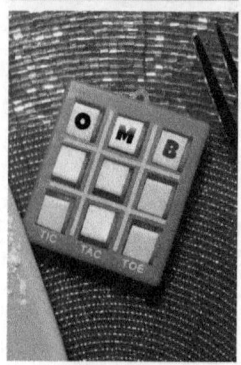

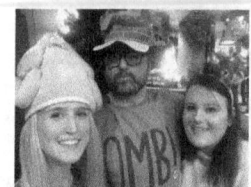

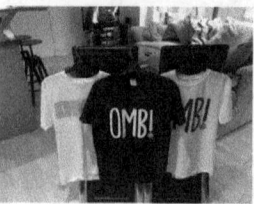

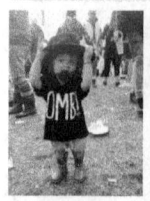

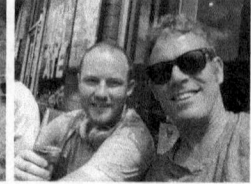

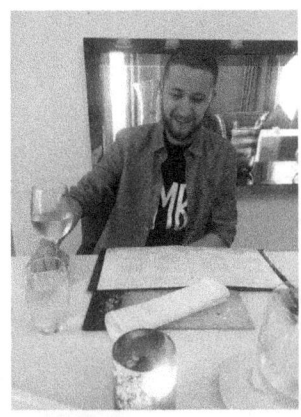
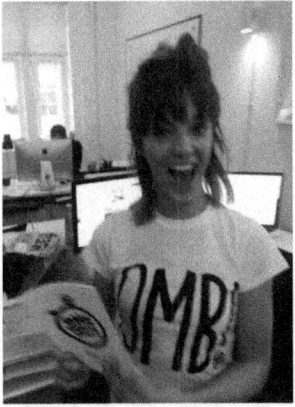
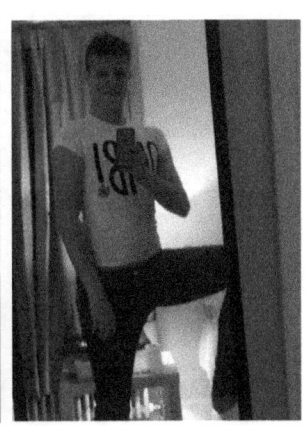
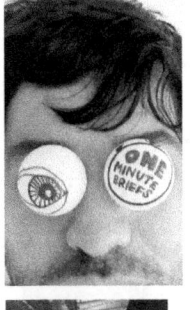
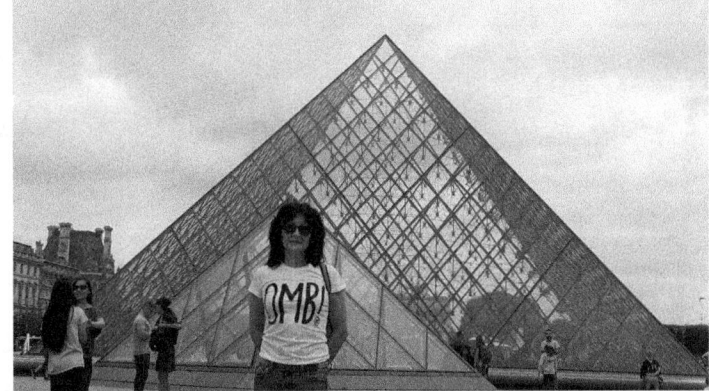
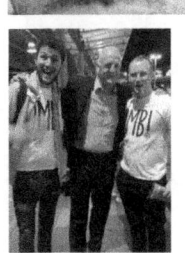
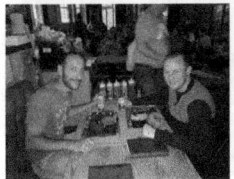
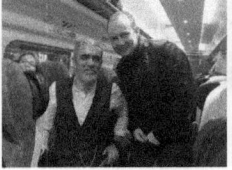
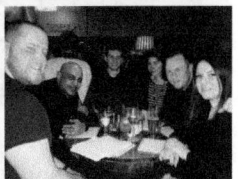
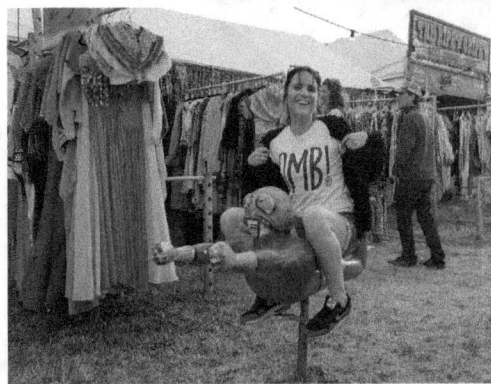
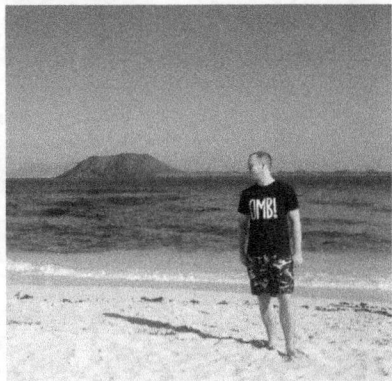

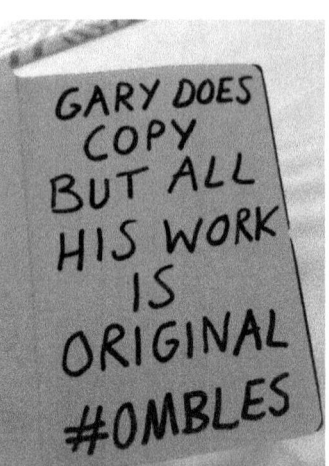

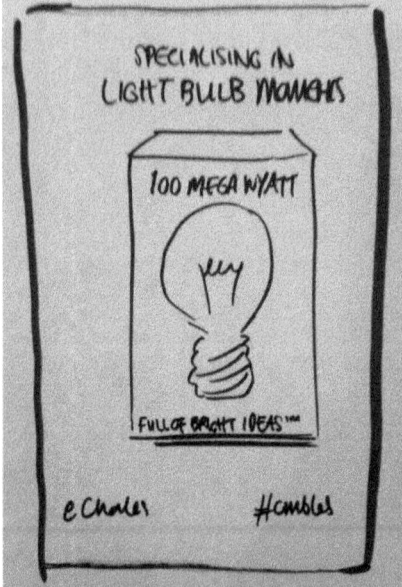

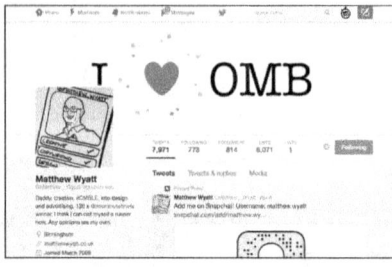

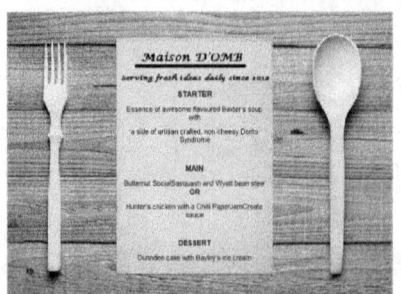

7,641

Notifications

Nick Entwistle's Lunch Hour

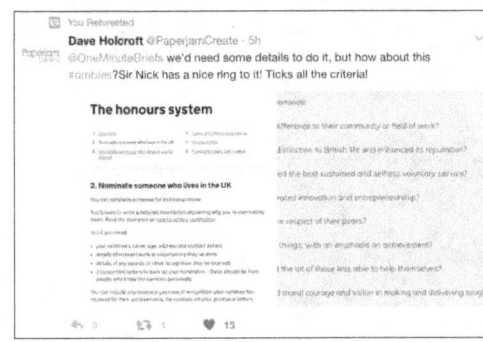

You Sian not pass

@SianEllenJ
oMBrilliant rising star

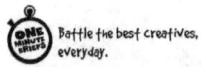
Battle the best creatives, everyday.

@Mac_Daddies

Bow down to the Bayley

@richbayley90
most consistent OMBle 2015

Battle the best creatives, everyday.

@Mac_Daddies

Chorles the first
(she usually is)

@charles
oMBies oMBle 2015

Battle the best creatives, everyday.

@Mac_Daddies

Who's your daddies?

@Mac_Daddies
oMBies of the year 2015

Battle the best creatives, everyday.

@Mac_Daddies

Wyatt didn't I think of that?

@Matthew_wyatt
133 x OMB winner

Battle the best creatives, everyday.

@Mac_Daddies

Keeping up with the Jones?

@beginnesjones
oMB veteran

Battle the best creatives, everyday.

@Mac_Daddies

OMB HALL OF FAME

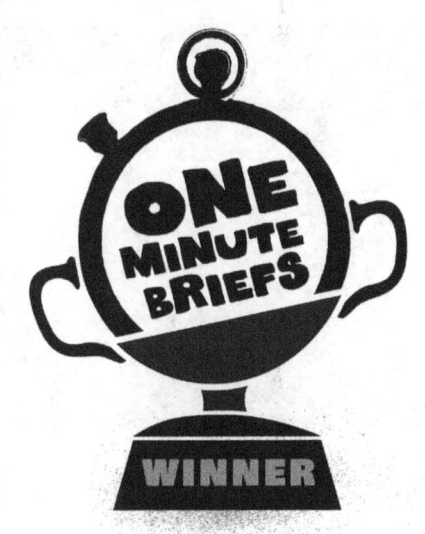

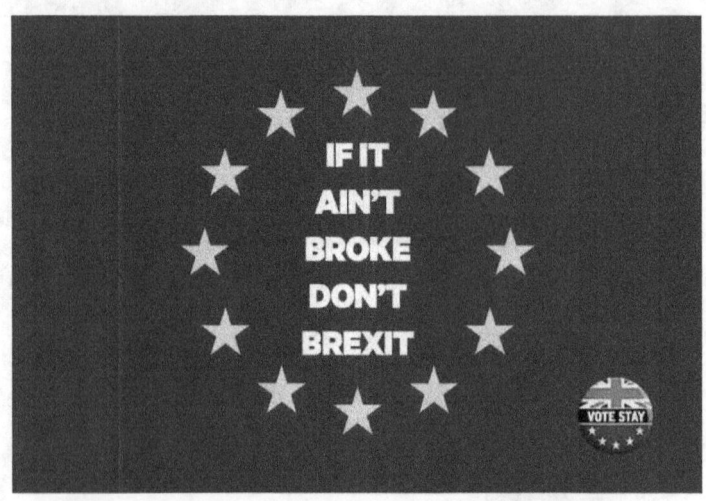

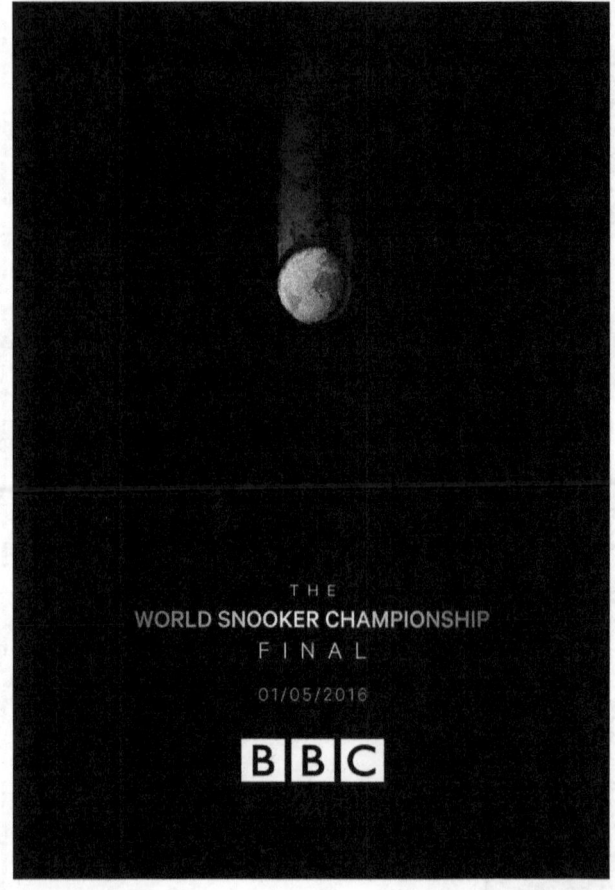

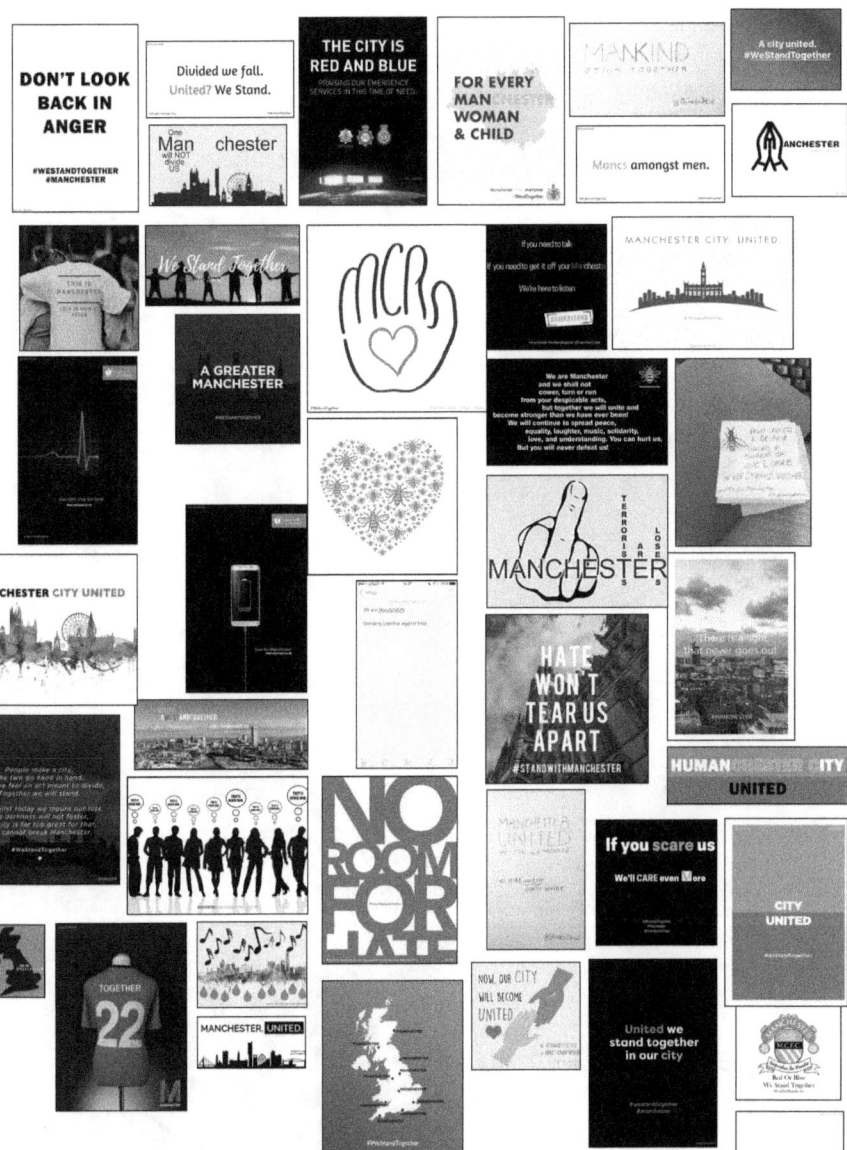

brokeLads

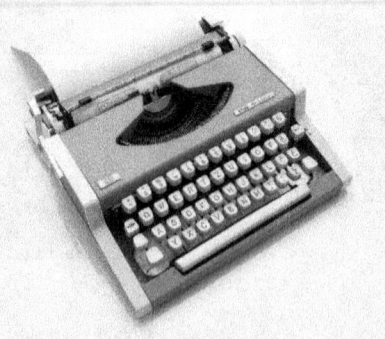

Paper. Thin. Display.

Lose 30 pounds a month, effortlessly

#Gyms   @Dissential

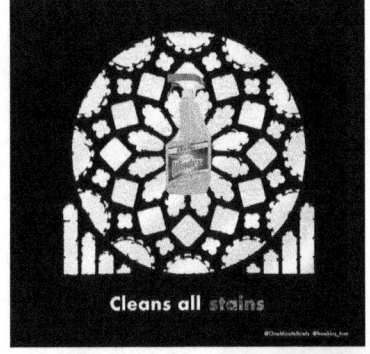

Cleans all *stains*

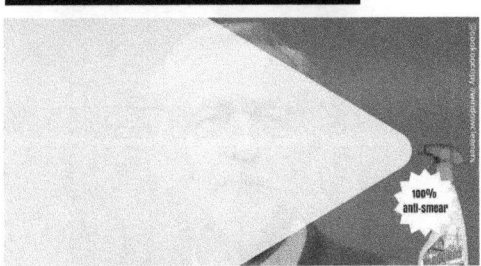

100% anti-smear

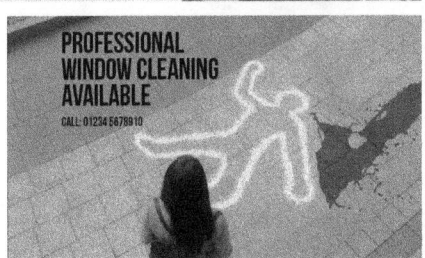

PROFESSIONAL WINDOW CLEANING AVAILABLE
CALL: 01234 5678910

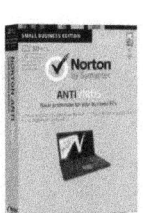

Professional Windows Cleaning Service

@Mac_Daddies

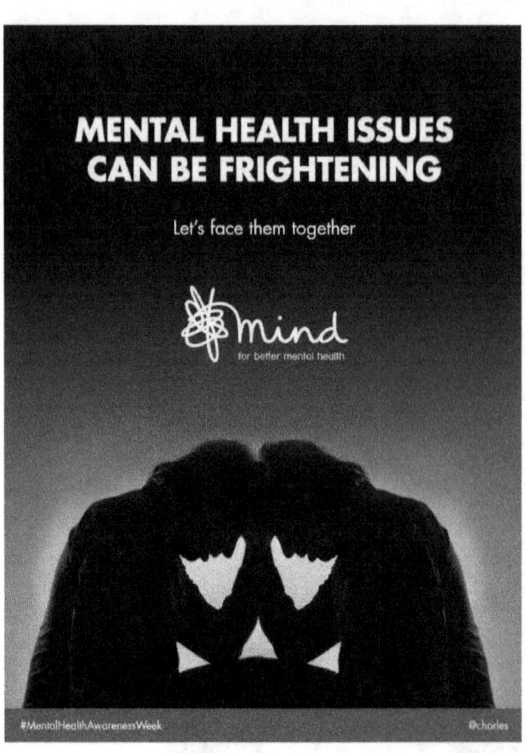

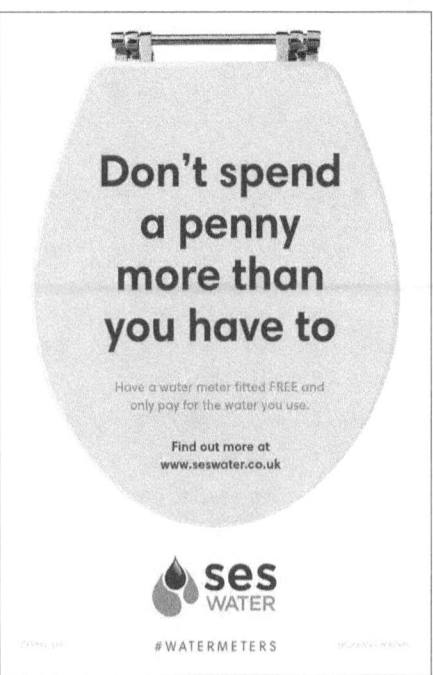

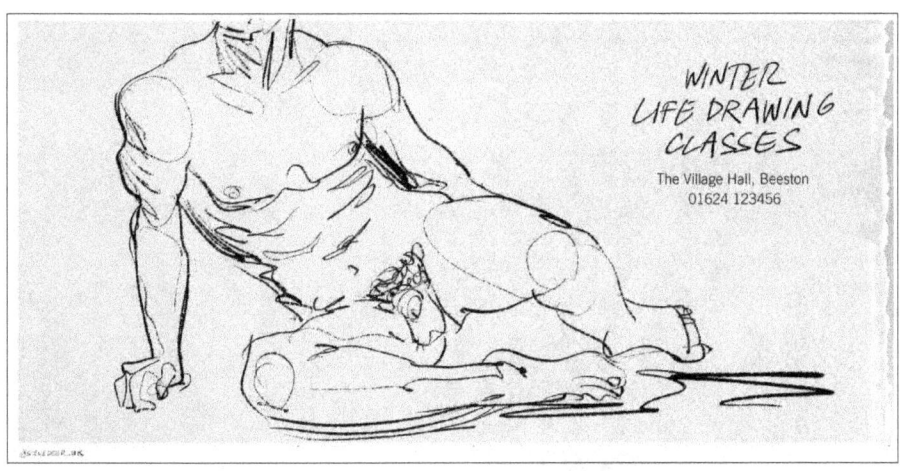

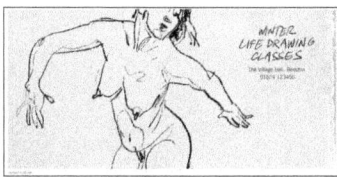

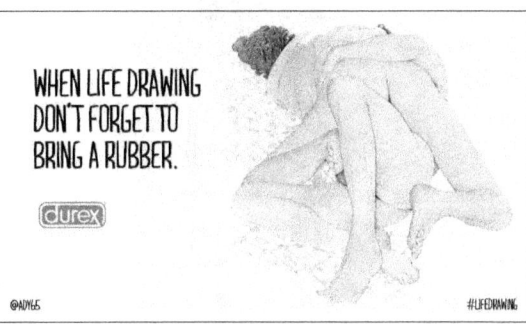

WHEN LIFE DRAWING
DON'T FORGET TO
BRING A RUBBER.

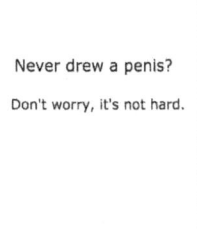

Never drew a penis?

Don't worry, it's not hard.

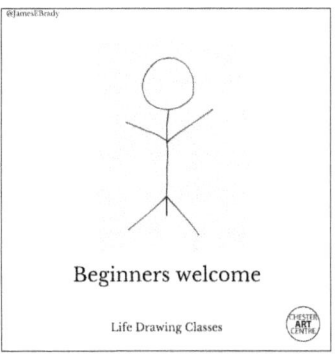

Beginners welcome

Life Drawing Classes

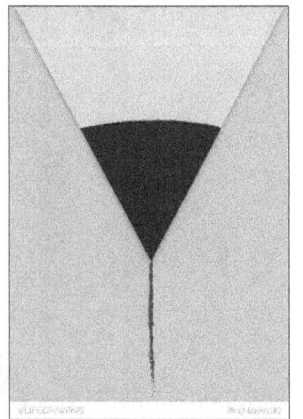

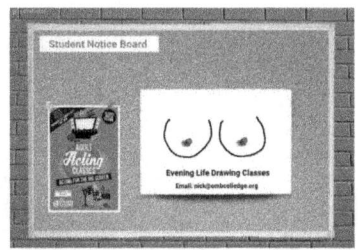

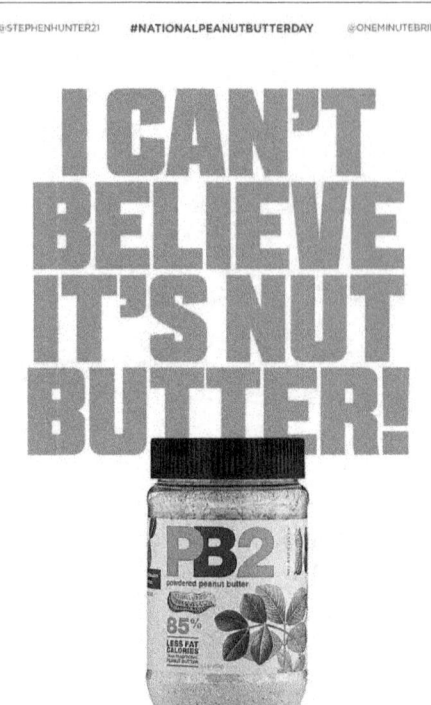

I CAN'T BELIEVE IT'S NUT BUTTER!

PB2
powdered peanut butter

85%
LESS FAT
CALORIES

VIRTUALLY FAT FREE PEANUT BUTTER

CATCH OF THE YEAR
Ann Summers

@johngocman
#Stockings

48.

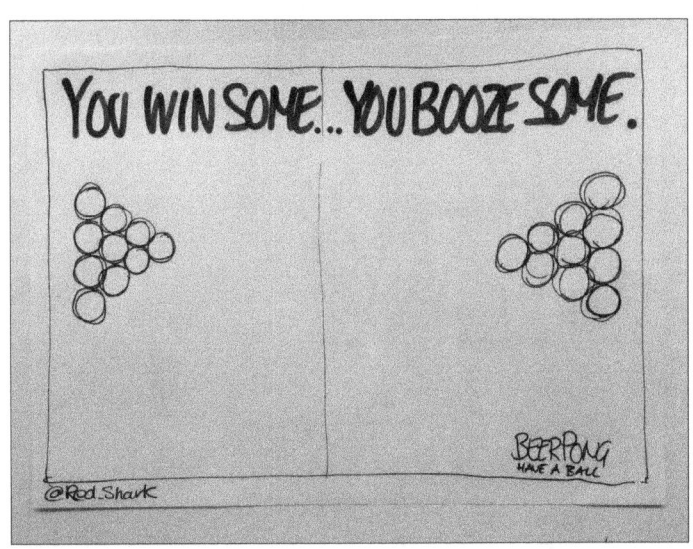

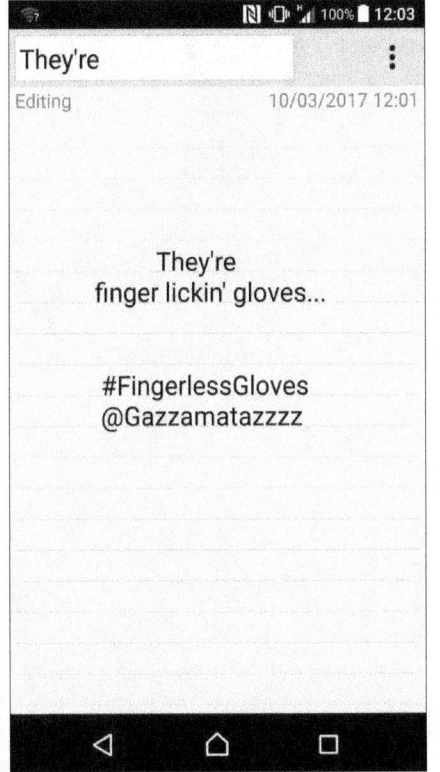

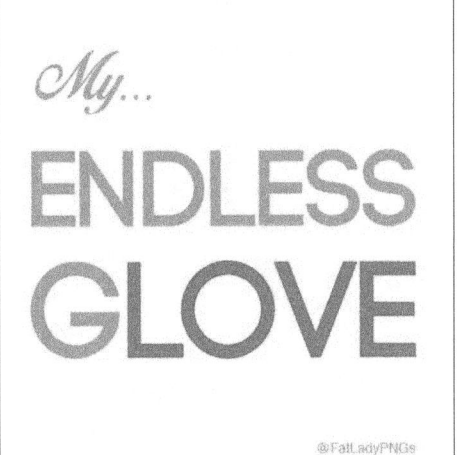

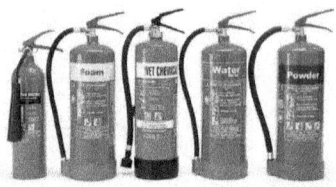

"SIR, MAY WE PRESENT THE DRINKS MENU?"

Merzetta Chillies. They're hot hot hot.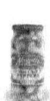

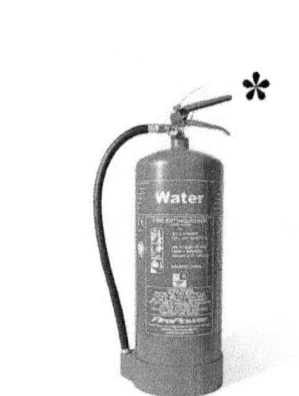

*SERVING SUGGESTION.

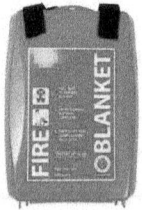

ALWAYS USE A SERVIETTE.

Merzetta Hot Chillies.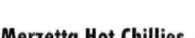

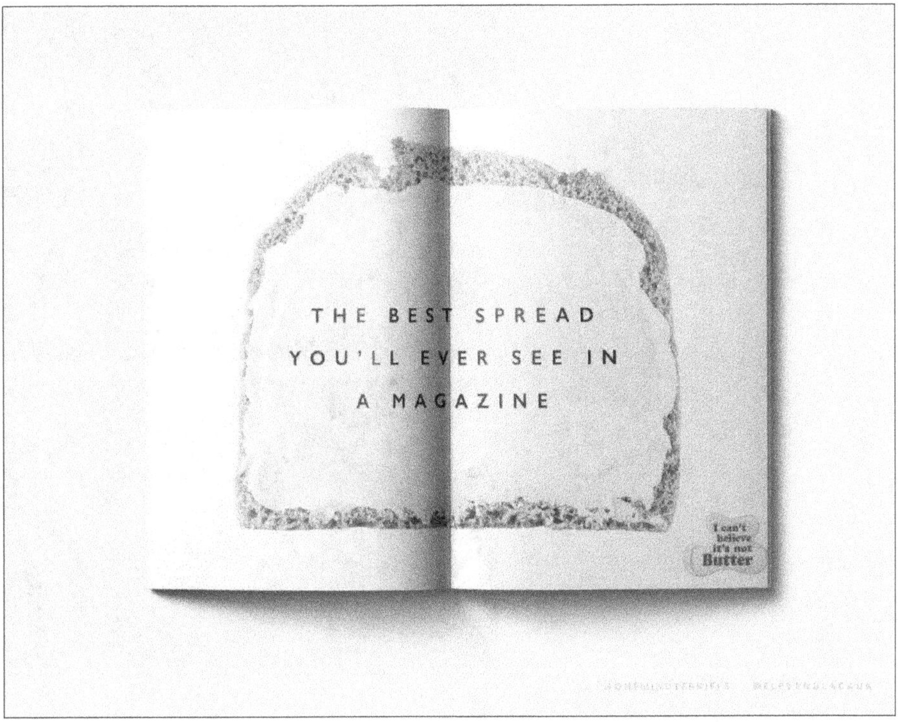

THE BEST SPREAD
YOU'LL EVER SEE IN
A MAGAZINE

I can't
believe
it's not
Butter

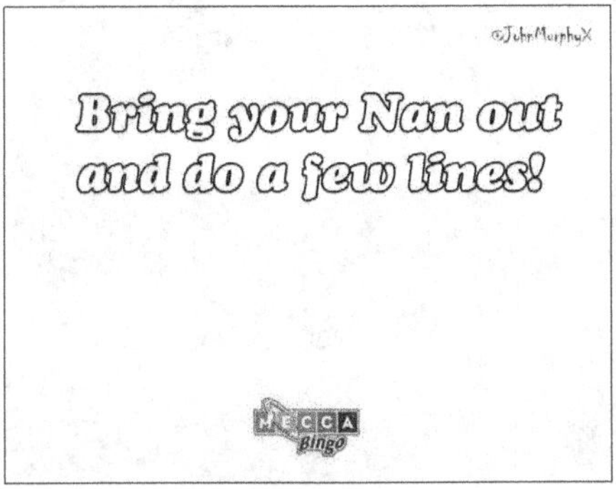

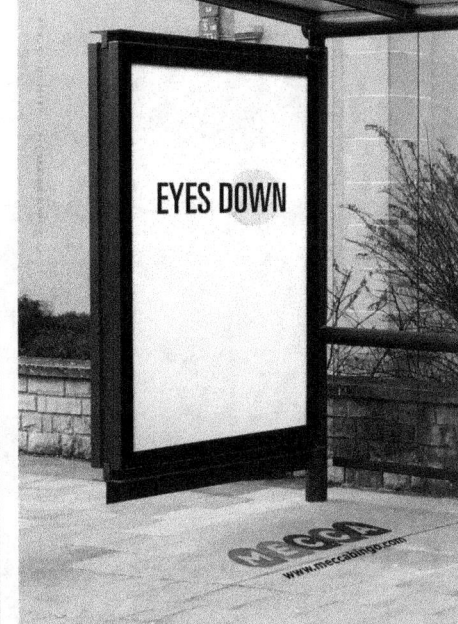

@JohnMurphuX

Bring your Nan out
and do a few lines!

EYES DOWN

mecca
www.meccabingo.com

Santa's not
the only one
working nights
on the 25th.

Thank you for being here at
Christmas time, and all year round.

#MerryXmasNHS

@Matthew__Wyatt

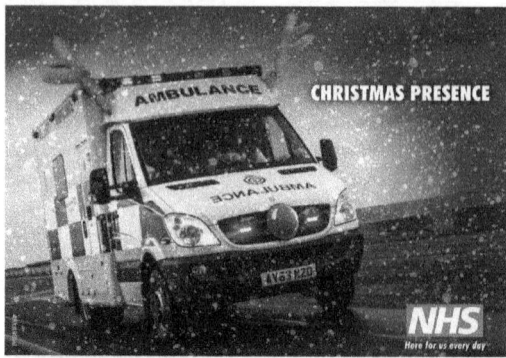

CHRISTMAS PRESENCE

AMBULANCE

NHS
Here for us every day

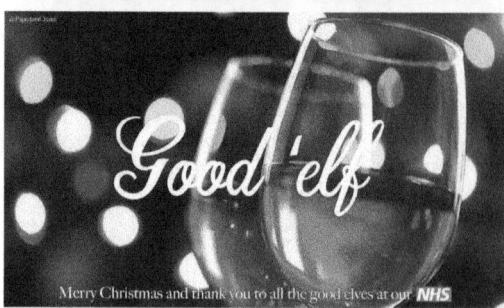

Good 'elf

Merry Christmas and thank you to all the good elves at our **NHS**

Wear a helmet.

It's not brain surgery

#HELMETS @GaryDoesCopy

Weakened health service?

The proposed 7 day NHS contract is both unsafe and unsustainable. Show your support at #Justh health

justice for health

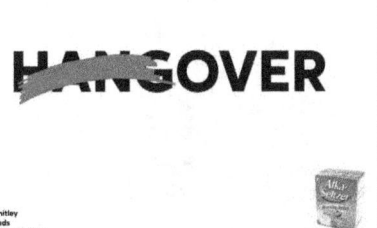

HANGOVER

@aidanwhitley
@hstringads
#HANGOVERTABLETS

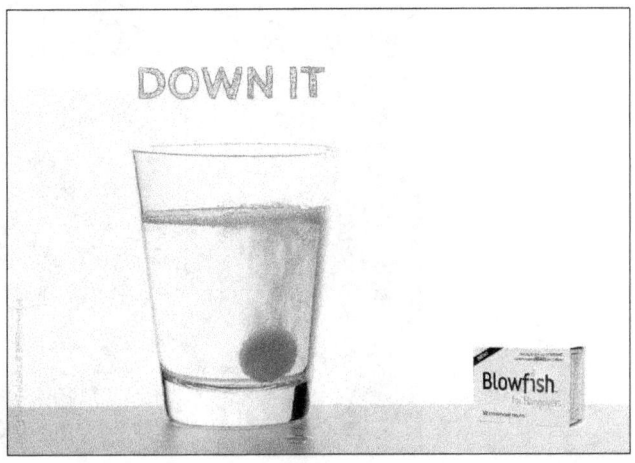

DOWN IT

Blowfish.

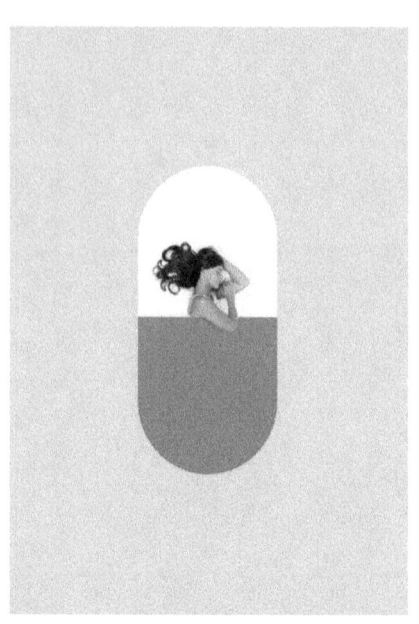

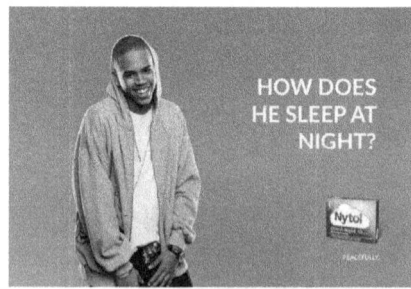

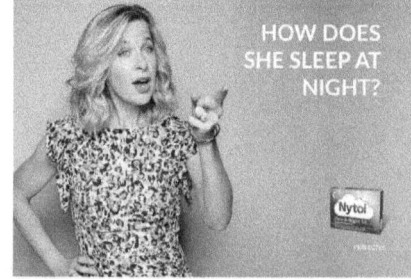

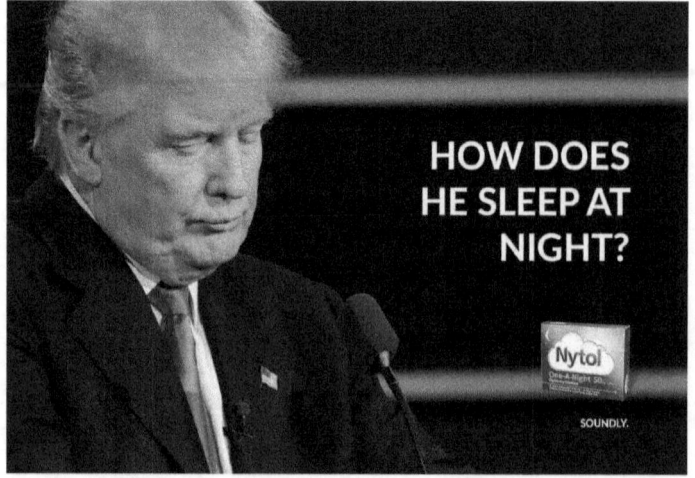

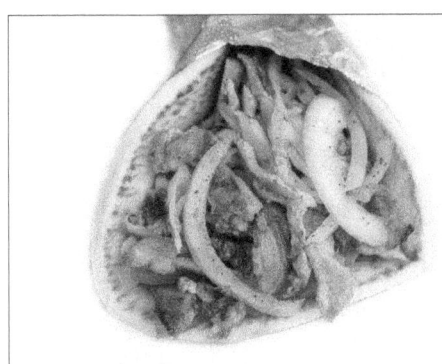

**HAVEN'T PULLED?
TAKE ME HOME INSTEAD**

doner kebabs - the 2am sure thing

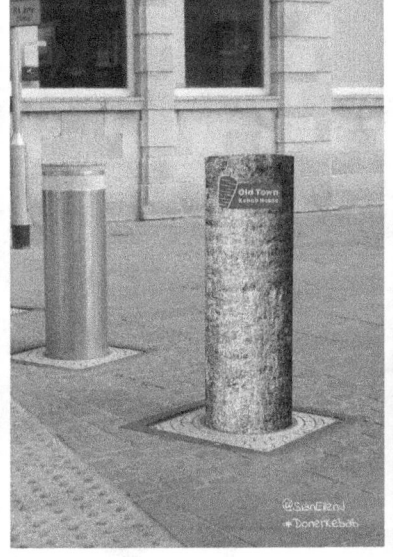

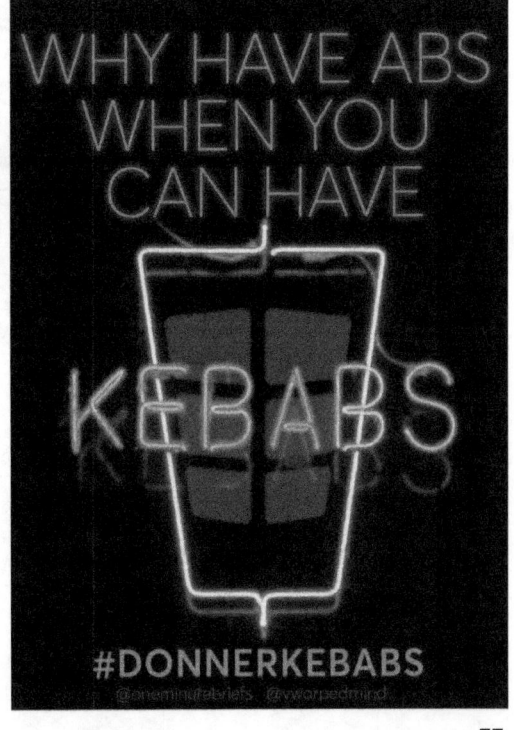

WHY HAVE ABS
WHEN YOU
CAN HAVE

KEBABS

#DONNERKEBABS

55.

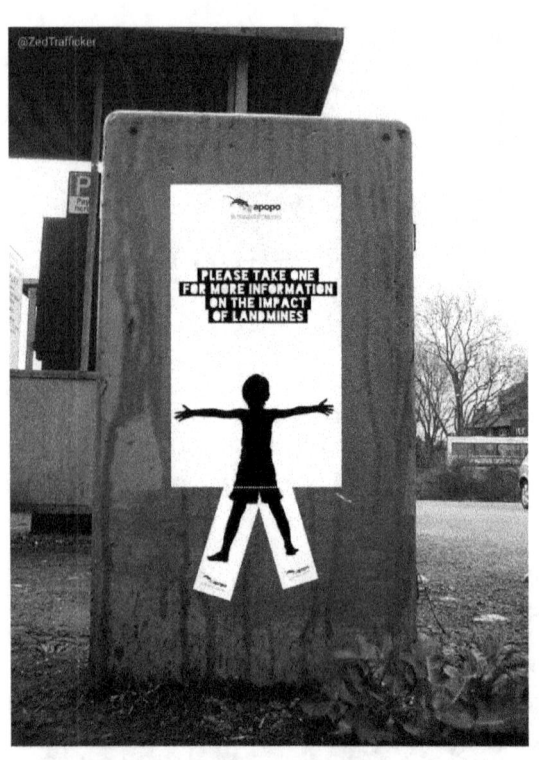

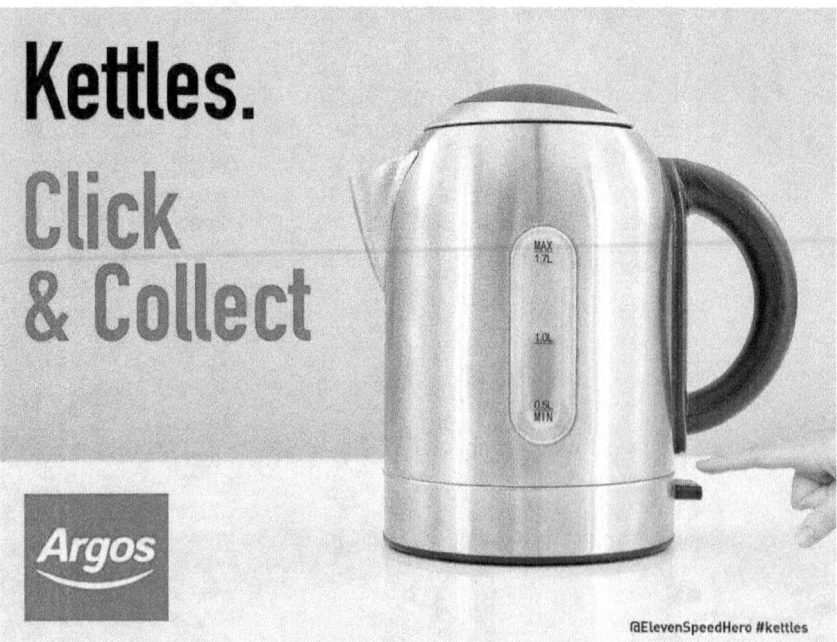

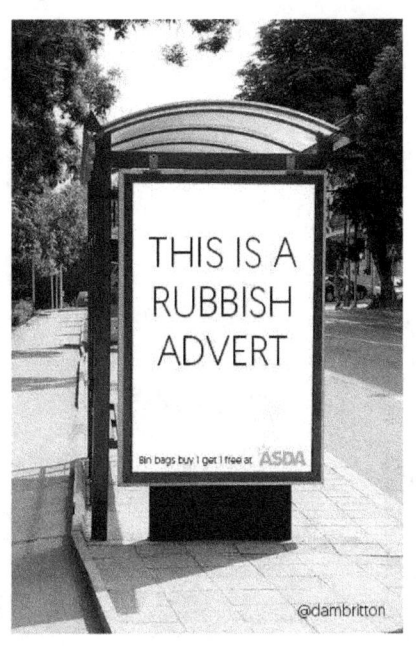

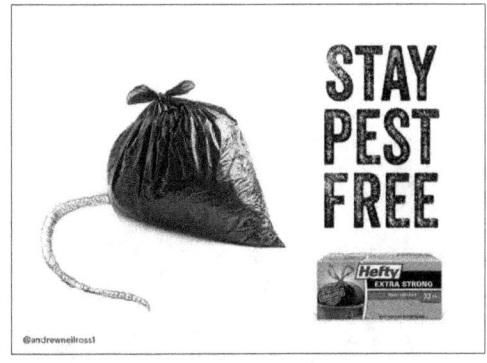

OMB #BinBags @williambaxter2

Buy our product. Put it straight in the bin.

Everyday Essentials from Wilko

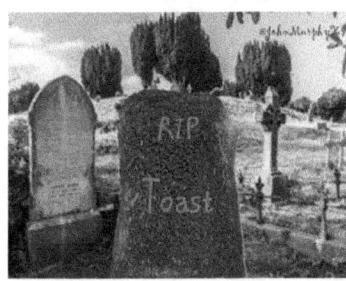

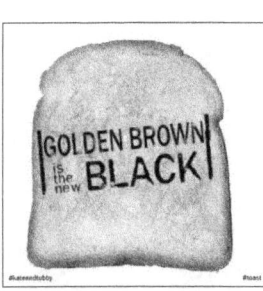

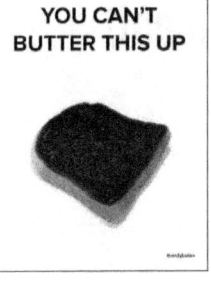

YOU CAN'T
BUTTER THIS UP

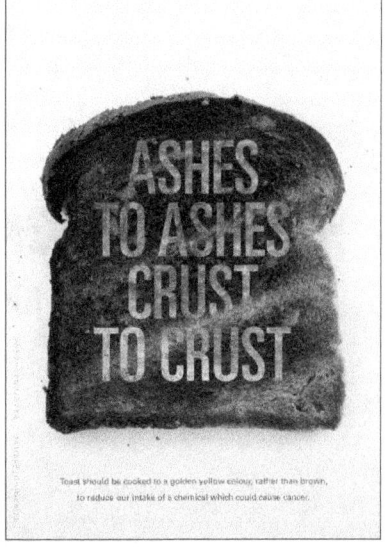

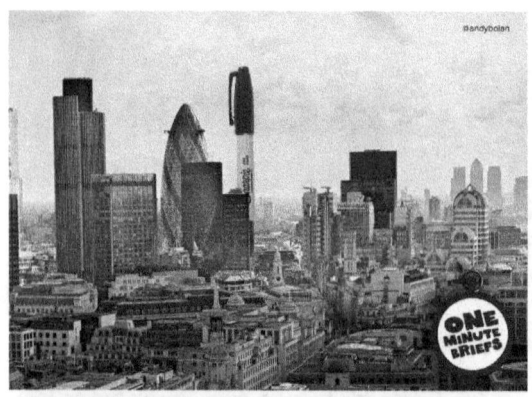

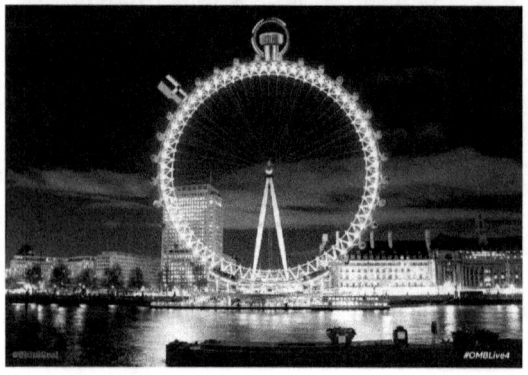

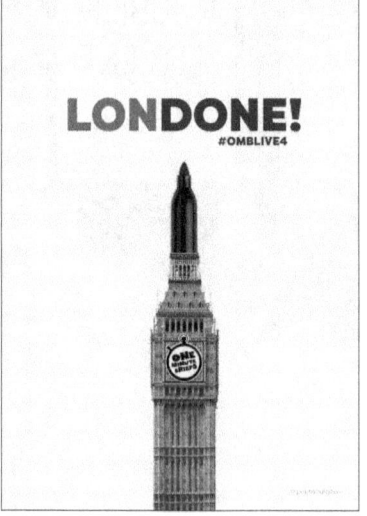

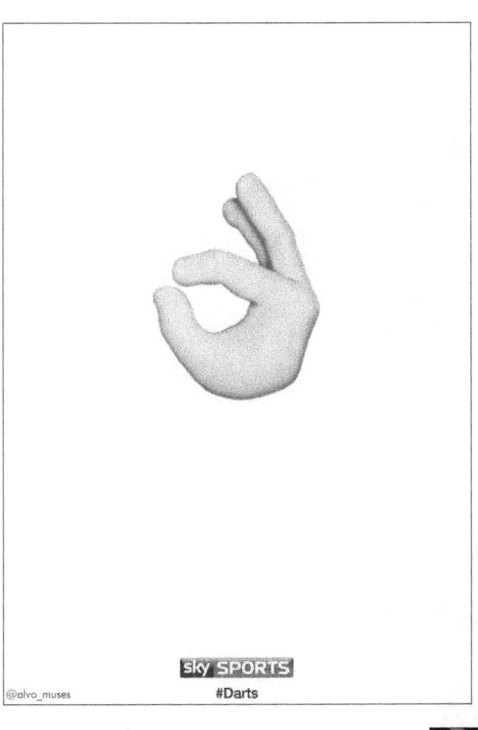

#Darts

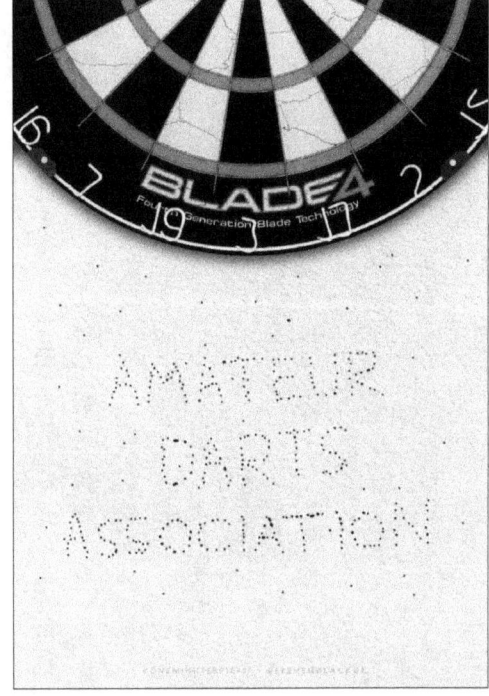

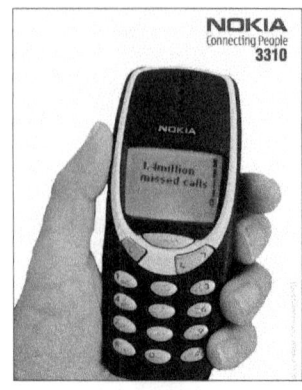

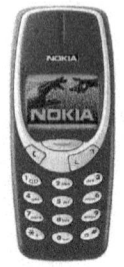

CONTACT YOUR LOCAL DEALER.

The Nokia 3310 is back.

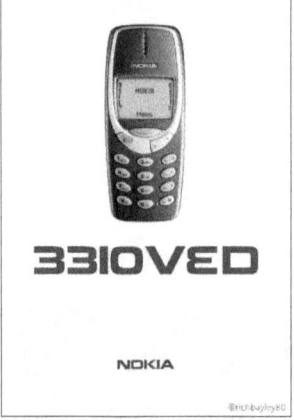

3310VED

NOKIA

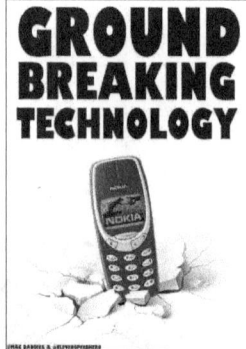

GROUND BREAKING TECHNOLOGY

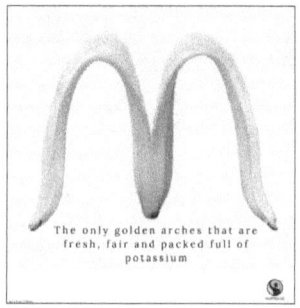

The only golden arches that are fresh, fair and packed full of potassium

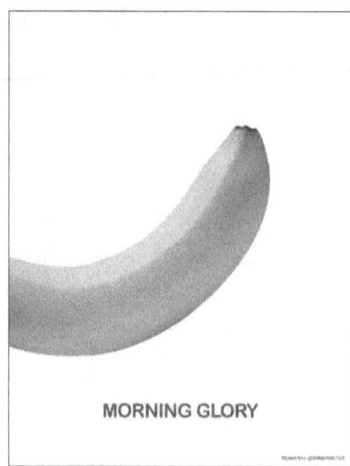

MORNING GLORY

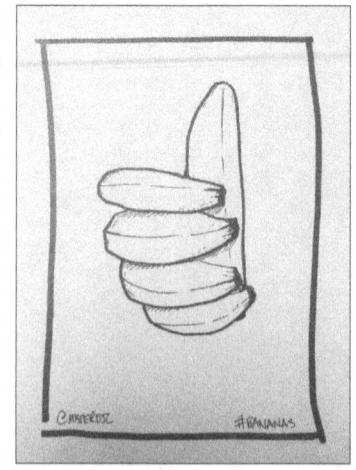

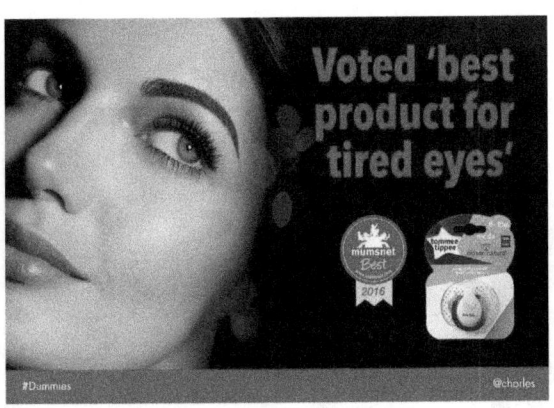

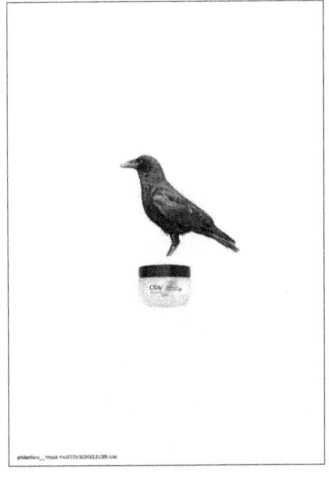

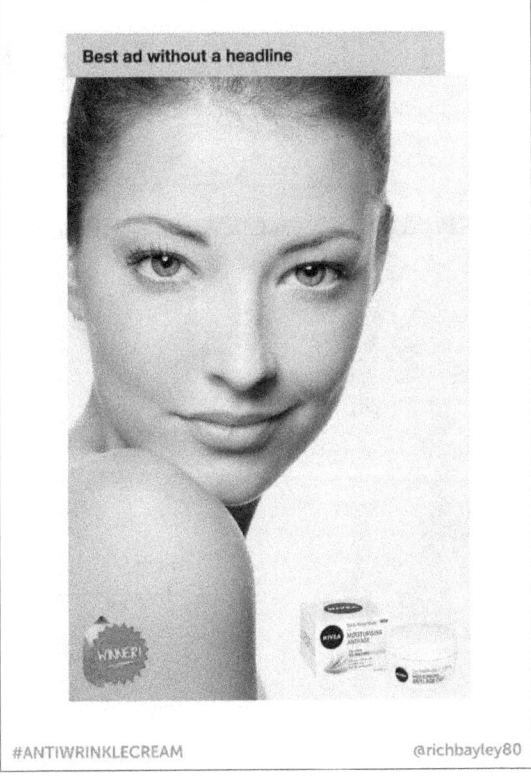

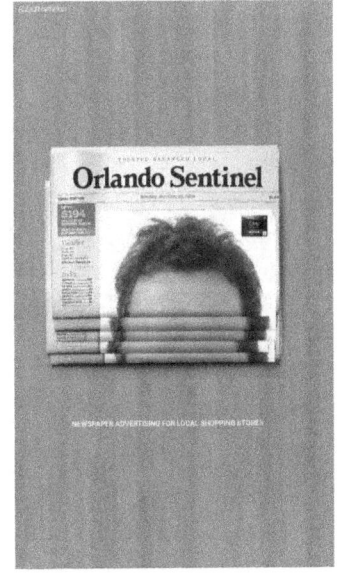

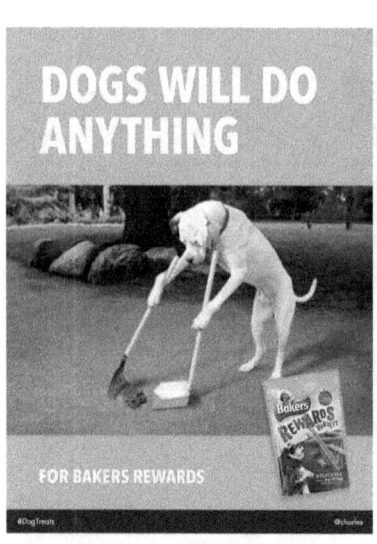
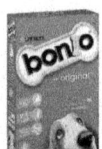
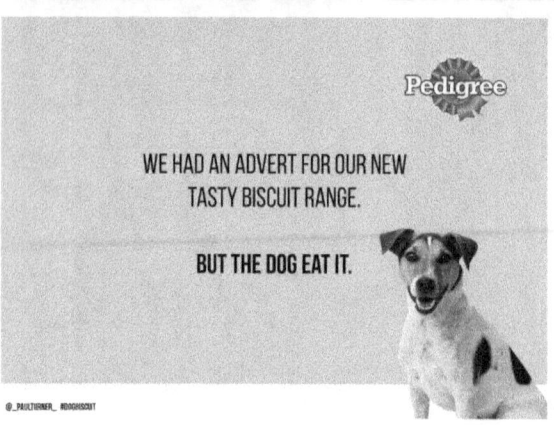
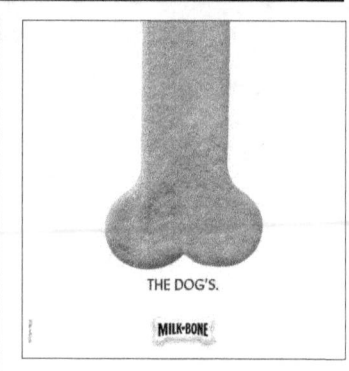

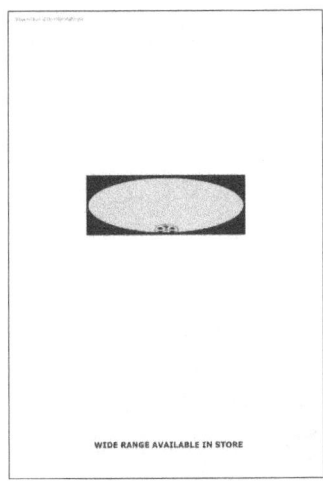

WIDE RANGE AVAILABLE IN STORE

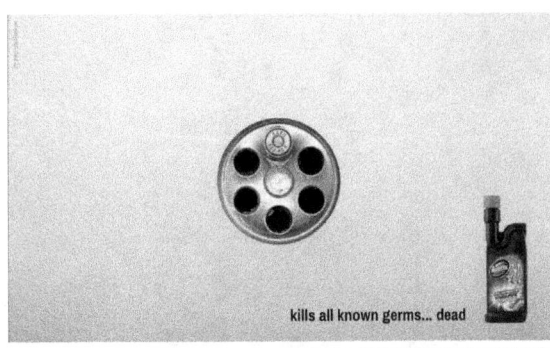

kills all known germs... dead

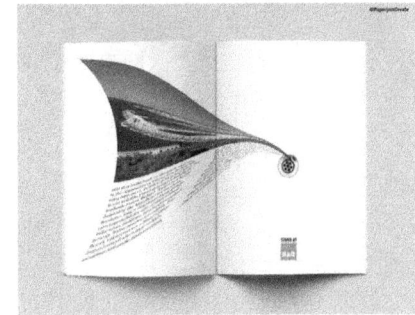

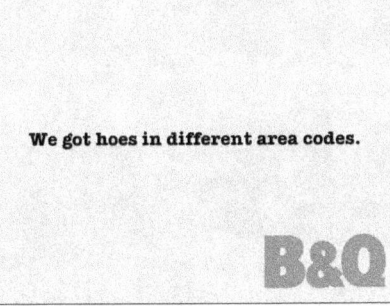

We got hoes in different area codes.

B&Q

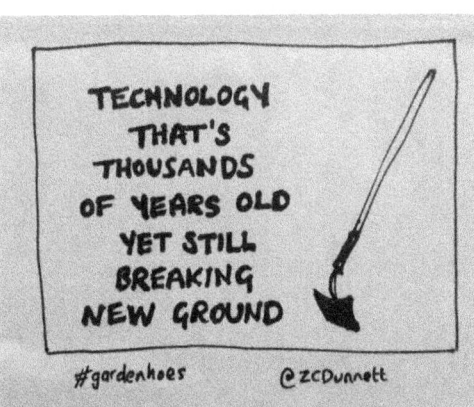

TECHNOLOGY
THAT'S
THOUSANDS
OF YEARS OLD
YET STILL
BREAKING
NEW GROUND

#gardenhoes   @ZCDunnett

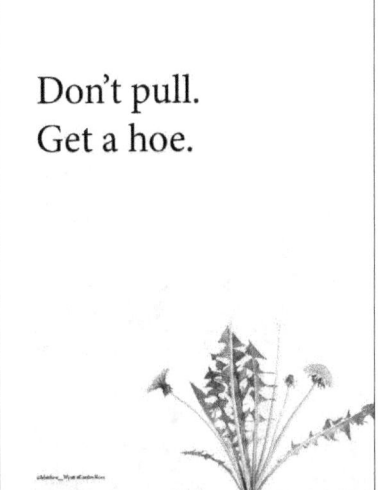

Don't pull.
Get a hoe.

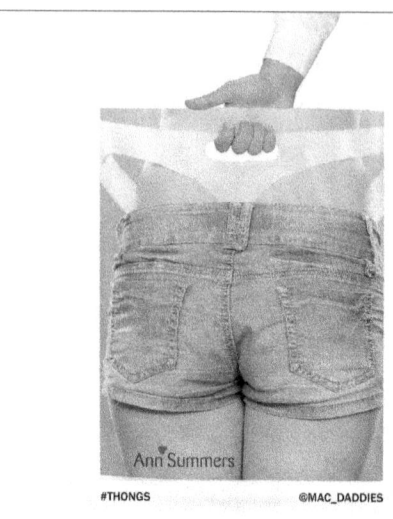

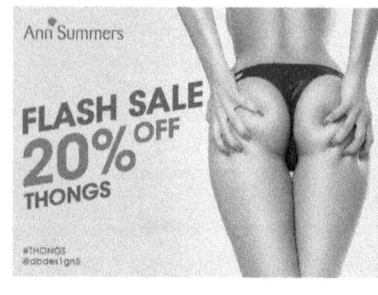

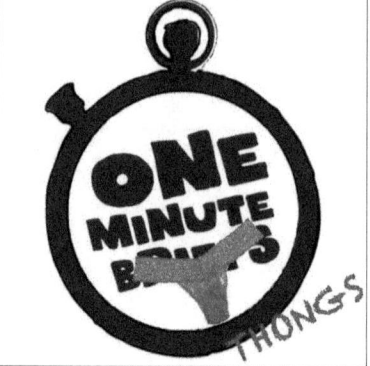

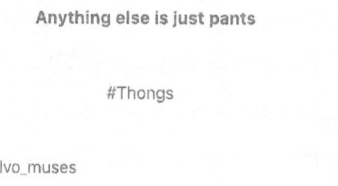

Anything else is just pants

#Thongs

@alvo_muses

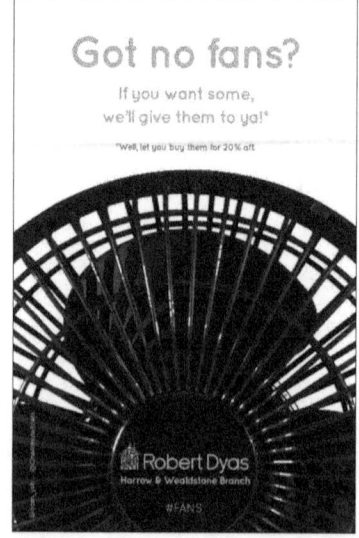

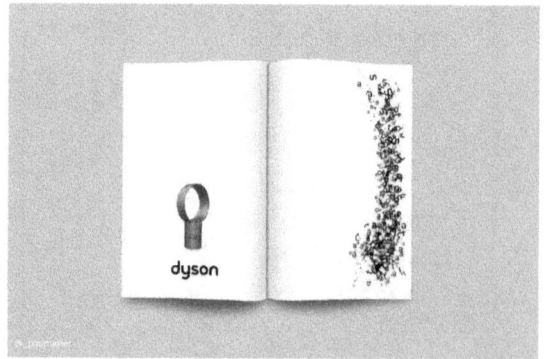

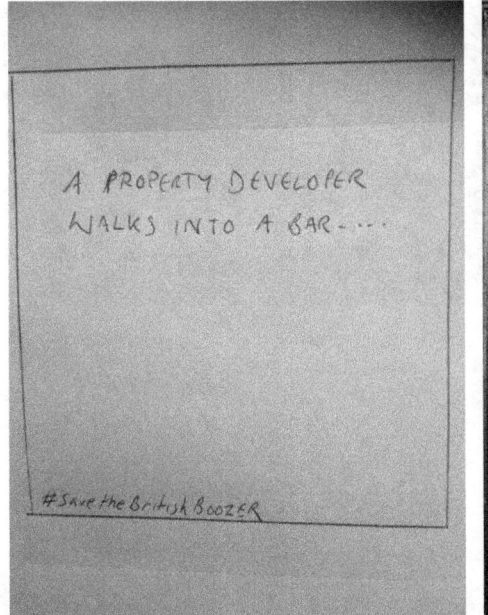

A PROPERTY DEVELOPER
WALKS INTO A BAR....

#Save the British Boozer

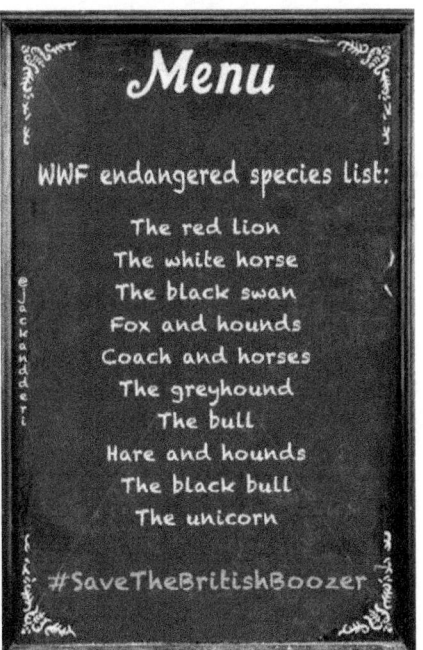

Menu

WWF endangered species list:

The red lion
The white horse
The black swan
Fox and hounds
Coach and horses
The greyhound
The bull
Hare and hounds
The black bull
The unicorn

#SaveTheBritishBoozer

@jackndderi

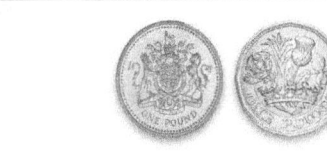

BETTER. POUND FOR POUND.

@olvo_muses   #PoundCoin

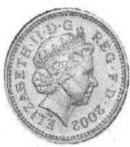

Get one before they're
dodecagone!

@_Lynton

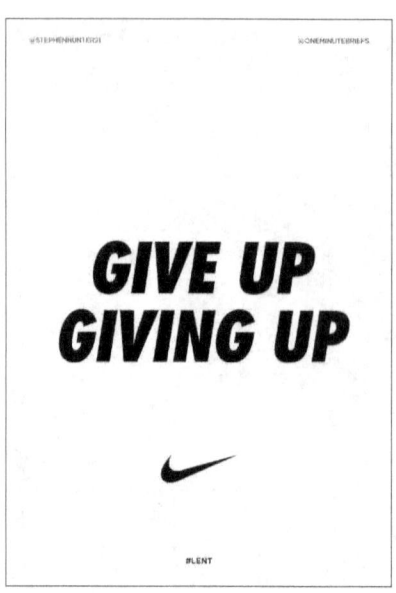

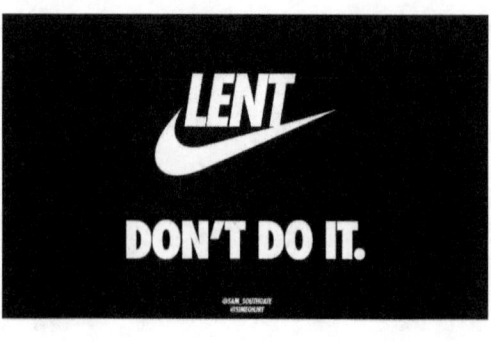

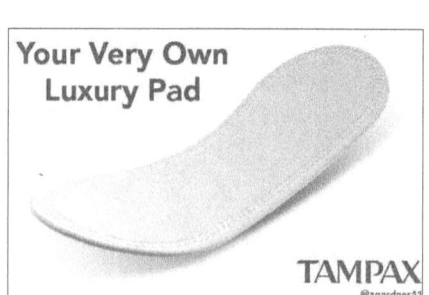

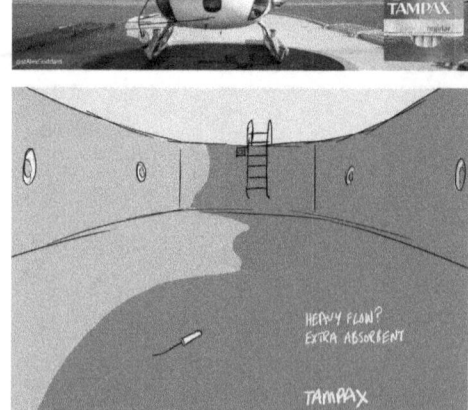

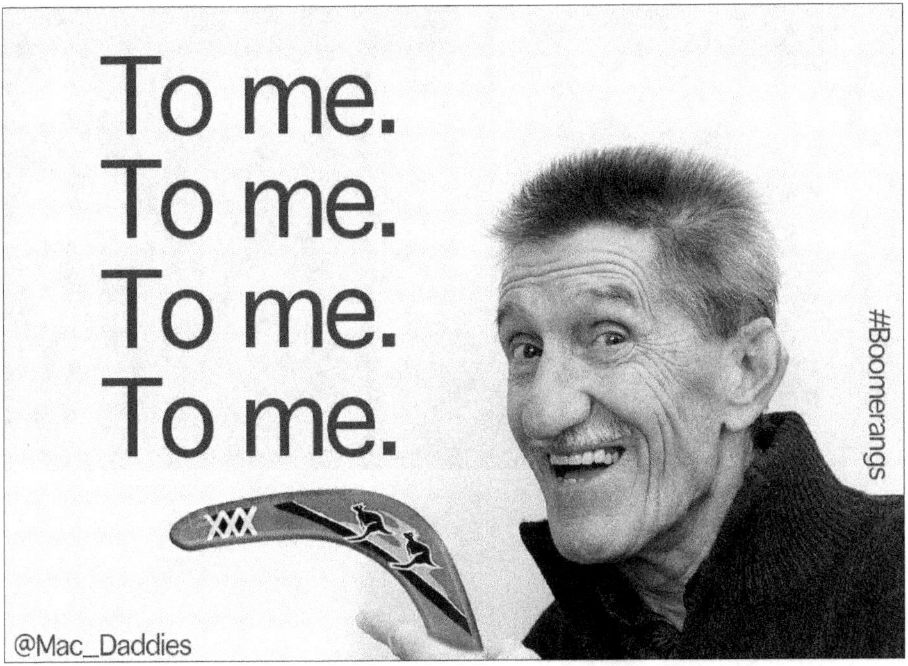

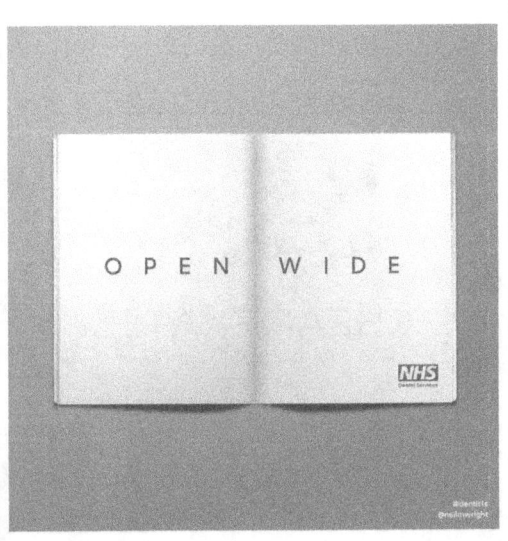

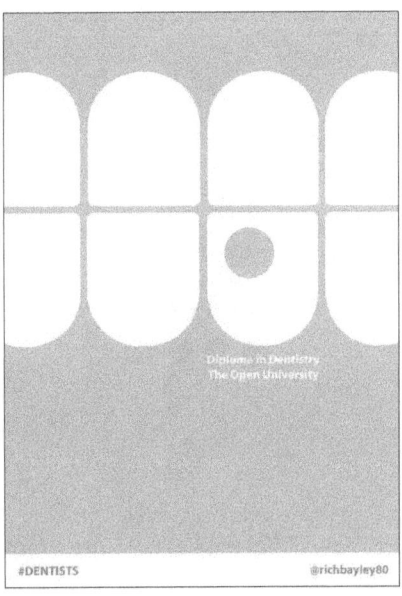

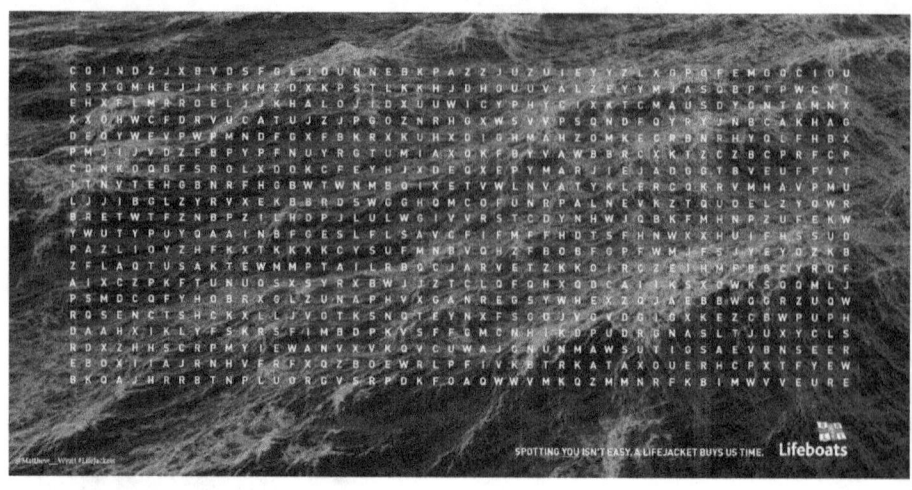

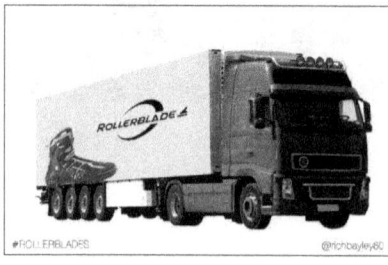

Get your skates on!
I day rollerblade flash sale

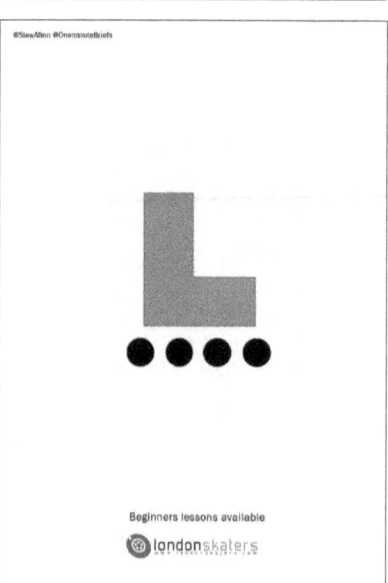

Beginners lessons available

londonskaters

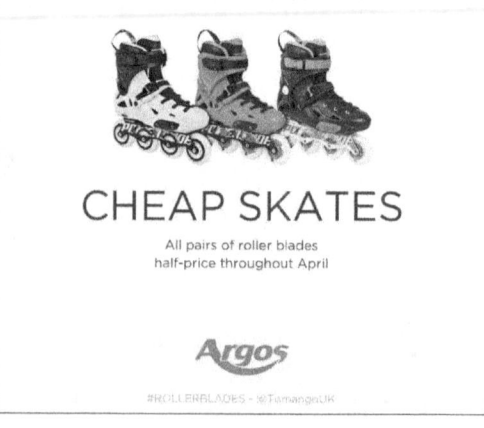

CHEAP SKATES

All pairs of roller blades
half-price throughout April

Argos

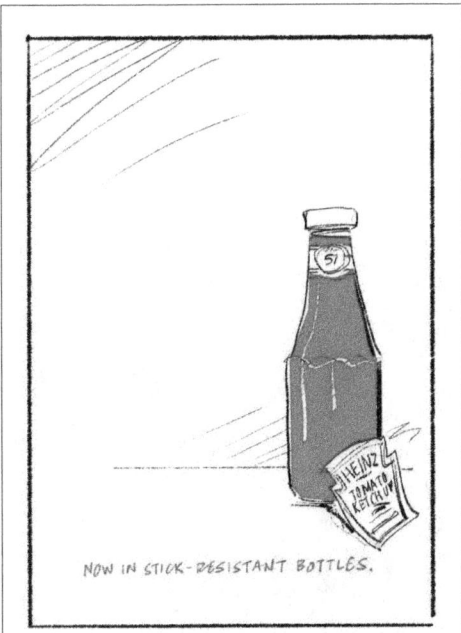

NOW IN STICK-RESISTANT BOTTLES.

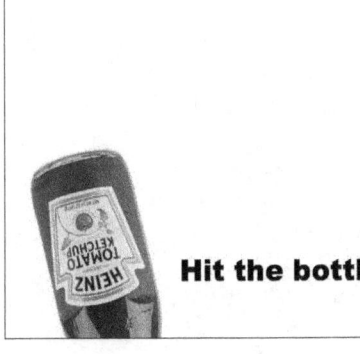

Hit the bottle

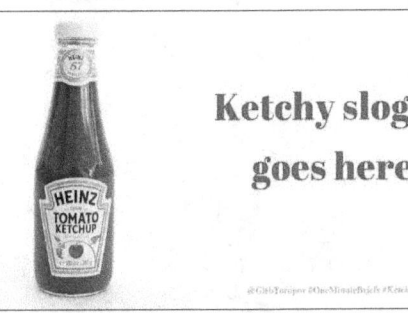

Ketchy slogan
goes here...

@GirlsEuropov 10neMinuteBriefs #Ketchup

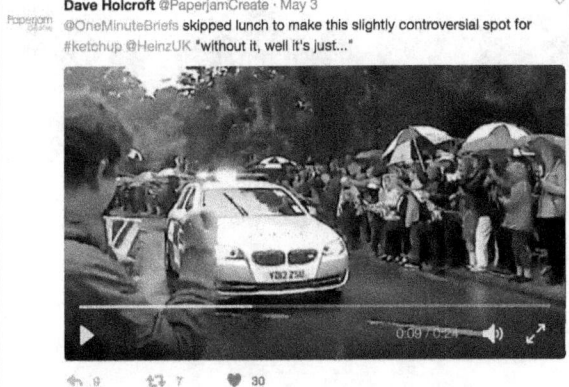

You Retweeted

Dave Holcroft @PaperjamCreate · May 3

@OneMinuteBriefs skipped lunch to make this slightly controversial spot for #ketchup @HeinzUK "without it, well it's just..."

0:09 / 0:24

9   7   30

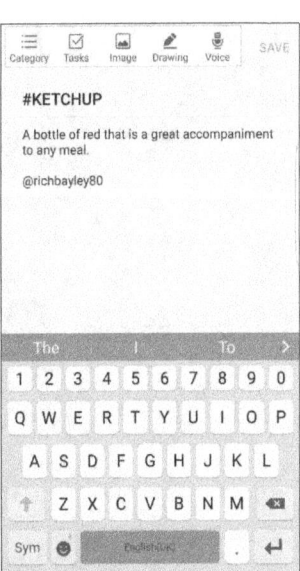

Category   Tasks   Image   Drawing   Voice   SAVE

#KETCHUP

A bottle of red that is a great accompaniment to any meal.

@richbayley80

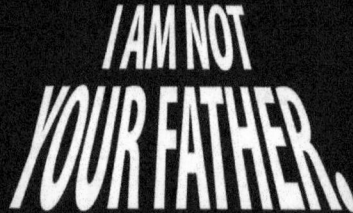

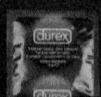

Pneumonia? Don't bother going to the doctors, those pills will only make you worse

You wouldn't speak to someone with pneumonia like this. So why should someone with anxiety or depression be any different?

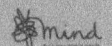

Parkinson's? I think it's all in your head

You wouldn't speak to someone with Parkinson's like this. So why should someone with anxiety or depression be any different?

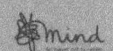

Diabetes? I'm not being funny, but is that even a real illness?

You wouldn't speak to someone with diabetes like this. So why should someone with anxiety or depression be any different?

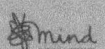

Cancer? Just try thinking positively and I'm sure you'll be fine

You wouldn't speak to someone with cancer like this. So why should someone with anxiety or depression be any different?

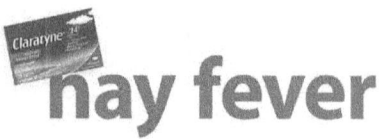

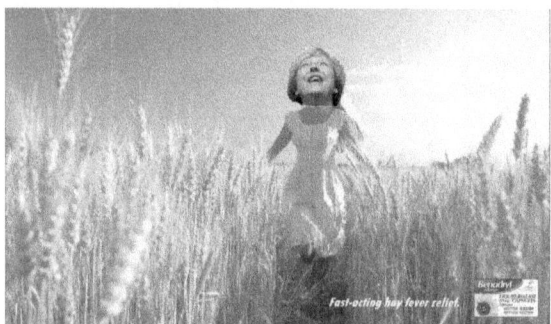

Fast-acting hay fever relief.

Aah...

Aahh....

Aahhhh...

ahhhhhhhhhh, that's better.

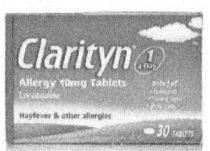

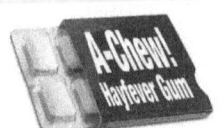

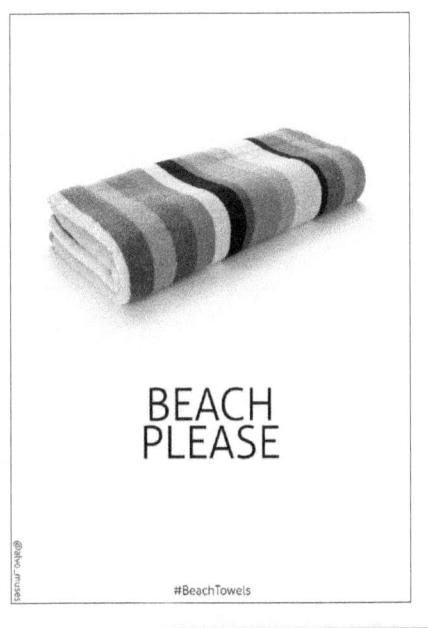

BEACH
PLEASE

#BeachTowels

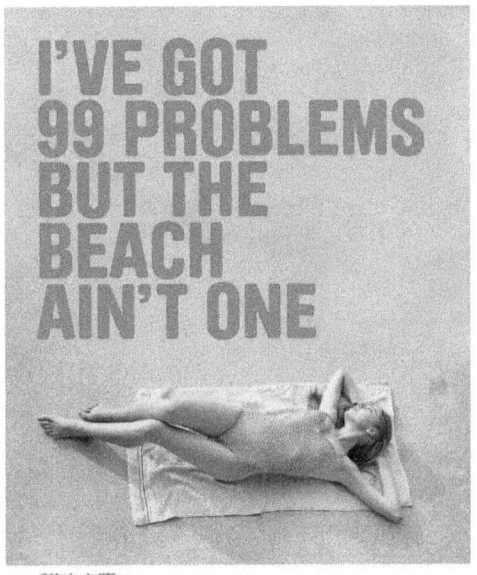

I'VE GOT
99 PROBLEMS
BUT THE
BEACH
AIN'T ONE

@timjsutcliffe

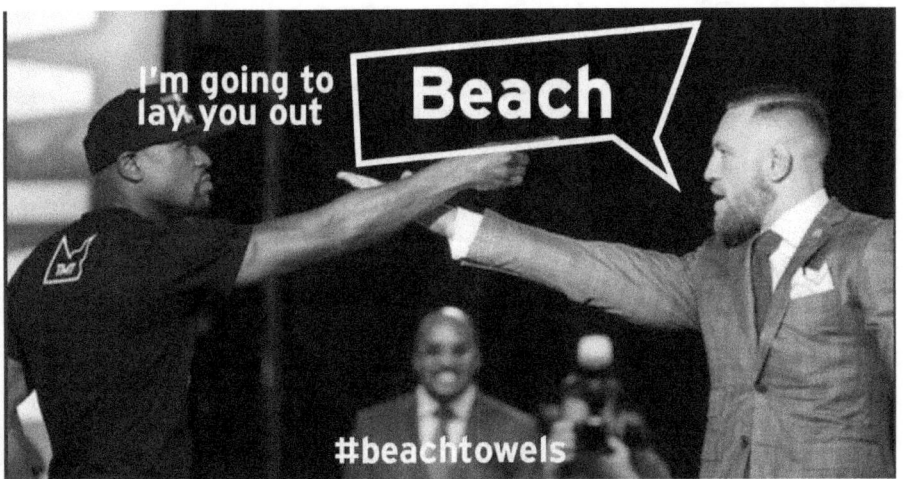

I'm going to
lay you out

Beach

#beachtowels

Geddit down yer

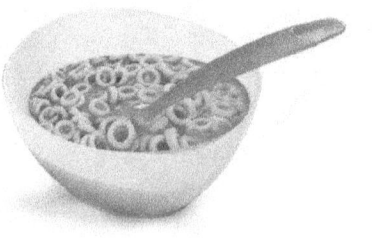

#bibs

@mattoakleymojo

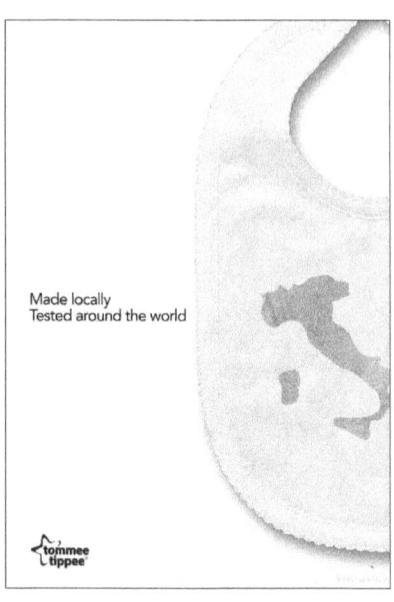

Made locally
Tested around the world

tommee
tippee

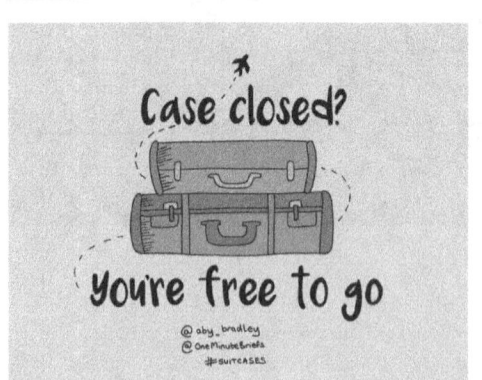

Case closed?

you're free to go

@ aby_bradley
@ OneMinuteBriefs
#SUITCASES

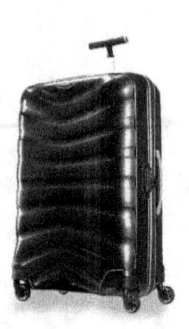

Best case scenario

Samsonite

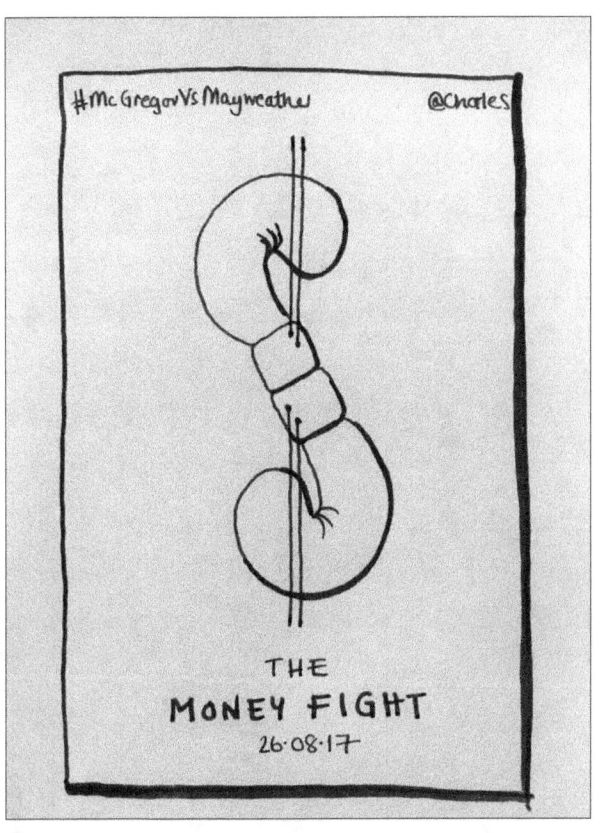

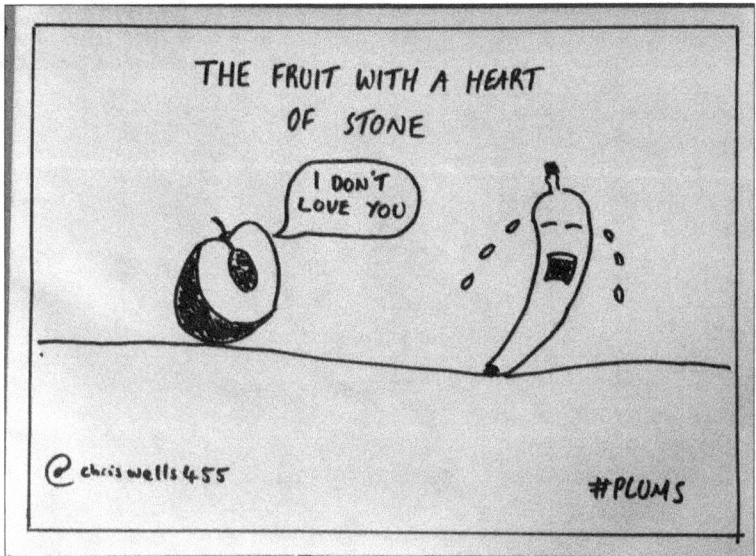

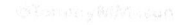

Roll on Amsterdam
Joint flights from £420

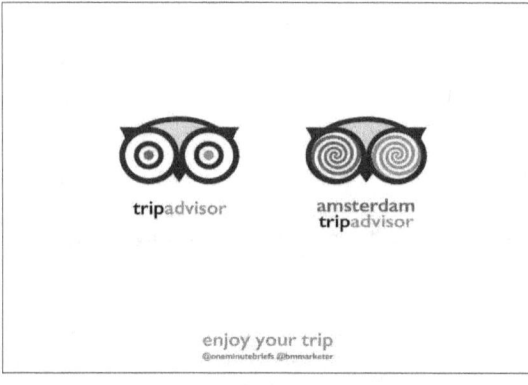

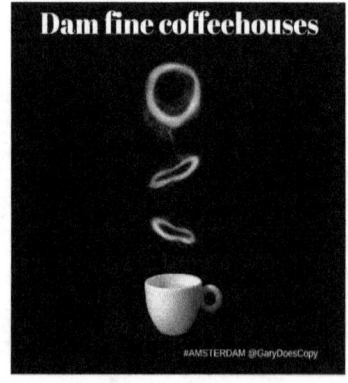

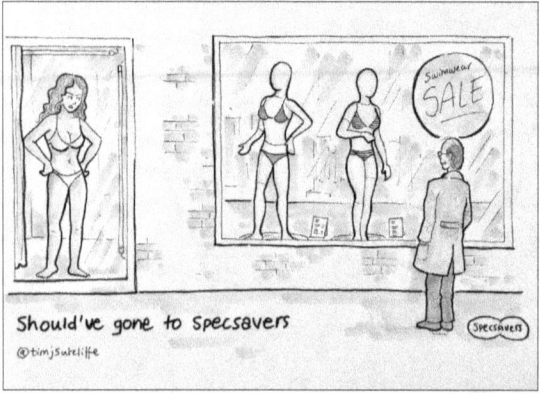

Four king good fun

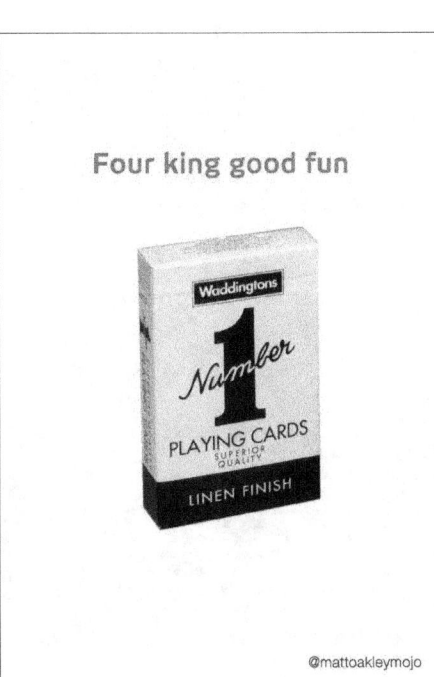

Waddingtons

Number **1**

PLAYING CARDS
SUPERIOR QUALITY

LINEN FINISH

@mattoakleymojo

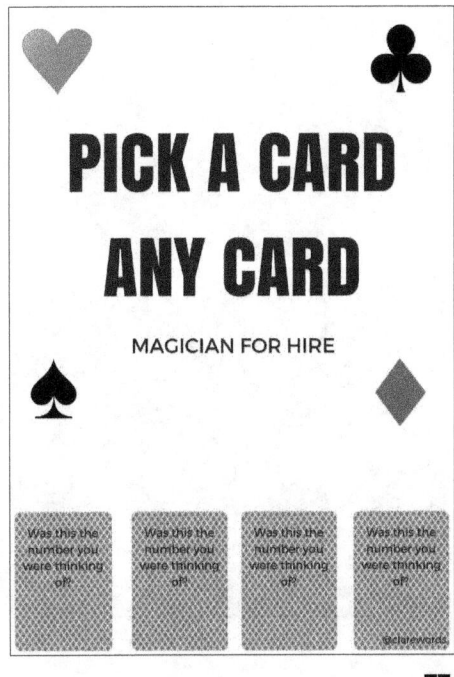

PICK A CARD
ANY CARD

MAGICIAN FOR HIRE

Was this the
number you
were thinking
of?

Was this the
number you
were thinking
of?

Was this the
number you
were thinking
of?

Was this the
number you
were thinking
of?

@clarewords

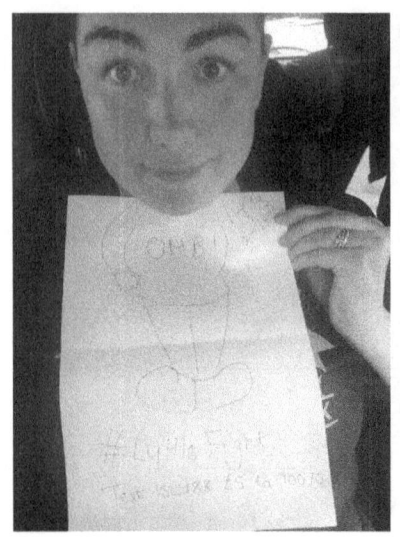

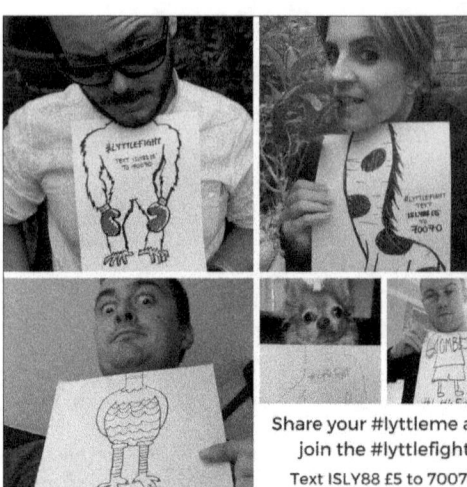

Share your #lyttleme and
join the #lyttlefight

Text ISLY88 £5 to 70070

@solvekidscancer

A Lyttle goes a long way

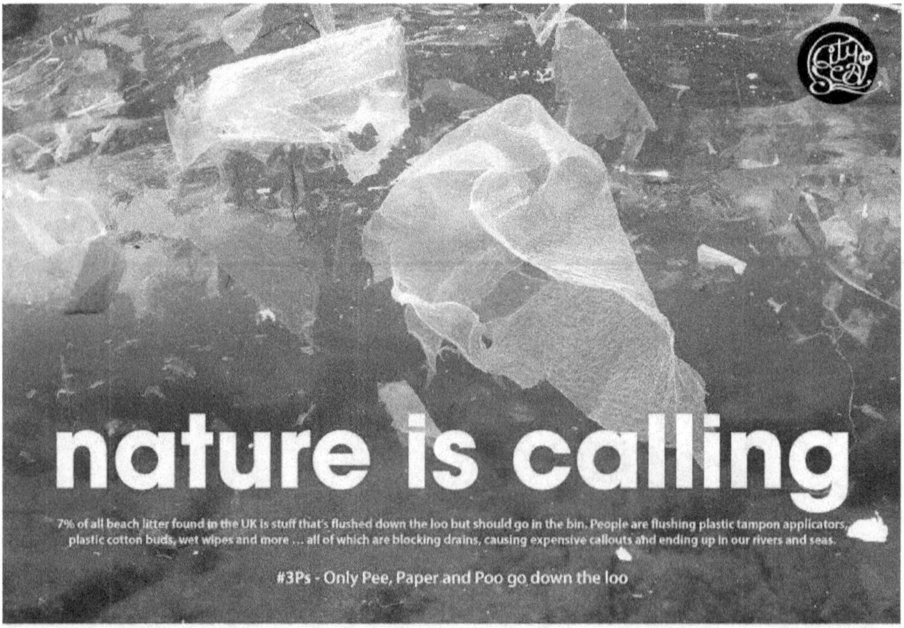

nature is calling

7% of all beach litter found in the UK is stuff that's flushed down the loo but should go in the bin. People are flushing plastic tampon applicators, plastic cotton buds, wet wipes and more … all of which are blocking drains, causing expensive callouts and ending up in our rivers and seas.

#3Ps - Only Pee, Paper and Poo go down the loo

@richbayley80

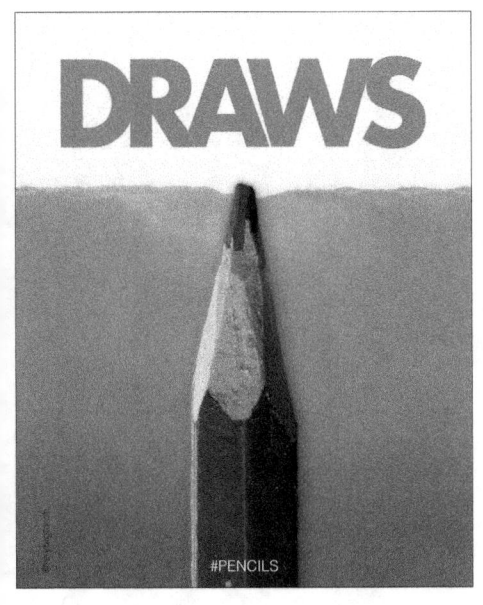

#PENCILS

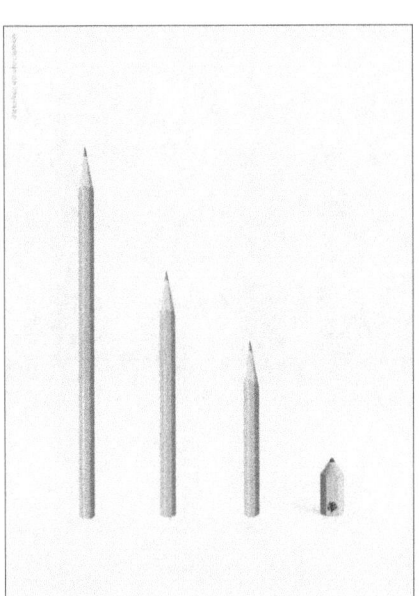

*Every great idea begins
and ends with a pencil.*

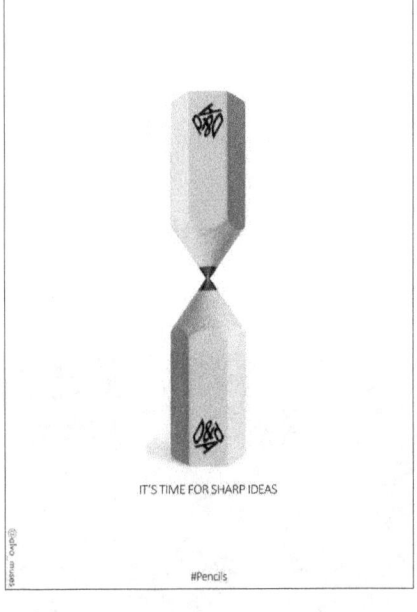

IT'S TIME FOR SHARP IDEAS

#Pencils

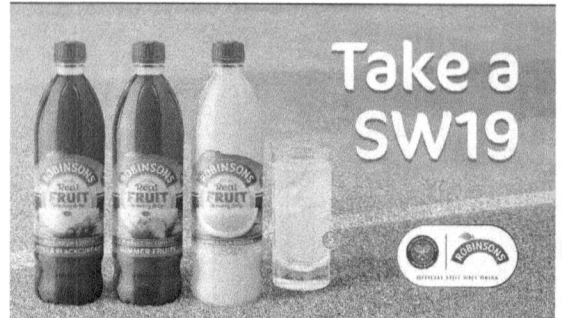

#Wimbledon
@chorles

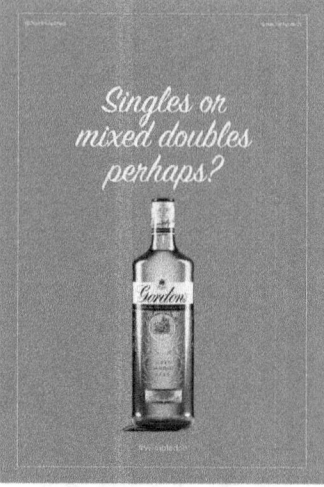

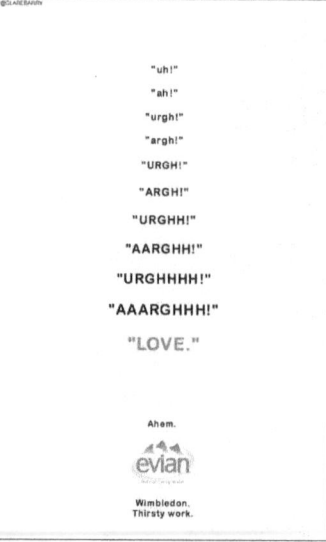

"uh!"

"ah!"

"urgh!"

"argh!"

"URGH!"

"ARGH!"

"URGHH!"

"AARGHH!"

"URGHHHH!"

"AAARGHHH!"

"LOVE."

Ahem.

evian

Wimbledon.
Thirsty work.

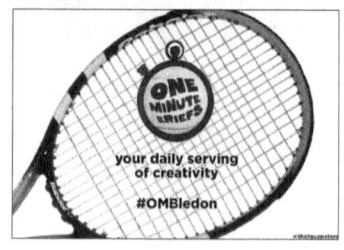

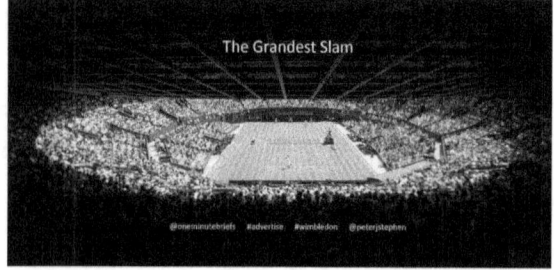

The Grandest Slam

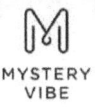
Customer satisfaction.
It is really important to us.

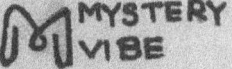

MYSTERY
VIBE

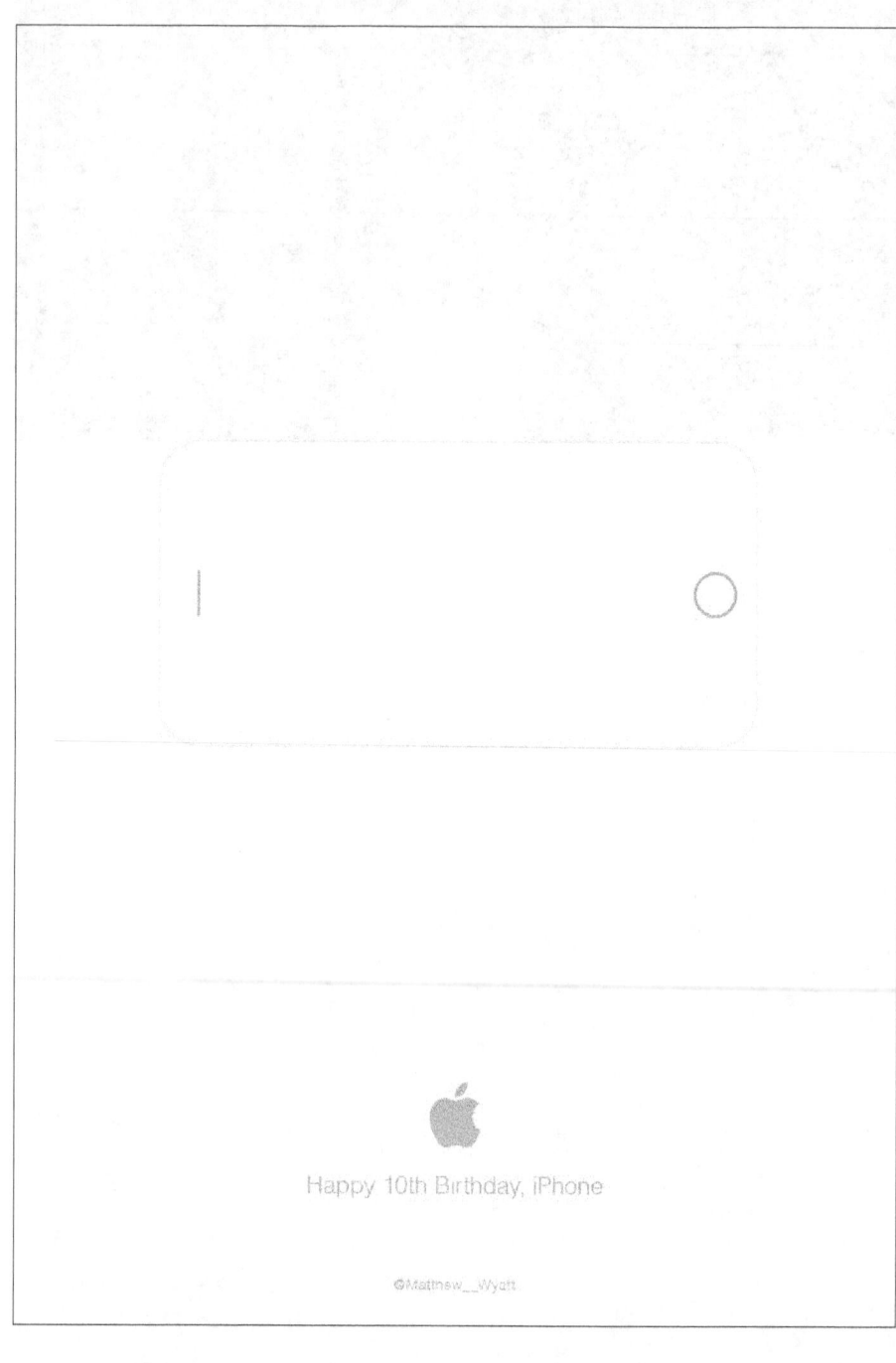

Happy 10th Birthday, iPhone

@Matthew__Wyatt

82.

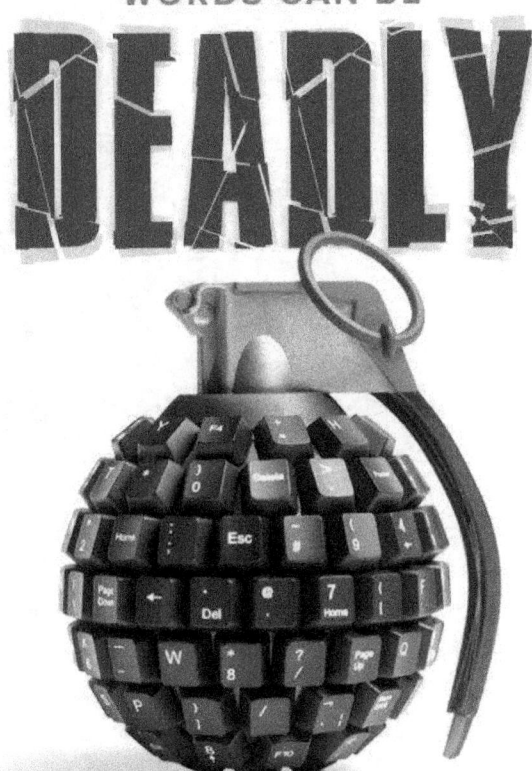

WORDS CAN BE

DEADLY

THINK BEFORE YOU TYPE

THE CYBERSMILE FOUNDATION

#STOPCYBERBULLYINGDAY   16 JUNE 2017

@ONEMINUTEBRIEFS   @CYBERSMILEHQ   @STEVESINYARD

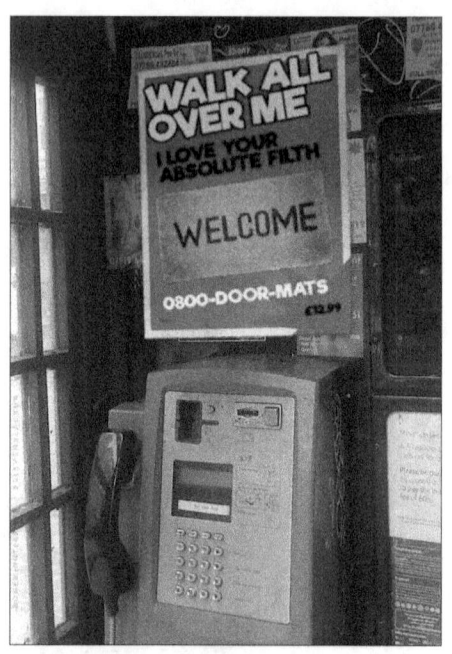

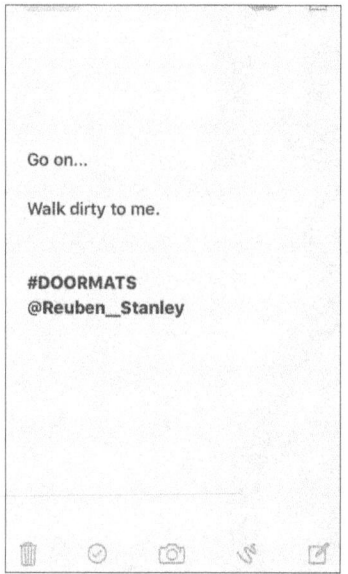

Go on...

Walk dirty to me.

#DOORMATS
@Reuben__Stanley

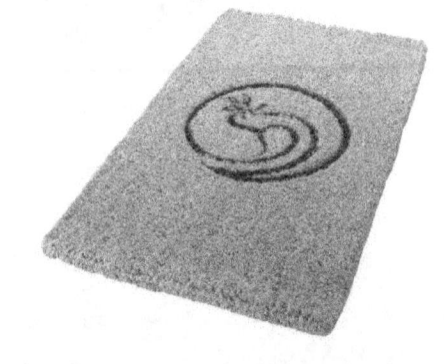

CLEANSE
YOUR SOLE

A robust, **fairly-traded** brush floor mat featuring a **dove of peace**.
Made in India from **environmentally-friendly** tough natural coir;
naturally damp-resistant.

AMNESTY SHOP

#DOORMATS   @chorles

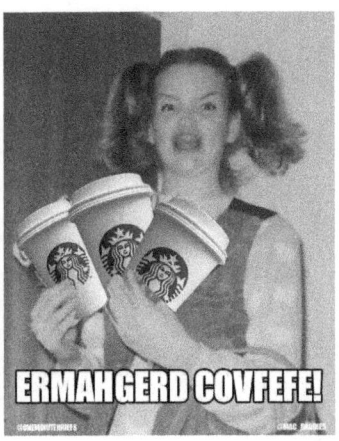

ERMAHGERD COVFEFE!

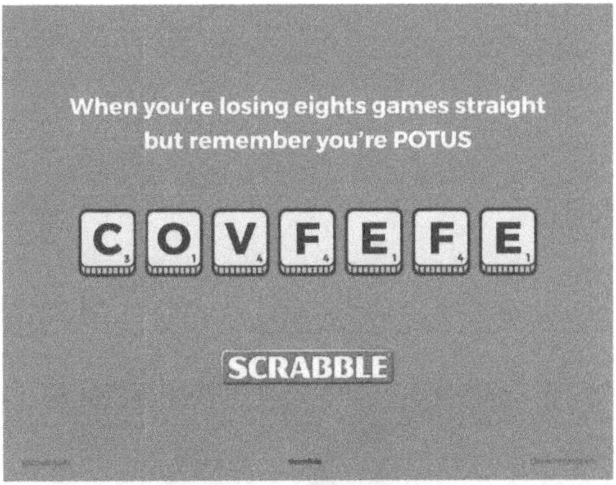

When you're losing eights games straight
but remember you're POTUS

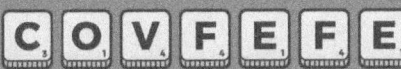

SCRABBLE

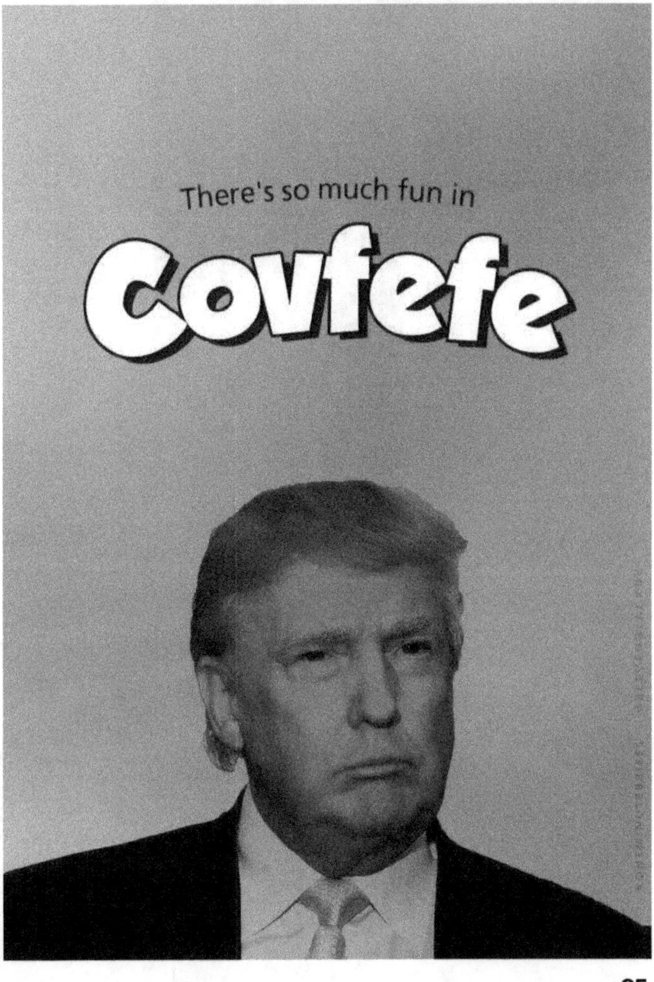

There's so much fun in

Covfefe

DOES MAY **END** IN JUNE?

#HUNGPARLIAMENT

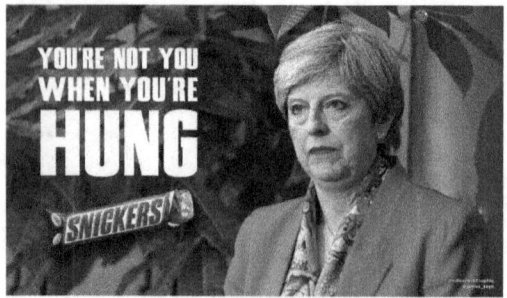

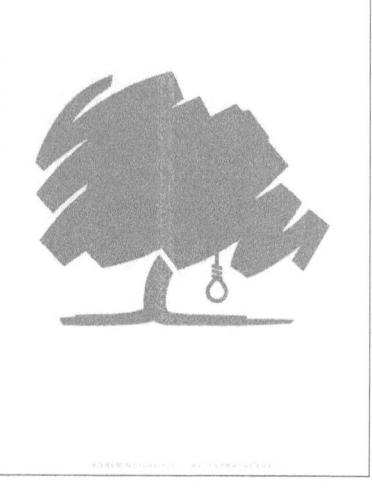

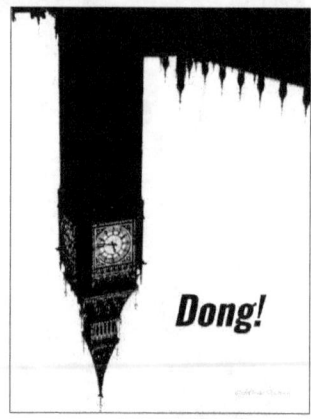

Dong!

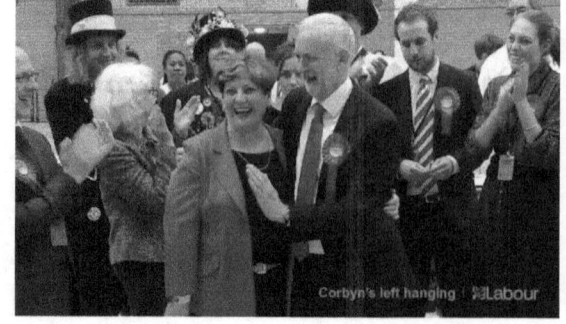

Corbyn's left hanging | Labour

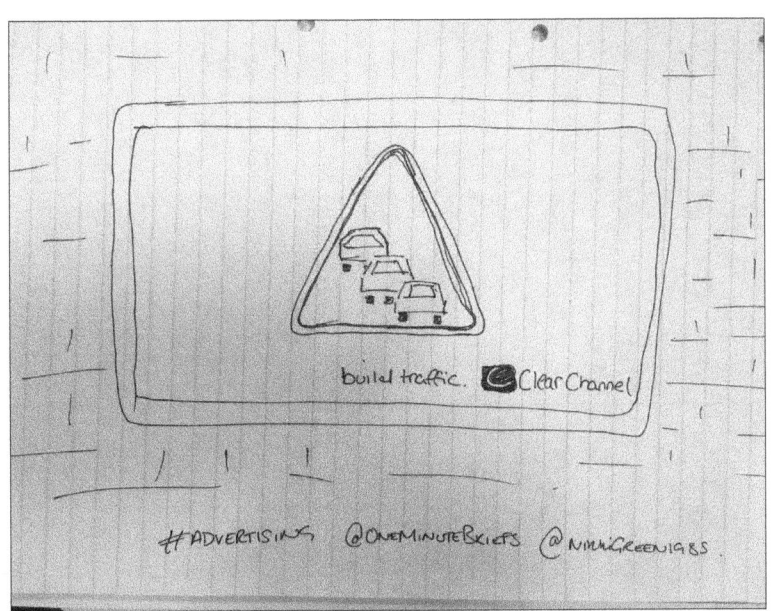

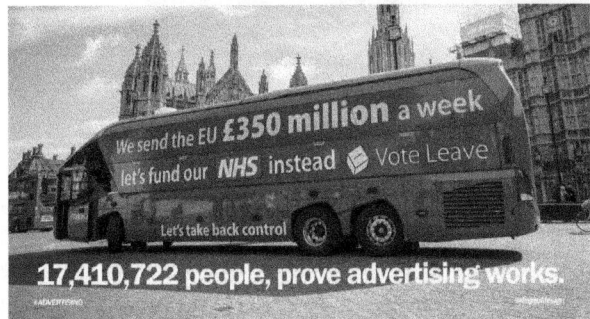

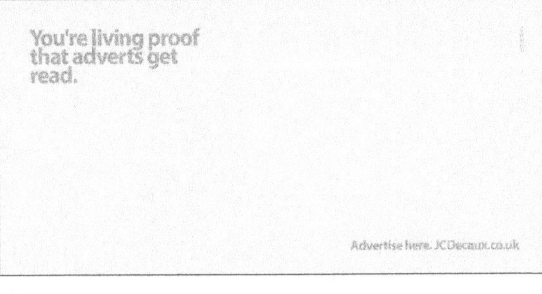

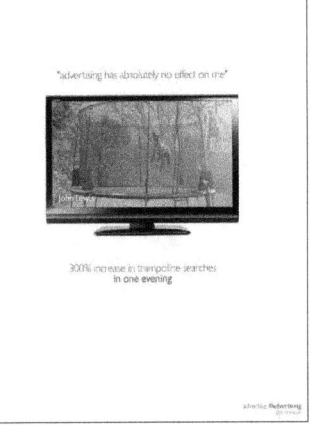

When shit was much simpler

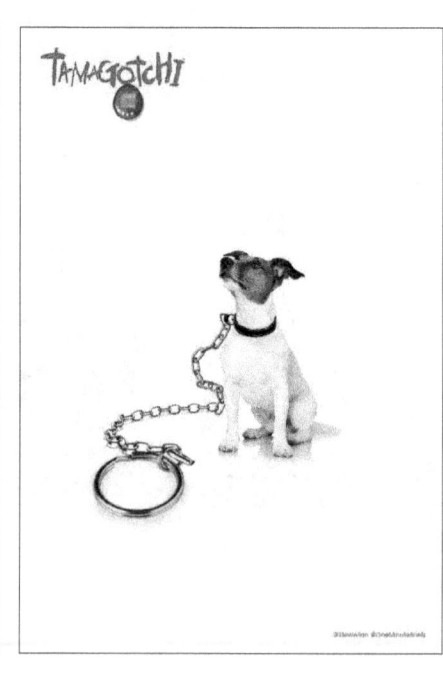

How can I get more vitamins, minerals & antioxidants into my diet?...

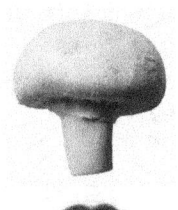

@GaryDoesCopy
#mushrooms

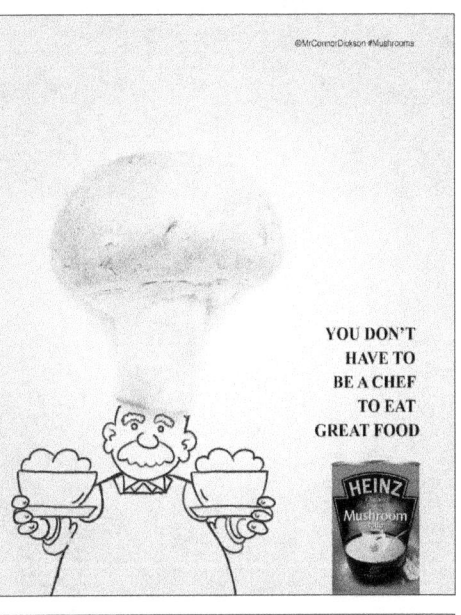

@MrConnorDickson #Mushrooms

YOU DON'T
HAVE TO
BE A CHEF
TO EAT
GREAT FOOD

IT'S THE SHIITAKE

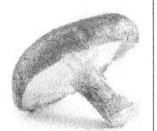

@alvo_muses

#Mushrooms

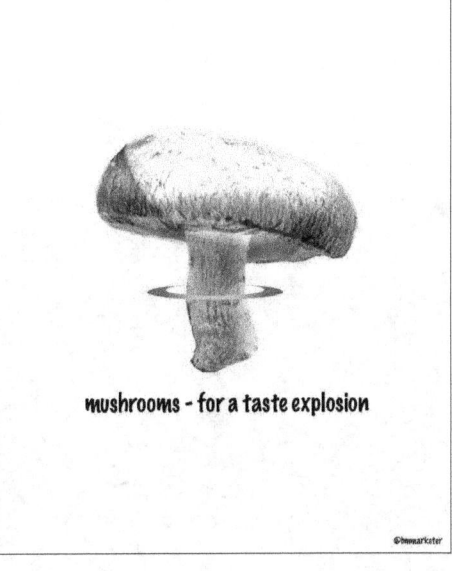

mushrooms - for a taste explosion

@bmnarkater

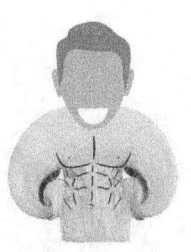

Fighting fat
Tasting great

@clarewords

#mushrooms

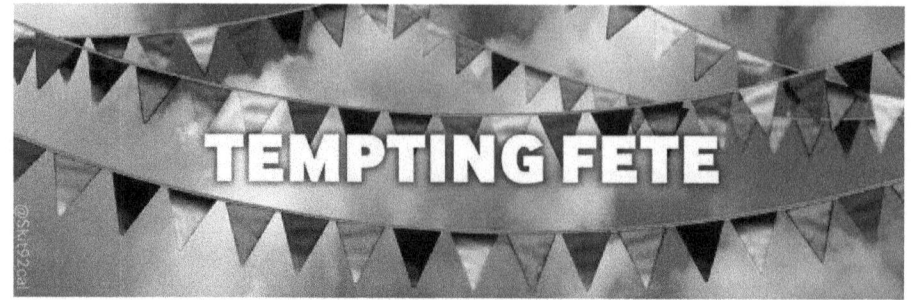

TEMPTING FETE

Bunting by **hobbycraft**

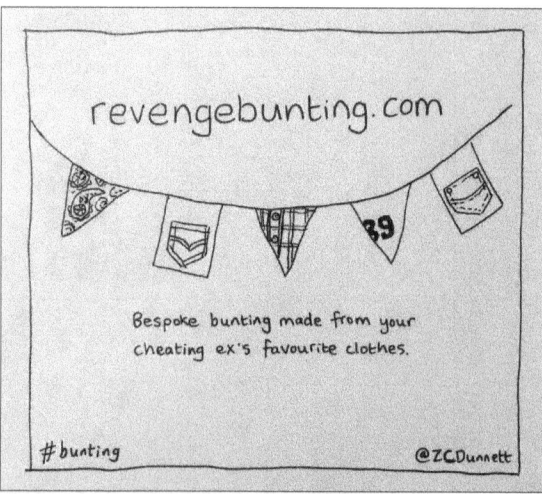

revengebunting.com

Bespoke bunting made from your
cheating ex's favourite clothes.

#bunting   @ZCDunnett

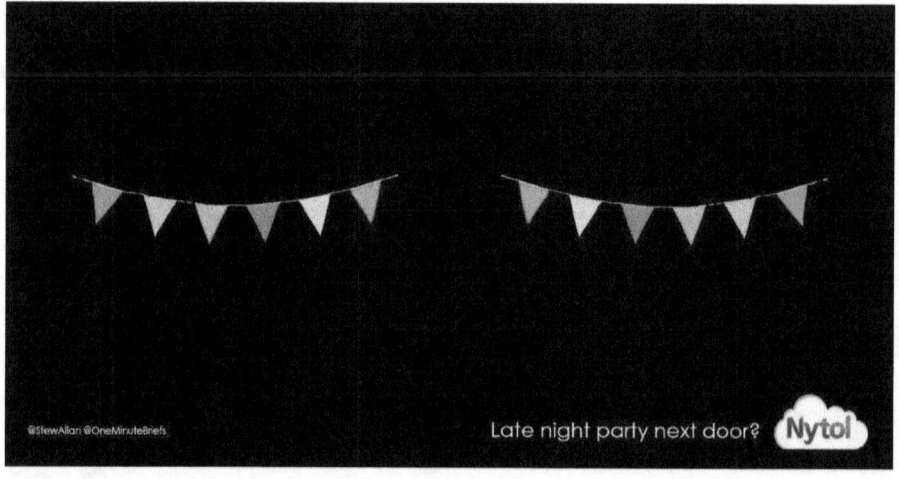

Late night party next door? Nytol

90.

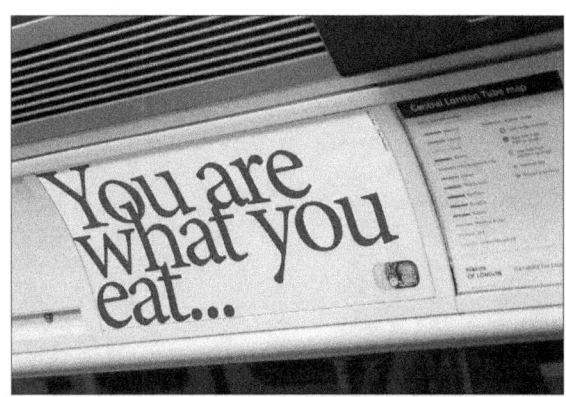

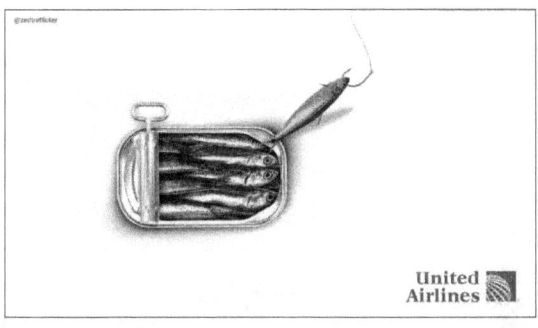

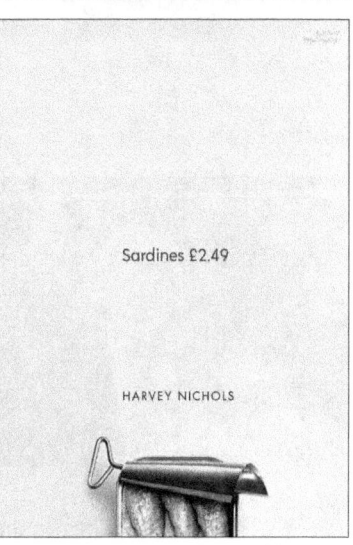

Sardines £2.49

HARVEY NICHOLS

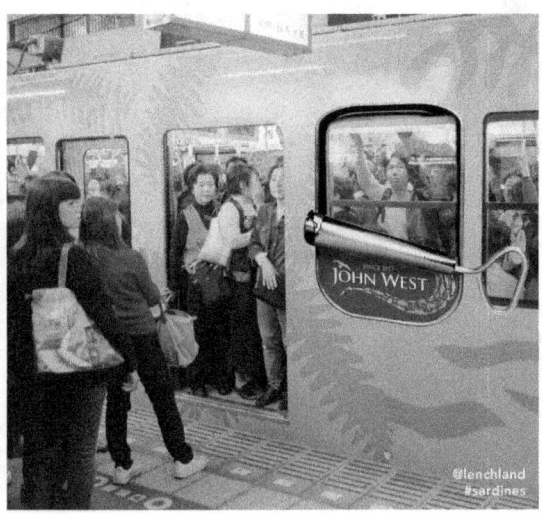

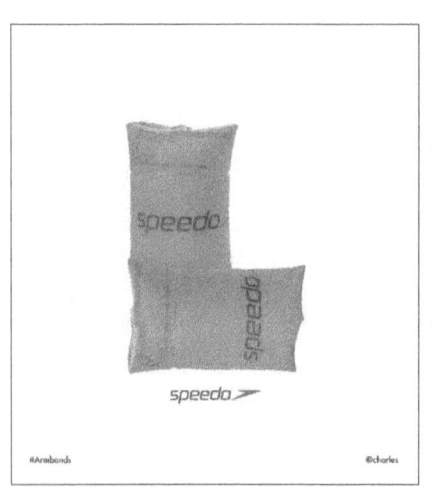

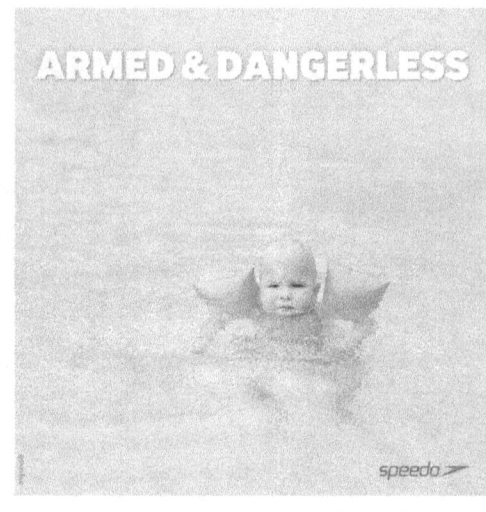

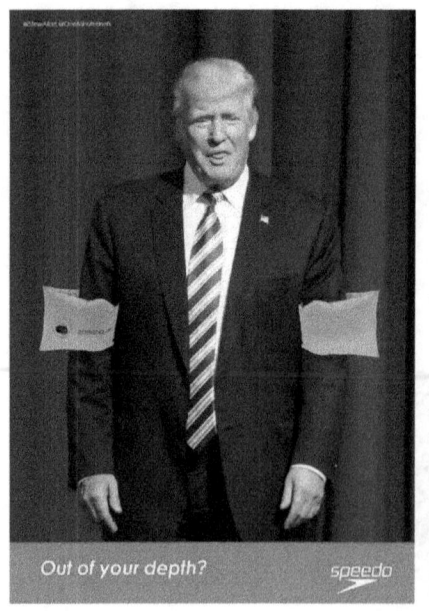

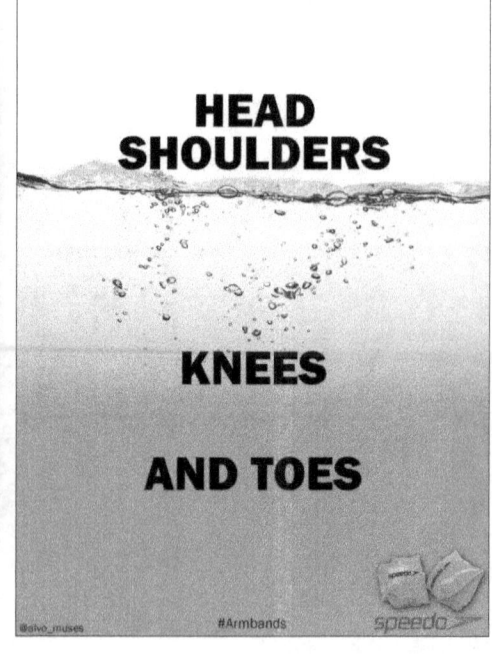

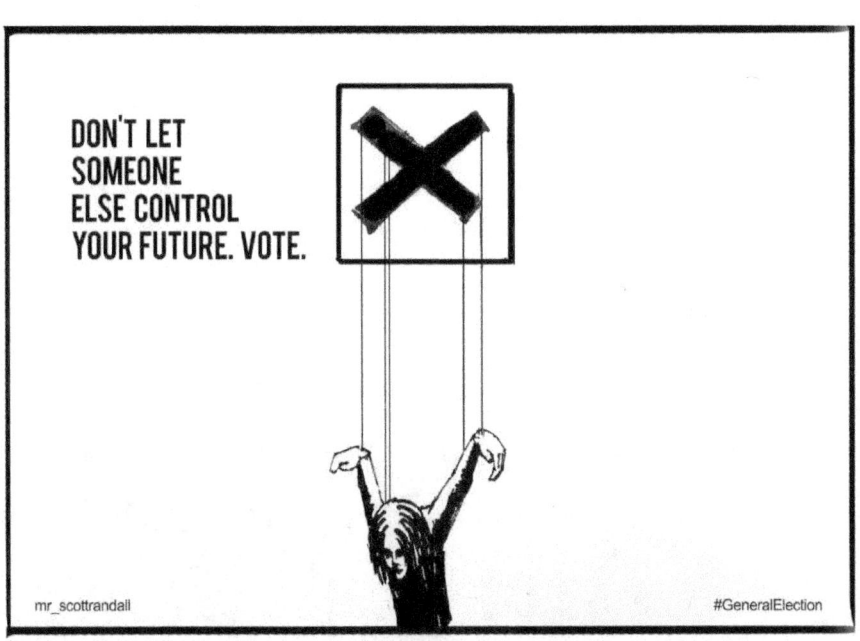

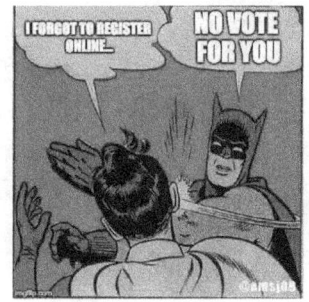

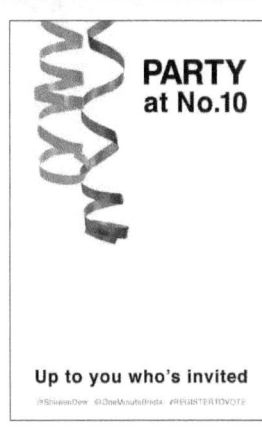

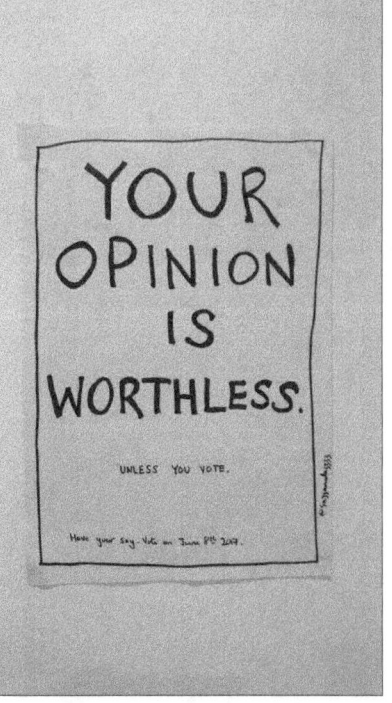

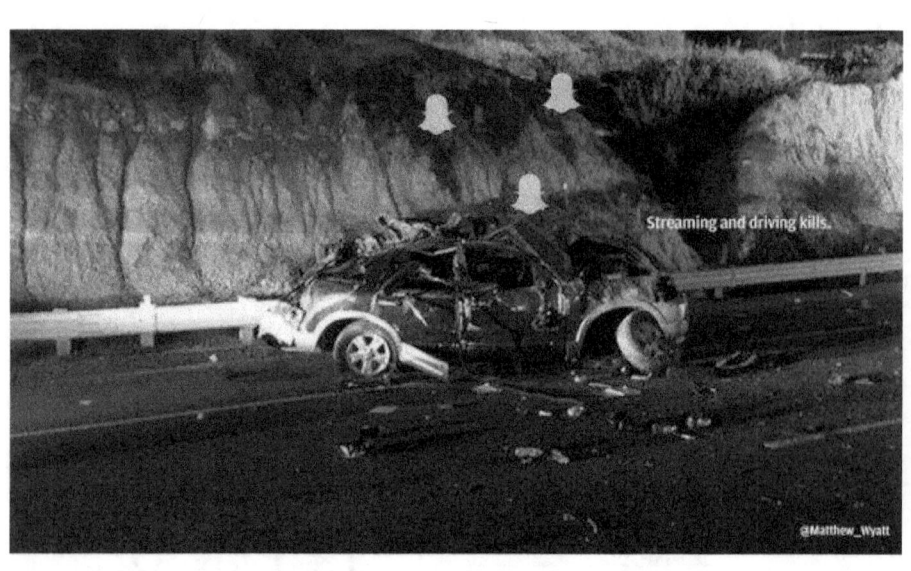

Streaming and driving kills.

@Matthew_Wyatt

94.

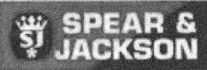

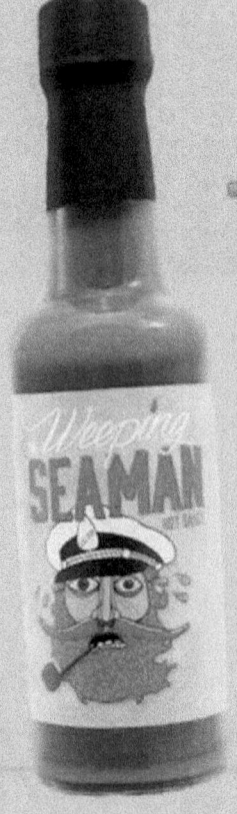

TIP:

KEEP A
SOOTHING
DRINK TO HAND

WE RECOMMEND
TABASCO

@pw_bond

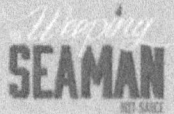

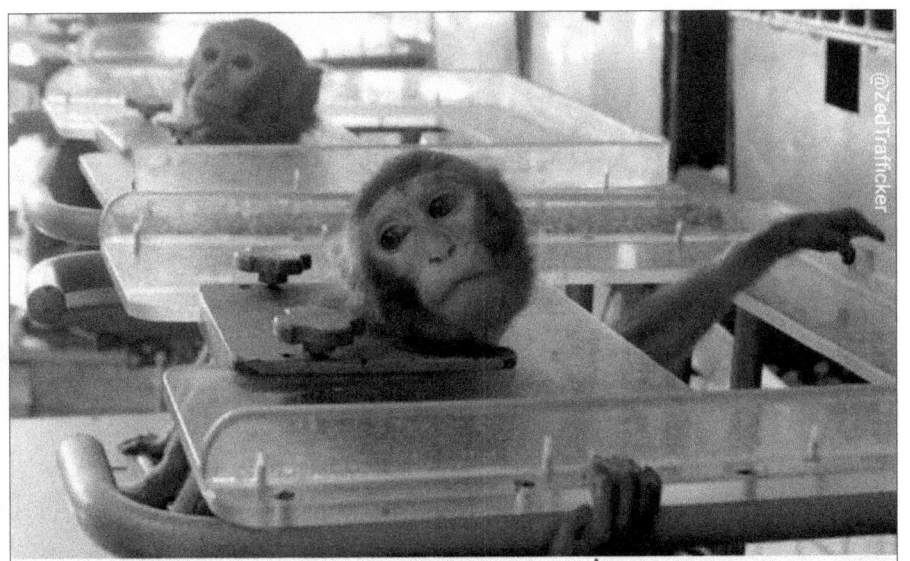

APPRENTLY... BECAUSE YOU'RE WORTH IT

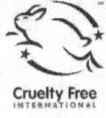

Cruelty Free
INTERNATIONAL

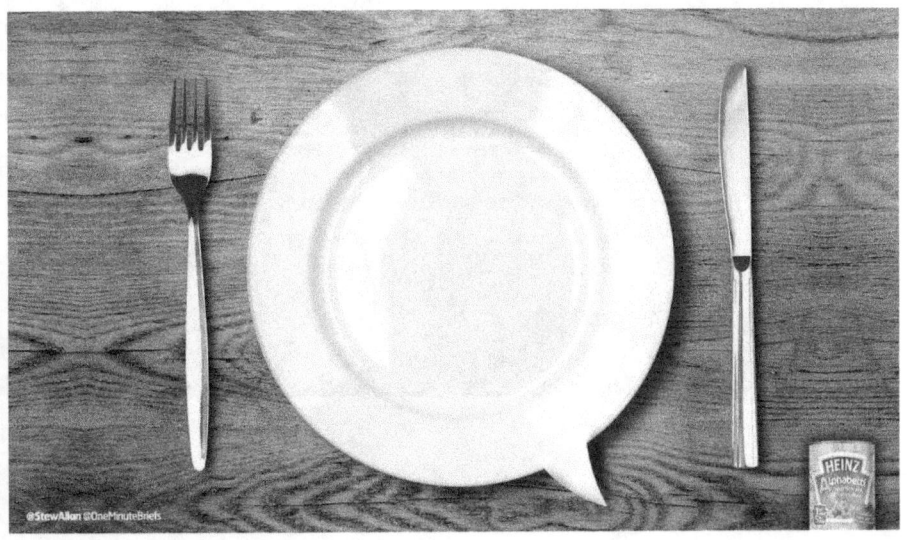

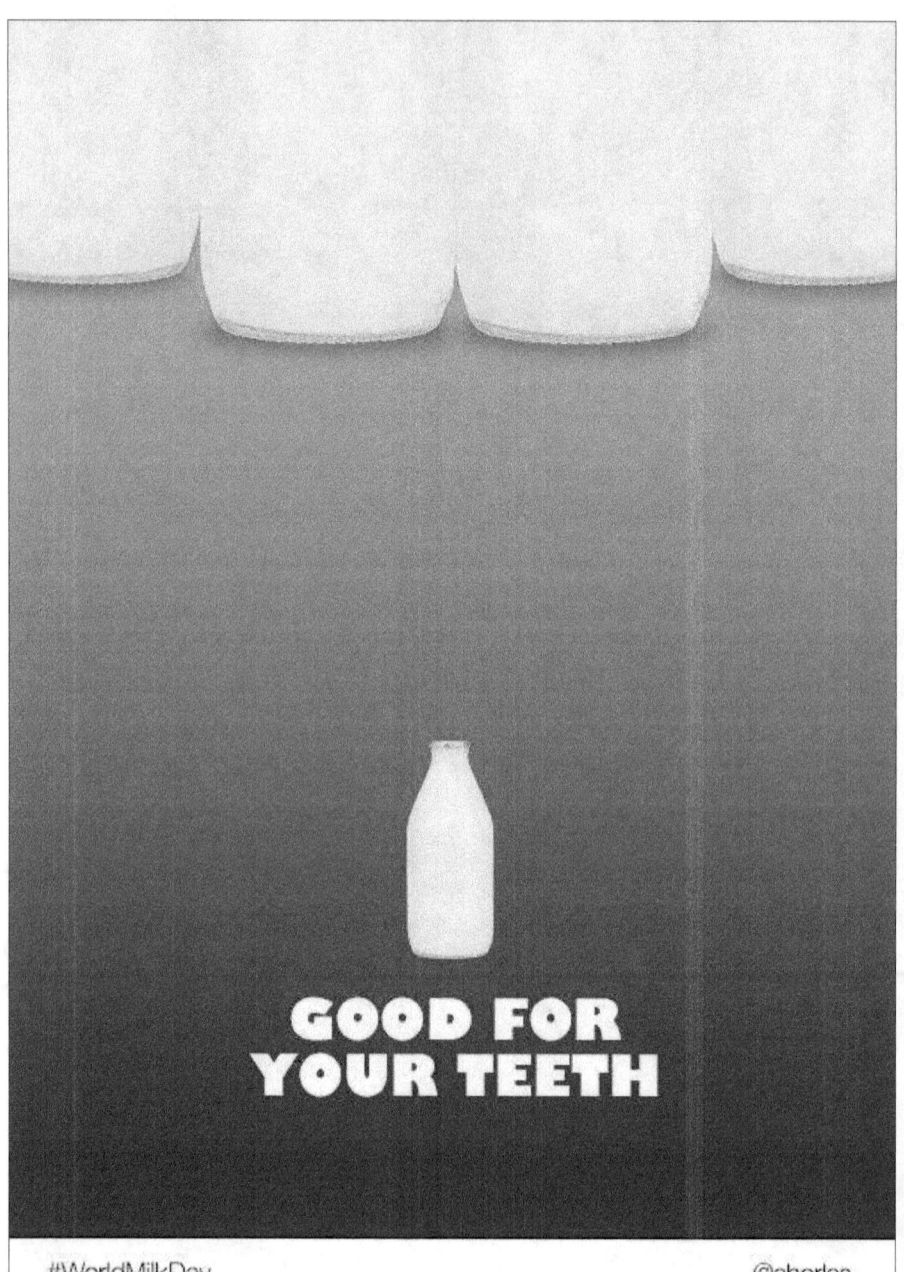

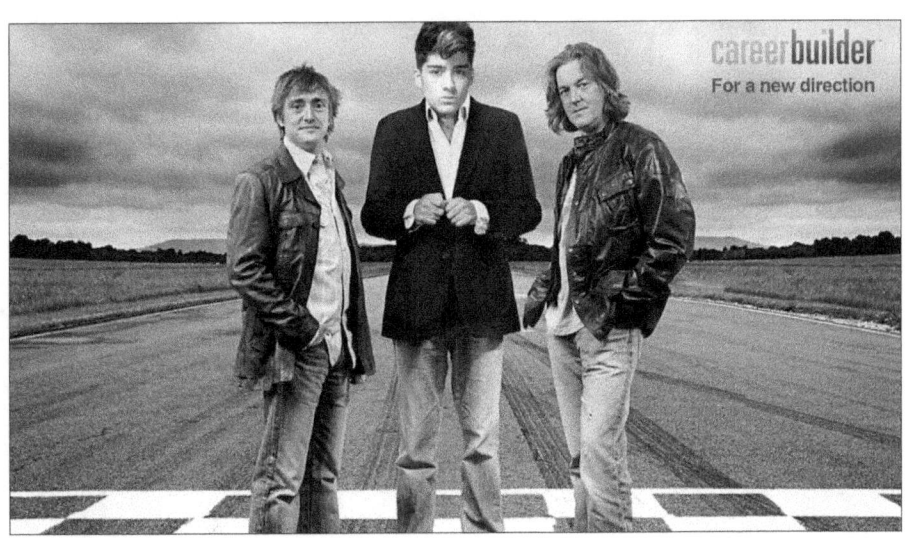

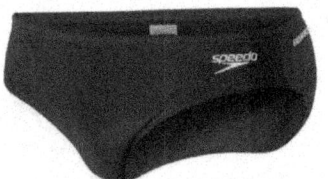

Top on the list when you're packing

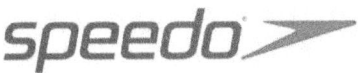

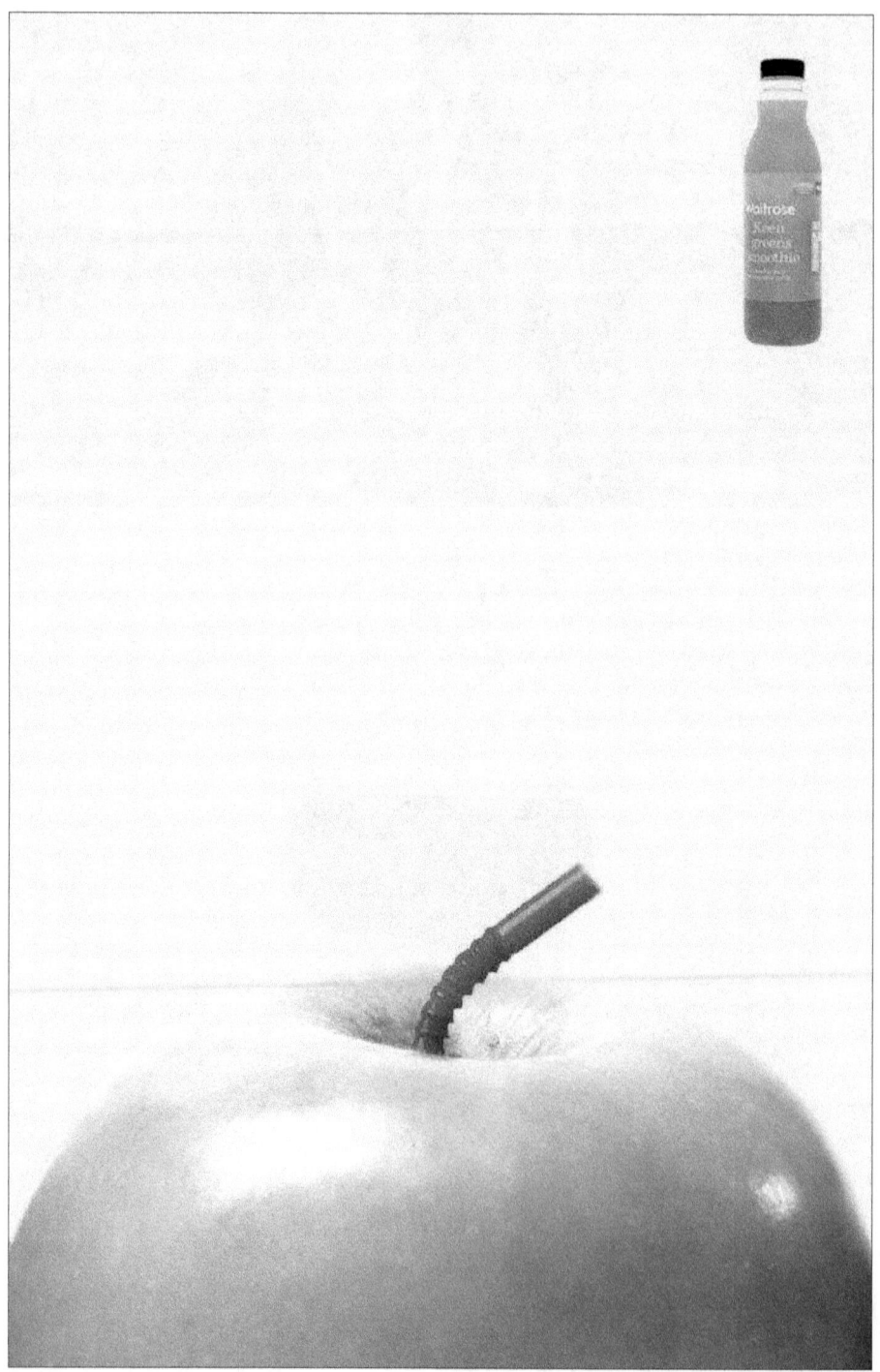

100.

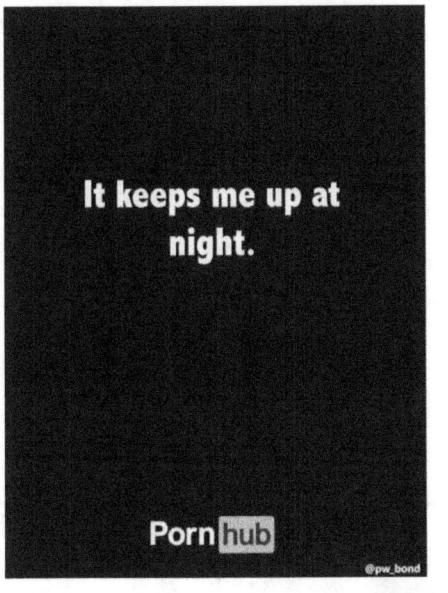

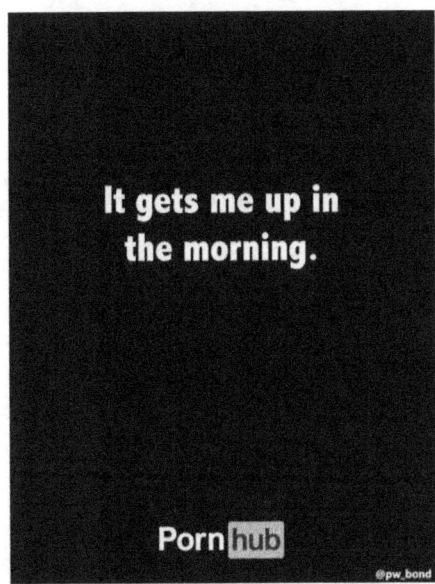

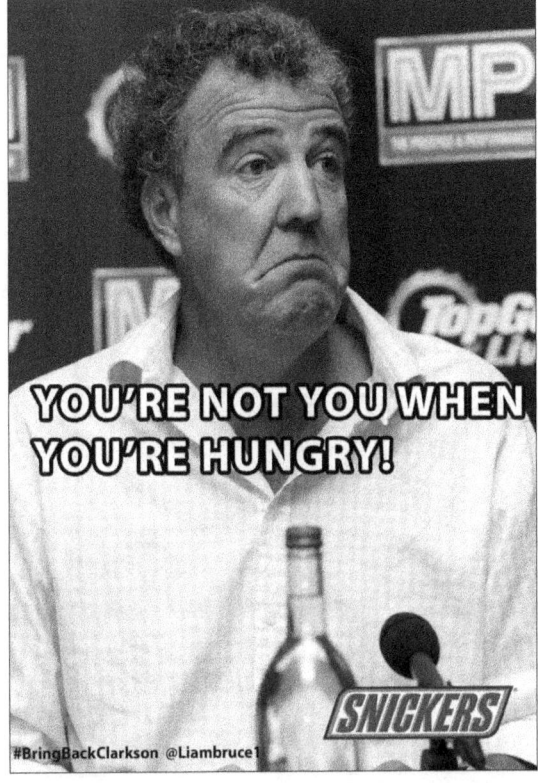

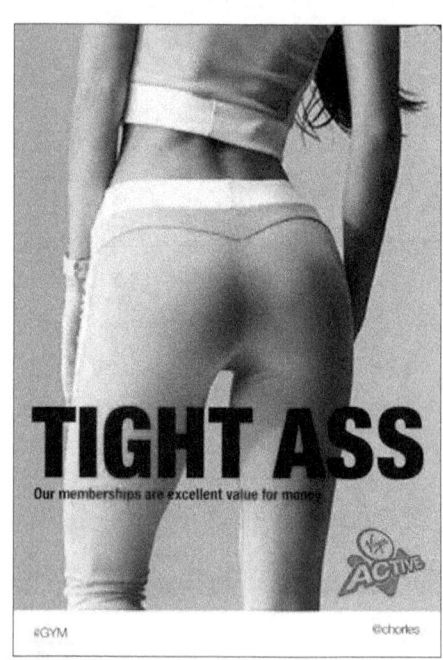

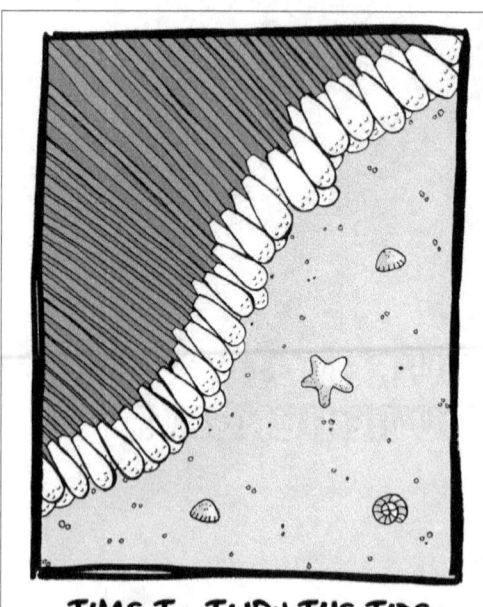

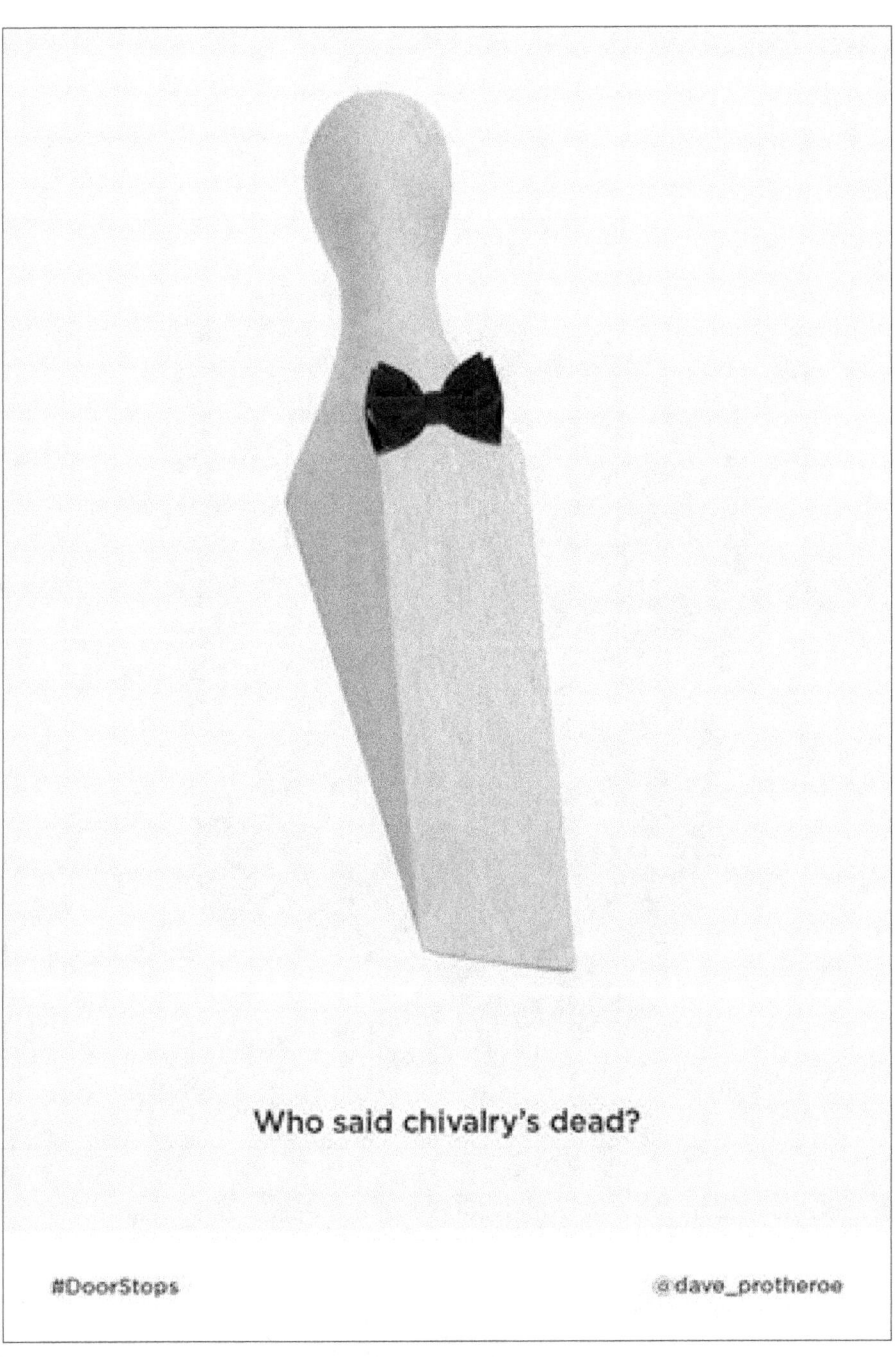

Who said chivalry's dead?

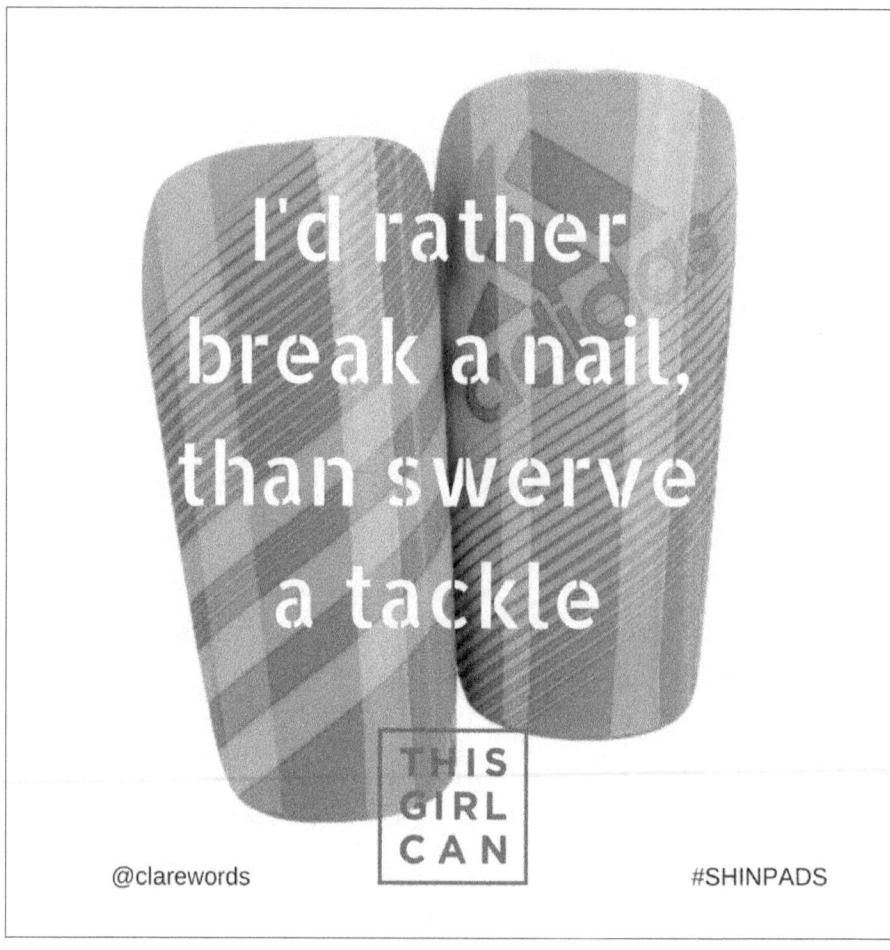

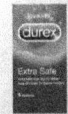

"Do you
feel
lucky,
spunk?"

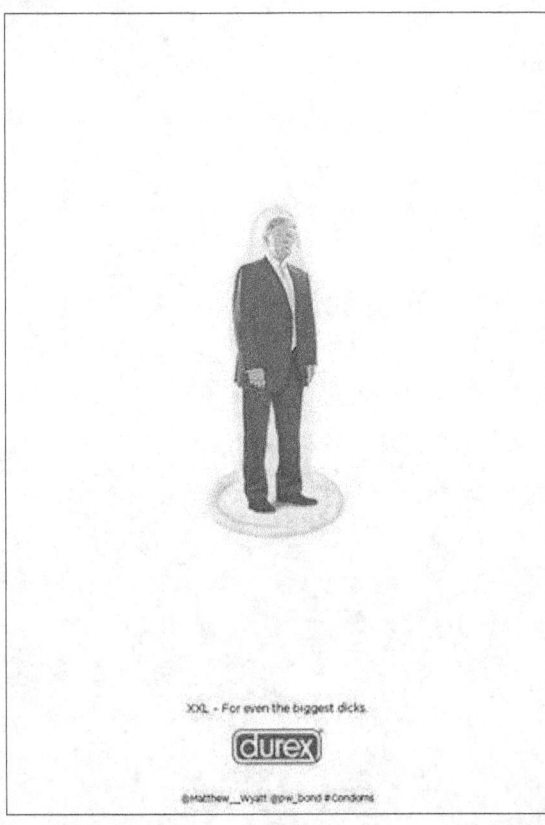

XXL - For even the biggest dicks.

durex

@Matthew__Wyatt @pw_bond #Condoms

TESTIMONIALS & TWEETS

Thank you, Thank you, Thank you.

Just wanted to let you know, I've just clicked send on a copy project for The Drum events team.

To me writing for The Drum represents a 'proper' copywriting job, so it was one of those heart-stopping 'what am I doing?' moments.

They'd remembered me from the DoItDay Brief so I just wanted to say, once again, thank you for providing the springboard into a career I really love.

I've also landed a small job with a local business off the back of OMB. A physio had seen some ads on my friend's Facebook timeline and had asked me to create some ads for her clinic front.

And (I'm not done yet) I've secured a retainer with a digital agency in Warrington to do their in-house copy for the next few months. I met their brand management guy, who had seen my OMBs and loved them.

It's been such a confidence boost and I'm just so grateful for OMB and all the OMBLEs. Thank you, thank you, thank you

@ClareWords

One Minute Briefs Transformed My Creative Process.

I'm so glad I went from watching on the sidelines to getting involved with One Minute Briefs almost every single day.
It has helped transform my creative process, and build a little spec portfolio, all in one fell swoop.

It's also the ideal writer's block remedy. I can get out of my own way and have some fun with words and pictures before I get back to the stuff that pays the bills. And when I do, it's often with renewed vigour and fresh ideas.

I can't wait to get to know the OMBLES better this year, and hopefully rack up a few more wins!

@iaingorman

OMB is an amazing community.

When I started OMB, I had no idea what a copywriter was. Now, a year later, I know it's what I want to be. One Minute Briefs has given me the opportunity to try new ideas, have fun and meet some amazing creative brains all over the country. The OMBLive event gave me a great chance to do some networking and meet real creatives doing what I want to do. Most importantly, OMB has given me the confidence to start applying for creative placements!

OMB is an amazing community. Whatever your background, whoever you are and whatever you do, it's a level playing field for creative ideas.

@williambaxter2

Creativity can come from anywhere.

One Minute Briefs has become a part of everyday studio life at The Hideout and there's no doubt it has made myself and the team better creatives.

Lessons learnt from the team taking part in OMB have not only had a positive effect on the person entering, but also on the studio as a whole. The skills and mindset created by taking on the daily creative challenges has forced its way into the way we create work for our clients. It's encouraged the sharing, development, and the discussion of ideas amongst the team and that in turn has got us creating better work.
OMB really is a true testament to the idea that creativity can come from anywhere.

@ElevenBlackUK

Thanks for existing OMB!

In advertising and marketing, your best ideas rarely get to see the light of day. One Minute Briefs let's you create the work you want without the limits of clients and well intentioned account managers (ahem). It's the perfect way to try out ideas, keep you creative, improve your day-to-day work, and showcase what you really got. OMBs is the dream client that you'll go to bed thinking about.

@MichaelTKeys

I am not miserable anymore. I'm happy.

The great Brian Clough once said, "It only takes a second to score a goal".

In my experience it only takes 60 to achieve all of your own.

Around 18 months ago I was miserable. Stuck in a dull, dead end job with absolutely no idea what I wanted to do, or where I wanted to go – it wasn't a creative rut, so much as a life one.

Then one day a friend of mine sent me a message saying – "Have a look at this, I think it is right up your street".

It was simply, advertise Diamonds on a twitter account called One Minute Briefs.

Fast forward a year and a half and I am currently finishing up my first placement at a creative agency, have a portfolio that includes live TV adverts, and freelance work already booked on the horizon.

But more importantly, I am not miserable anymore. I'm happy.

I'm not a prolific winner really, but I've won a few. What has been more valuable is the fantastic community found, the ambition rediscovered and the spring put back into my step.

My advice to anyone, advertising orientated or not, would be to take the minute because you have no idea where that minute will take you.

Oh and the agency where I'm having a placement? It just so happens the creative director runs One Minute Briefs.

Do it.

@ZGardner11

I now enjoy my job and don't dread work days anymore.

One Minute Briefs is a daily twitter competition for followers with an interest in advertising.

That is what OMB seems to be from first glance. It's actually many different things for many different people. For me it started as something to keep me from giving up on my career as a designer and looking for another path. I was stuck in what was more of a mac operator job and I was hating it. I wanted to be more creative and I wanted to be challenged but I could do my job with my eyes closed.

It then became a great place to see how other people answered briefs, how other people took on the OMB challenge. It was learning from people who entered regularly and something I was amazed by every day (this is still the case today). It was then that I realised that I wanted to work in advertising not just any old design role.

I decided to go to OMBLive2 even though I had never met anyone there before (apart from Nick at the Range :)). This is something that I wouldn't usually do but I'm really glad I did. I met some great people who really inspired me to stop moaning about my job and to do something about it. I filled my portfolio with One Minute Briefs, put some of my work online and sent the link out to a few agencies. I got a really positive reaction and 2 agencies asked me to meet them. The first offered me some freelance work and the second a full time job.

I now enjoy my job and don't dread work days anymore. I still do One Minute Briefs everyday and enjoy seeing new and regular OMBLES taking part. I always try and look through all the final entries on Facebook and I'm always really impressed by the high standard of ideas. The 2 live events that I have attended have been really well organised and I've met some great people. That's the best thing about OMB, the OMBLE community.

Thank you Nick and the OMBLES. See you all soon.

@RichBayley80

I would not be where I am today without One Minute Briefs.

I remember doing my first OMB so clearly. It was the end of my first year at uni and I was moving out of halls. I was sat on the floor in my room surrounded by boxes and I was definitely not procrastinating when I came across the account…!

I was really nervous sending my first entry in because it was just a sentence written on a torn up piece of paper, and I thought I was going to get absolutely slated. But I didn't. Everyone was really supportive and I immediately felt welcome, something that I think still rings very true today.

Fast forward four years I'm in disbelief at how much it has grown and the amount of opportunities it has given everyone involved in it. Some people have achieved some truly amazing things and come up with some incredible ideas that it's hard not to be really jealous of! The standard is constantly getting higher, and I think it's rare not to be inspired or learn something every time you visit the OMB page now.

I can 100% say that I would not be where I am today without One Minute Briefs. Through it I've:
-Got placements.

-Found an awesome art director.

-Attended the NHS Number One thank you party.

-Had work featured on The Drum, Adweek and Campaign after collaborating with fellow OMBLES to create Merry Critmas.

-Done a terrible one-minute talk at OMBLive3.

-Made some great connections and friends (even if I've never met some of them!)

-Made some amusing memories with the ones I have met (one of my favourite's being when Nick dropped his Chip Shop Award, reducing it to a Chipped Shop Award).

-Got into a bit of an argument with a CD at a large London agency during a book crit….

"True ideas take days or weeks, even months. I don't understand this One Minute Briefs thing and don't see the point in it."

"Well it got the NHS to No1 last year so I think it does have its place."

I could never have done any of this without One Minute Briefs, fellow OMBLES and obviously Nick. I'm so grateful for everything and really couldn't recommend OMB enough!

@atAlexGoddard

It's 17:24 on my Creativity Clock...

No. These are not the ravings of a Twitter lunatic (we have @realDonaldTrump and his alter ego @POTUS for that).

Let me explain.

It's been 4 years (April 2013) since I submitted my first OMB (toilet roll)... Midnight on my Creativity Clock.

This was a dark time. I didn't have a clue what I was doing but I knew it was fun. I didn't know how to create an ad, but I enjoyed trying. I never won, but I took inspiration from those that did.

It may have been a dark time during this Creative Twilight, but it's always darkest before the dawn (Yeah... That was slightly vomit-inducing).

Thanks to OMB I learned how to use Photoshop (it provided me with enough practice!)... Thanks to OMB I have had work featured in The Drum and Campaign Magazine... Thanks to OMB I have won prizes, worked with some very talented people, developed a diverse portfolio and made friends with people with whom I have never met.

By my calculations I have worked on approximately 1044 briefs (but this is a conservative estimate). That's 1044 minutes (at least).

So now it's tea time on my Creativity Clock.

And I still can't get enough of OMB. It is such an outlet of no-holds-barred creativity that has developed into a really supportive community, that I can't imagine a weekday without it.

So as the clock ticks its way towards the evening, One Minute Brief at a time, I guess it's time for some Jager bOMBs to celebrate the creative awesomeness that is OMB.

@Alvo_Muses

One minute, every day, changes the way you think.

Working in the health and wellbeing sector, we see all kind of faddy diets and bogus claims about how various routines can change your life overnight.

We also see, that if you take incremental changes every day, it genuinely can benefit you.

This is true of OMB.

One minute, every day, changes the way you think and the way you work.

It's removed the fear of failure that creatives can often succumb to.

It gives us a platform to create ideas without having to prove an ROI, or debate with a committee about "ways to improve the work".

And it's fun. You get to collaborate with like-minded folk who have an unrivalled passion for creativity.

Since we've joined OMB, the combination of healthy competition and challenging briefs has improved our creative output. No doubt.

So, if you get a minute, you should give it a go.

@Mac_Daddies

Penis reductions, stockings and pole dancing**

OneMinuteBriefs has killed my Google search history in the office. But it has also:
- cured my lunch hour;

- given me a chance to explore and try ideas I'd NEVER encounter in my day job;

- genuinely made me far better at that day job;

- inspired me to train and develop my team differently;

- introduced me to lots of really cool and talented people;

- shown me the true meaning and potential of social media; and, most importantly of all...- made me happy. Thanks Nick & OMBLES

@BMMarketer

Dropping OMBS since Jan 2017

Hi, my name's Emma and I'm an OMB-a-holic! It's been two minutes since my last OMB....

I decided in January 2017 that teaching 'the youth' of today was no longer for me and what I actually wanted to do was be a copywriter. So feeling like a bit of an imposter I created my first ad for OMB and nervously pressed the send 'tweet' button. Did anyone bat an eyelid? Laugh me off twitter? Tell me 'you can't sit with us'? No, because that's not what it's about. You don't need to be a graphic designer or a copywriter to take part. There's no such thing as a typical #omble. What is typical about an #omble is they'll welcome you in, no matter who are. They'll laugh with you and they'll pat you on the back when you've done a good job. I'm not entirely sure how I discovered One Minute Briefs but thank God I did.

Thanks.
Emma
p.s. with it running Monday - Friday, I actually look forward to the weekend ending! Who'd have thought?

@cookoocopy

Make blank pages less intimidating.

One minute briefs helps to make blank pages less intimidating and allows me the creative outlet to approach subjects in a different wa to how I need to in my job. It's an amazing confidence boost when you see the fellow OMBles liking and commenting on your ideas. Makes me think "Hey, maybe I'm actually ok at this designing lark."

@emsj09

Creativity at its democratic best

As an agency, One Minute Briefs is a really great tool for us to exercise our creativity. Having a limited amount of time to respond to a variety of briefs keeps us on our toes which, in turn, improves idea generation. The OMB concept is creativity at its democratic best, allowing advertising students, creatives and freelancers a platform to shine and grab the attention of agencies and brands alike.

@S3Advertising

WARM UP THE BRAIN

One Minute Briefs should be every creative's breakfast in the morning, it gets you going, pumps you up, warms up the brain for a creative day ahead.

I would like a marker and a pad please, and make it snappy!

But how has it affected me? Well ever since I decided I wanted to do advertising I have been on OMB; you could say it was my first taste of real intense creative thinking, giving me the energy to break into Watford.

Also, OMB marries the two things I love, sport and creativity, I use boxing as a metaphor in my career, and OMB lets me unleash that in head to heads, I love it.

@CreativeBrummie

1440 minutes in a day. Create a One Minute Brief.

The first time I submitted a OMB I ran with a dad joke about doughnuts. Since then I've been hooked. With over 40 wins in my back pocket, it really does give you that daily creative boost.

It really is the best channel to try out new ideas that you don't always get to roll with. It challenges you to create concepts quickly. Plus, OMB gives you the opportunity to work on briefs for big named clients.

Over the last 2 years OMB has definitely helped me progress as a designer, landed me interviews, expanded my portfolio, as well as even got me a job. It exposes you as a designer, copywriter or just someone with a passion for advertising. It makes networking fun. I seriously could not recommend it more to anyone who has a minute spare, there's 1440 of them in a day after all.

Cheers to Nick and the OMBLES!

@_paulturner_

Gary Does One Minute Briefs...Every Day.

One Minute Briefs. It's not just a game-changer. It's a life-changer.
As far back as I can remember, I always wanted to be a copywriter. Actually, scrub that, not true. I had no idea. I wanted to be a film script writer, or, ahem, a film studies teacher, or a primary school teacher, or..... I dunno. Jobs came and went and I still had no idea. I felt anxious that time and age was against me.

I finally worked it out. I love writing. I love pop culture. Media. Politics. I have outspoken views. A mildly abrasive socialist streak. I've always been a massive cultural sponge of sometimes useful knowledge. How to apply it all?
I took the plunge after my last career (education) came to a natural end in 2014 and broke my copywriting cherry on some friends' start-ups. They were happy. I was jubilant inside.

After that, a lot of free content for lifestyle websites, 'for the portfolio'. Some little jobs here and there, and then I lucked out after some local networking, and worked with an amazing CD at a local agency on a rebrand for a national company, for nigh on a year. A toasty baptism of fire, and to carry on the heat analogy, it lit a fire under me that continues to spur me on. And then...

In my trawling of the net for #freelance #copywriter jobs, contacts, etc. I came across a tweet by a guy called Nick. We had a bit of an offline chat. He was looking for somebody to work with. Very nice chap. Nothing happened, but yes, you guessed it. He turned me on to ONE. MINUTE. BRIEFS.

Just to contextualise, having not really been a part of The Industry via the traditional route (first career, courses, placements, junior roles), this one word, 'creative', monopolised everything I was seeing, learning and taking in. And here's the rub: I didn't know how to be 'creative'. I knew I had skills; I love wordplay, puns and writing lines, but not how to generate IDEAS. "Go on Gal! Write a book! Write this.... Write that...." Ummm. I would if I was inspired.

And this is where, after the generous pre-amble, the real focus of this piece comes in to play, and I get to the 'write a bullet list for your readers to make it more digestible', bit about OMB.
Here's what One Minute Briefs has inspired me to do, get involved with and eulogise about (sorry wife, a win doesn't mean money, not yet). It's been a slinky fit from the start.
23 OCT 2015 I won on my very first OMB (#JagerOMBs)
...and went to OMB Live 2

I knew nobody and was a Southerner in a strange land, but came away uber hyped, and chatted to some amazing people

After one of said chats, in 2016 I was referred by an OMBle to an agency and have had regular, paid work from the introduction. Now (Feb 2017), I've won 41 ... and counting. I've also been on 10 shortlists (including some great campaigns)

7 Oct 2016 OMB LIVE #3 - I'd made a video (but wound up giving an emotional, garbled speech instead), was first to get knocked out of the Live OMB, had a amazing adventure with a fellow OMBle and travel companion, bowed down to my OMB idols, and stood proud when I got a mention for one of my wins
I've asked for help, and collaborated with fellow OMBles

I did star jumps for a minute, a la Joey from Friends (many layers of clothes on), and filmed it for a brilliant SM idea from a fellow OMBle

Did a book crit for two talented, lovely creative students, and got roasted myself by Father Critmass (invaluable advice which I'm working on)

Have gained a lot of followers on Twitter, clocked up likes, had some very nice comments from my peers and international 'conversations"
Met fellow OMBles in the flesh at Copy Cabana and #copywritersunite nights - delightful

The buzz from winning and getting likes from peers is like creative crack
Feverishly checking and refreshing your feed is perverse fun
WARNING: Can create green-eyed envy, but you know, in a good way

Have created a body of work from scratch – a portfolio, yes, with actual conceptual ideas for products and campaigns

Oh, and BOUGHT THE T-SHIRT and book (you don't get more dyed in the wool OMBle than that).

To surmise, OMB is an amazing tool for unlocking parts of you that maybe didn't exist, were suppressed due to confidence, or have been sharpened due to its medicinal, 'take one daily' approach. It's made me feel like I can tackle anything creative.

Am utterly addicted, and am continually spurred on by other OMBles' amazing work. It's an essential tool in any creative's toolkit.
I know my strengths (wordplay, puns, and lines) but am learning so much from being on there about visual style, what works, what doesn't, that I genuinely believe I'm improving.

We are part of an industry that can take an understandably risk-free approach at times, and god knows we see some dross out there, but at Casa OMB you can relax knowing that every idea lives and breathes with no rules, within a fully embracing community that's as nice in real life as they are online. Nick and all the OMBles, we salute you.

@GaryDoesCopy

A sense of community.

One morning, a few weeks after graduating from university, I sat down at my computer in a state of slightly lost frustration and googled "how to get a job at an advertising agency".

My degree in marketing was great; I learned all about segmentation, targeting and positioning, the 4p's, 4e's and all the other acronyms. But we didn't do any actual work. You know, real, tangible work that you can show people.

"Hey I'd like a job please, I'm creative"

"Ok, can you show me something to prove it?"

"Uhhhh"

Anyway, it was that morning I stumbled across a blog started in 2006 by a man called Will Humphrey called Confessions of a Wannabe Ad Man. I went right back to the first page and began to read. This 2006 edition Will Humphrey talked about a variety of things (like the exciting new technology of blogging!) but mostly it was about the struggles of being a recent grad, trying to break into the ad industry. It was also full of great advice. The 2006 Will sounded a lot like me, and I really wanted to speak to him. I had a poke around the blog until I found what I was looking for, there is was, nestled away like a fossil of the Web 2.0 era, a @yahoo.com email address. The blog hadn't been updated since 2013, and I thought " This guy's a big shot now, there's no way he still reads this inbox, does Yahoo even exist anymore?" But what the hell. So I emailed him a few lines about myself and my ambitions, and attached my CV for good measure. To my surprise, I received ack 3 paragraphs of the best advice I could've asked for titled read, create and learn.

Will explained what I had already guessed, that I needed to prove that I can actually do the job. Then he wrote "Start answering the 'One Minute Briefs' on twitter." So I did. To my absolute surprise, my first ever entry (advertise summer solstice) was a winner. There were 7 other winners of that particular brief. Some were well established creatives from big boy agencies, others were like me, freelancers and young hopefuls.

Now, OMB is fun, a kind of daily brain training for creatives, it's not super-serious, but it is also a lot more than that. It is absolutely a legitimate platform for creative excellence and successful collaboration. I've only been following for 3 weeks and already the sense of community is fantastically evident. So when Nick proposed the idea of an OMB board I jumped at the chance. Obviously, I'm way too new in the world of advertising (I haven't even got a job yet) for the notion of any kind of board, but I expressed my interest to get involved on any level, despite my junior status. Nick's reply surprised me "We don't do hierarchy here. All on the same level mate." So I told him straight "That's fucking cool, seriously, as a fresh out of uni grad that's just about the most encouraging thing to be told". As soon as I sent it I regretted swearing, but it had been an honest, in the moment response, and it worked. In fact, it's the reason I'm writing this. As a first timer, being on a level playing field with some of the best in the game is a rare gem in any industry. OMB is a place where you can have a go, where you can see ideas from people who really know their stuff, and, perhaps most importantly, where people who really know their stuff can see you. Keep on OMBLING

@JordonKing

One Minute Belief

My OMB story starts with an interview. An interview for a graphic designer position working alongside mighty OMBLE and Chip Shop Award Winner Paul Bond. Completely oblivious to the OMB phenomena on Twitter I was asked to work on some OMBs to present at my interview the following day. Subjects included 'Pickled Onions' and 'Glamping', I didn't get the position in the end but I appreciated the experience and introduction to the OMB community.

Since then OMBs have helped me through breakups, redundancy, the big 3-0 and general creative drought whilst working uninspiring graphic designer roles. Cue the violins! Anyway, for someone who has struggled to find the right fit creatively, OMBs have helped me tap back into my creative thinking and reinvent myself. I'm still searching for that perfect role but for the time being I've got OMBs!

For anyone with a lack of belief in their creative ability, I would strongly urge you to get involved you'll surprise yourself and inspire your peers. Quoting a piece of graffiti I walked by today here in Brighton... "sucking at sumthin' is the first step towards being sorta good at sumthin'". Be persistent and confidence will follow.

@AndrewNeilRoss1

Paul Bond @pw_bond · 15m
@SianellenJ @OneMinuteBriefs @BOC_ATM No problem! It's a nice concept - and I love the OMBLE agency! Haha.

🔁 1   ♥ 1   •••   View conversation

Lidl UK @LidlUK · 2m
@henhouse_uk @OneMinuteBriefs @BOC_ATM Nice Lidl ad :)

RETWEET   FAVORITE
1   2

4:35 PM - 1 Oct 201[5]   Undo favorite

↩   🔁   ★   •••   Hide conversation

ZED @ZedTrafficker · 42s
@clarewords @OneMinuteBriefs @TheDrum @thedrumdoitday thank you, you have been such a inspiration and a important friend to me xxx

↩   🔁 1   ♥ 1   •••

ZED @ZedTrafficker · 27m
@OneMinuteBriefs @TheDrum @thedrumdoitday I'm so excited... Thank you Nick and a big thank you to all the #ombles xxx

↩   🔁   ♥   •••

One Minute Briefs @OneMinuteBriefs · 12h

OMB Prizes: Mon: £100 Tues: £100 Thurs: £200 Weds & Fri: Chance to have your OMB in Times Square New York. All for one minute's work.

↩   🔁 3   ♥ 14   ılı   •••

Brian @BMMarketer · 45m
@OneMinuteBriefs by the way - serious respect intended here - I have no idea how you get through the OMB volume. #AmazeBalls #SoImpressed

↩   🔁   ♥ 1   •••   View conversation

Paul Turner @_paulturner_ · 3m
@OneMinuteBriefs @GaryDoesCopy @ZedTrafficker every interview I had the interviewer wasn't interested in my other work, only my OMBs.

The Social Sasquatch @hairyhandshake · 14h
@Chorles @OneMinuteBriefs @Anchor_Dairy Wow, good entries! Queen of OMB!

🤍 2

David Felton @doritosyndrome · 11h
@richbayley80 @Chorles @OneMinuteBriefs @Anchor_Dairy I've got an OMBLE4LYFE tattoo. Just don't ask where.

🔁 2   🤍 5

Brave The Shave @Brave_The_Shave · 8m
We absolutely LOVED all of these. Thank you to everyone for your creativity & support on Brave! @OneMinuteBriefs @pw_bond @macmillancancer

🔁 1   🤍 1

ZED 😑 @ZedTrafficker · 6h
@alvo_muses @OneMinuteBriefs @BMMarketer @CopyAndCats @Chorles @gypsy_jangle @ElevenBlackUK credit to you too sir, OMBLES are inspiring

Owen Evans @owenjevans · 6h
@richbayley80 @OneMinuteBriefs When Owen saw the breadth of his OMB goody bag he wept, for there were no more briefs to conquer. #OMBlive3

🤍 2

Matt Dunn @Mr_Matt_Dunn · 2m
@OneMinuteBriefs @thedrumdoitday This isn't an entry, but all of the creative contribution today to such a cause is absolutely amazing.

Stephen @stephenhunter21 · 19s
@ZedTrafficker @OneMinuteBriefs @thedrumdoitday @TheDrum We can't go making special rules for me that'll lead to OMBLE anarchy

🔁 1   🤍 1

James Sharp @Sharp_1988 · 9m

18 months
5 days taking over OMB
101 wins (thanks to tonight's 2)
£100's of prizes won
1 minute
@OneMinuteBriefs

James Sharp @Sharp_1988 · 5m
Mentioned @OneMinuteBriefs in the interview #TheRestIsHistory

Adam Playford @little_scamp85
I HIRED THIS MAN. That is all. twitter.com/sharp_1988/sta…

  1   1   ...

Shireen Dew @ShireenDew · 4h
Speaking about @OneMinuteBriefs: "Time constraints free the mind from
restrictions" – Nick Entwistle @glug @GlugMCR @BOC_ATM @magnafication

 1   4   ...

Daniel Forni @DanielForni · 23m
woop, one more under the belt, congrats all, frickin love OMB-time

One Minute Briefs @OneMinuteBriefs
I posted 7 photos on Facebook in the album "OMB WINNERS: ADVERTISE
#GINGERBREADMEN" fb.me/4p33g3U60

 1   1   ...

ZED @ZedTrafficker · 5m
@windupmerchant @Matthew__Wyatt @OneMinuteBriefs @richbayley80 every
single OMBLE!

 1   1   ...

David Felton @doritosyndrome · 1h
@OneMinuteBriefs OMBLES changing the world through the power of ONE
MINUTE!

      ...

Joe Clark @PensandPostIts · 10m
@williambaxter2 @OneMinuteBriefs @bigbrandideas
OMBLAD!!!!!!!!

↩   ↻ 2   ♥ 2   •••

Alex Goddard @atAlexGoddard · 3m
Cannot believe some of the adverts made over the last fortnight, the standard is so so high, amazing work being made! @OneMinuteBriefs

↩   ↻   ♥   •••

Louise Chorley @Chorles · 2h
Another week of great work on @OneMinuteBriefs, standard just keeps getting better #omb #ombles

↩   ↻ 2   ♥ 4   •••

John Vingoe @ElevenBlackUK · 2m
@clarewords @OneMinuteBriefs Ha! I'm just a creative like you with an appreciation for good work. That's what makes #OMB, an equal chance.

↩   ↻   ♥ 1   •••

AMPERSAND WRITING @clarewords · 57s
@OneMinuteBriefs at the risk of sounding like an Oscar speech, it means so much to me & I want to thank t'OMBLEs, getting there bit by bit

↩   ↻   ♥   •••

Gareth Alvarez @alvo_muses · 2h
@clarewords @OneMinuteBriefs Taking part in OMB every day is the greatest way to learn & improve. Some absolute masters contributing daily.

↩   ↻   ♥ 2   •••

Daniel Forni @DanielForni · 5h
@ZedTrafficker @OneMinuteBriefs ditto, OMB is pretty much saving my brain from eating itself

↩   ↻ 1   ♥ 2   •••

The Blackpool Tower @TheBplTower · 2h
@SianEllenJ @OneMinuteBriefs We love One Minute Briefs here in The Blackpool Tower :)

↩   ↻ 1   ♥ 2   •••

David Felton @doritosyndrome · 55m

@OneMinuteBriefs Being part of One Minute Briefs is my absolute favourite thing on twitter.

Dave Holcroft @PaperjamCreate · 8s

@OneMinuteBriefs @ChipShopAwards @lenchland @MrMartinSo this is one of the best days ever!! #OMB is spoiling me! Awesome work everyone

Lauren Torr @lrennn_ · 11m

Replying to @OneMinuteBriefs @BMMarketer and 4 others

#ProudMoment, my first win! Congrats everyone

 1   3

Emma Cook @cookoocopy · 2h

@emilySOUP @OneMinuteBriefs YES Emily! Welcome to the most addictive thing on twitter x

 1   1   1

Hannah Willis @_hannahlw · 20h

Love the @OneMinuteBriefs concept - promoting brands and causes via one minute ad ideas Need to have a go one day!

     1

Jack Rivers @jrivers1987 · 20h

I can see us becoming a little bit addicted to @OneMinuteBriefs

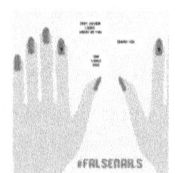

S3 Advertising @S3Advertising

Today's attempt at @OneMinuteBriefs by our creative team. #FalseNails

 1   1   2

Stephanie Alys @StephanieAlys · 9m

Random chuckling in the @mysteryvibe office today can be completely and utterly attributed to @OneMinuteBriefs. Bravo

John @notvalerossi · 17h
There's only one Twitter account I've turned on notifications for: @OneMinuteBriefs. Essential if you're in any creative role.

    1   •••

Rich Bayley @richbayley80 · 4m
@OneMinuteBriefs @LoveYourNHS @magnafication OMB makes things happen, congratulations to everyone involved

            •••   View conversation

Dave Holcroft @PaperjamCreate · 1h   ∨
Replying to @OneMinuteBriefs

No trouble Nick, proud to be an #Omble and owe #OMB a lot like so many others. Least we can do

○   ↱ 1   ♥ 2   ✉

Louise Chorley @Chorles · 3m   ∨
Replying to @OneMinuteBriefs
Nice one Nick! Thanks for all the hard work you put in so that we can be part of such a brilliant Twitter community #omb #ombles

    ↱   ♥

Brian @BMMarketer · 22m   ∨
Massive shout out to @OneMinuteBriefs @BOC_ATM for giving me and others the confidence to enter the @ChipShopAwards
Cheers brother Nick

↰   ↱   ♥ 3

ZED @ZedTrafficker · 3m   ∨
Replying to @OneMinuteBriefs
Cheers Nick! It sure did and man thank you for the chance x OMB mean a lot to me, from the ideas, to the community love to all ombles xxx

↰   ↱ 1   ♥ 1

Joe Jeffries @_joejeffries · 18m   ∨
Replying to @OneMinuteBriefs
Best thing on Twitter, bar none, case closed. Only wish I'd got involved sooner!

↰   ↱   ♥ 1

Brian @BMMarketer · 1h   ∨
Replying to @GaryDoesCopy @OneMinuteBriefs
OMB is literally made for creative team sessions (even for marketers!). Love it! First pint on me Nick!

↰   ↱ 1   ♥ 1   ✉

↱ You Retweeted
Brian @BMMarketer · Jul 6   ∨
I just filmed a few hours of Nick's twitter notifications...
#DontMissItIfYouDontGetaRT

#StrongScrollAction
@oneminutebriefs

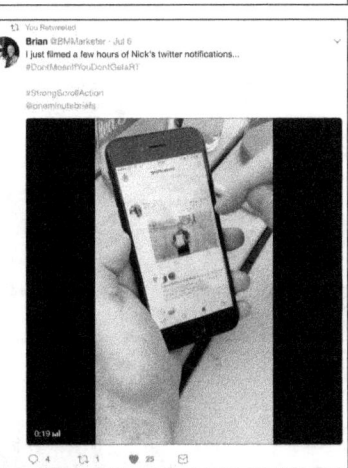

0:19   ○ 4   ↱ 1   ♥ 25   ✉

Elisabeth Ellis @ElisabethMEE · 13m   ∨
Very engaging session at @LeedsUniBiSchool this morning. I'll definitely be doing more @OneMinuteBriefs from now on!

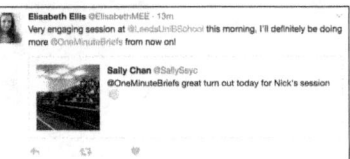

Sally Chan @SallySsyc
@OneMinuteBriefs great turn out today for Nick's session

↰   ↱   ♥

AMPERSAND WRITING @clarewords · 2h

I'm over the moon - thank you so much to @GrantThorntonUK @OneMinuteBriefs for the opportunity to take part.

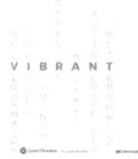

Grant Thornton UK @GrantThorntonUK

Congratulations to @CLAREWORDS, who won the @OneMinuteBriefs #VibrantWestMidlands competition with her amazing poster!

  2   4

ECHO @echoukcharity · 1h

@OneMinuteBriefs further info on successful DLA campaign - you've helped make this happen!: m.facebook.com/echoukcharity/…

ECHO @echoukcharity · 1h

@OneMinuteBriefs we've done it! The DWP have confirmed guidance on CHD is to be given to DLA assessors! We've won! Thanks for supporting us!

Rich Bayley @richbayley80 · 2h

Thanks to @OneMinuteBriefs I can now go to the cinema with clean ears for the next 12 months. 😄😄😄 Much appreciated 👍

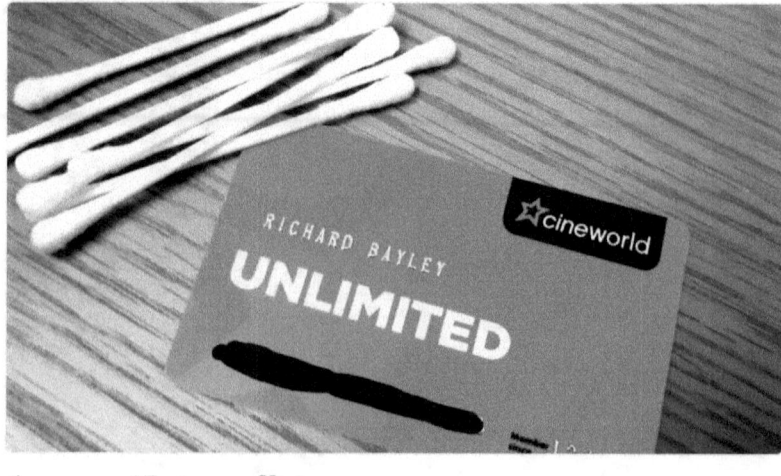

  1   ♥ 6   •••

John Ford @_johnford · 22m
@SianEllenJ @richbayley80 @OneMinuteBriefs Cool beans. There's definitely going to be a few book-worthy OMB stories 10 years from now.

↩ ↻ 1   ♥ 2   ●●●   View conversation

Sian James @SianEllenJ · 10m
@_johnford @richbayley80 @OneMinuteBriefs Thank you! Everything has been go recently and that's thanks to OMB. Can't recommend it enough :-)

↩ ↻ 1   ♥ 1   ●●●   View conversation

John Ford @_johnford · 48m
@richbayley80 @OneMinuteBriefs Nice one, Rich! Great to see OMB positively impacting an OMBLE's life. Another one for Nick's talks, too ;)

↩ ↻ 1   ♥ 1   ●●●   View conversation

Sian James @SianEllenJ · 11m
@richbayley80 @OneMinuteBriefs ...it's so much more than a creative tool. It's a life changer. :-)

↩ ↻   ♥ 1   ●●●   View conversation

Sian James @SianEllenJ · 12m
@richbayley80 @OneMinuteBriefs OMB recently helped me get a new job too. It's all thanks to everyone here for the feedback and confidence...

↩ ↻   ♥ 1   ●●●   View conversation

The Mac Daddies @Mac_Daddies · 8m
@Matthew__Wyatt @OneMinuteBriefs @pw_bond @SianEllenJ @alvo_muses sure it's

1 Min Briefs
Scamp-ton
Adville
M4C D4DD135

↩ ↻   ♥ 1   ●●●   View conversation

GaryLewis-Copywriter @GaryDoesCopy · 42m
@richbayley80 @OneMinuteBriefs Nuff respect to all OMBles, but you make it look easy. Love your work, and MEGA congrats!

↩ ↻ 1   ♥ 1   ●●●   View conversation

GaryLewis-Copywriter @GaryDoesCopy · 19m
@OneMinuteBriefs Anybody else using Twitter pretty much just for OMB these days??

 1   3   ● ● ●

Brian @BMMarketer · 4h
@richbayley80 @OneMinuteBriefs I think @SianEllenJ said it already today - I am loving the creativity on show. I'm in awe
#ProperKudos

RETWEET   LIKES
0   3

5:45 PM - 3 Dec 2015 · Details

    ↩   ♥   ● ● ●   Hide conversation

Reply to @BMMarketer @richbayley80 @SianEllenJ

ZED @ZedTrafficker · 4h
@SianEllenJ @OneMinuteBriefs @richbayley80 yeah agree, rich and many other OMBIES, been very creative and very helpful #nuffrespect

 1   3   ● ● ●   View conversation

The Mac Daddies @Mac_Daddies · 7m
@Chorles @OneMinuteBriefs Will you still be OMBing once the bOMBle is born or will you be giving everyone else a chance? ;)

 1   1   ● ● ●   View conversation

Sian James @SianellenJ · 9m
@pw_bond @OneMinuteBriefs @BOC_ATM hehe it's probably somewhere on Nick's to-do list, along with OMBLEgeddon!

    ↩   ♥   ● ● ●   View conversation

Sian James @SianEllenJ · 6h
@Matthew__Wyatt @Gazzamatazzzz @OneMinuteBriefs @CreativeBrummie your power rating is like the Charizard of OMBles :-P

    ↩   4   ● ● ●

Rich Bayley @richbayley80 · 22m
Sent out some @OneMinuteBriefs to a few creative agencies recently. I was offered and accepted a position at one of them. I just wanted to..

↩   ⟲ 1   ♥ 4   •••

Rich Bayley @richbayley80 · 21m
say thanks to Nick and the ombles for all your comments that inspired me to go for it. #powerofomb @OneMinuteBriefs

↩   ⟲   ♥ 3   •••

Sian James @SianEllenJ · 4h
@ZedTrafficker @OneMinuteBriefs @richbayley80 @pw_bond @Mac_Daddies I love how all these nice words are under a picture of tits #ClassicOMB

RETWEET   LIKES
1   5

Dave Holcroft @PaperjamCreate · 3m
Brilliant idea! @OneMinuteBriefs the home of advertising genius!

> **One Minute Briefs** @OneMinuteBriefs
> One Minute Brief WINNER: Advertise #STANDREWSDAY
> @Richbayley80 facebook.com/OneMinuteBrief... RT

↩   ⟲   ♥   •••

BioSure UK @BioSureUK · 6h
@OneMinuteBriefs thank you so much everyone for the incredible ideas yesterday. #Fanbloodytastic! We're reviewing everything now....

RETWEET   LIKES
1   3

4:49 PM - 2 Dec 2015 · Details

↩   ⟲   ♥   •••   Hide conversation

Sian James @SianEllenJ · 22m
@onaysapatel @OneMinuteBriefs OMBles are the ultimate team. Everyone made it happen :-)

↩   ⟲ 1   ♥ 1   •••   View conversation

OMB ON TOUR

Some of the places we've been or been featured with some great stories along the way.

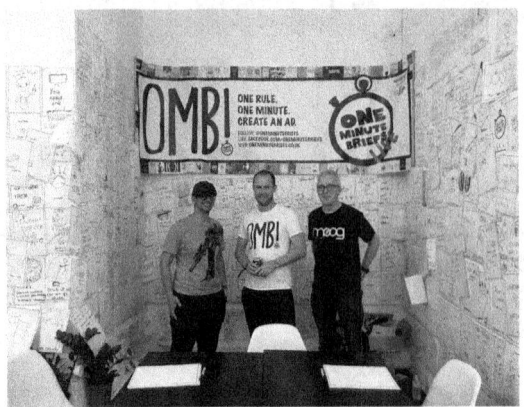
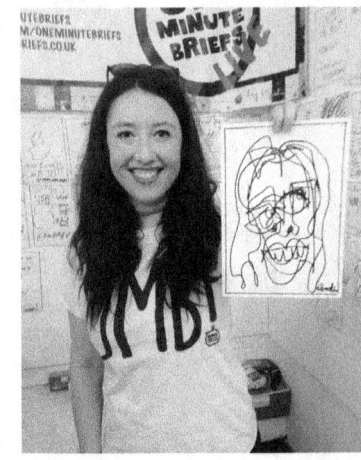
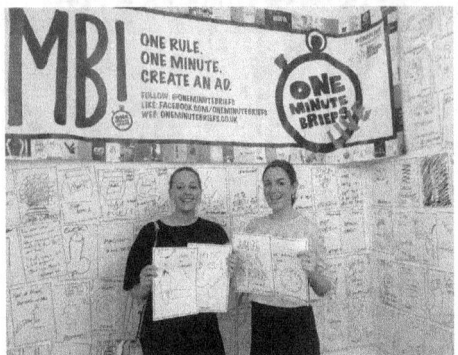
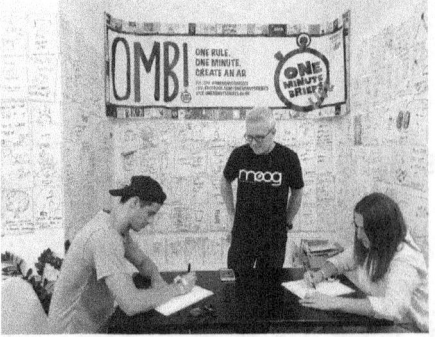
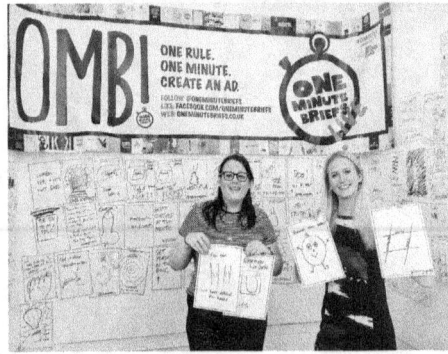
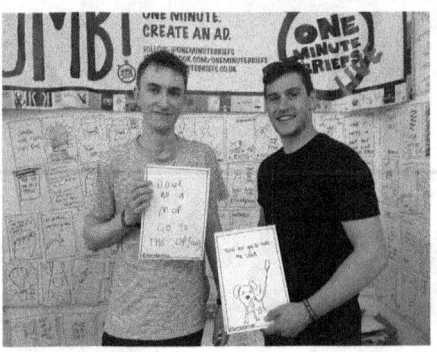

D&AD NEW BLOOD

For the 4th year running, we ran a One Minute Briefs stand at D&AD's exhibition for creative graduates. And, this year it was better than ever. A huge amount of people got involved and we saw lots of great talent. Thanks to Brian, Alex and David for helping me on the stand!

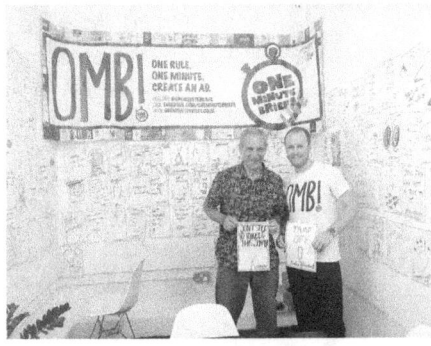
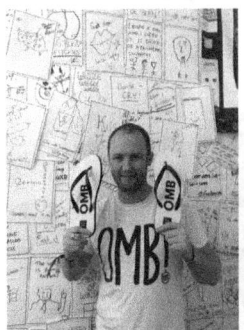
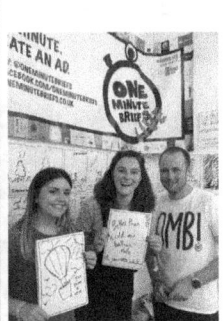
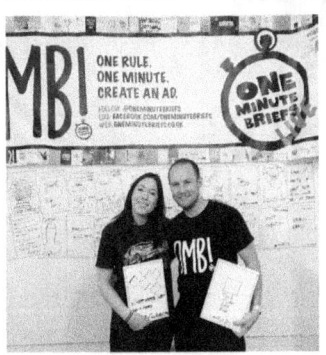
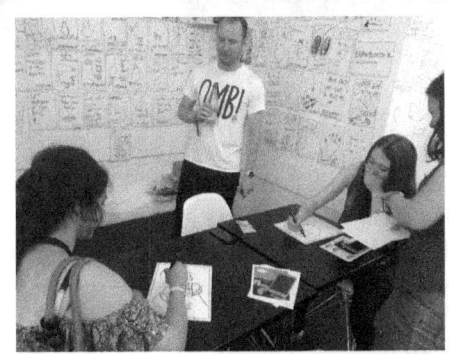
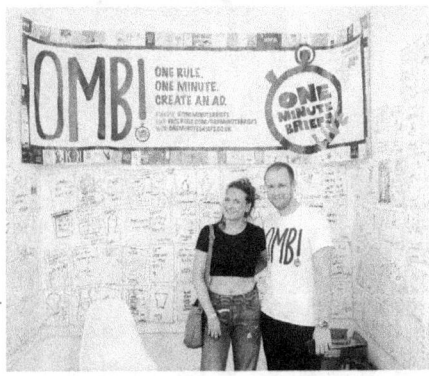
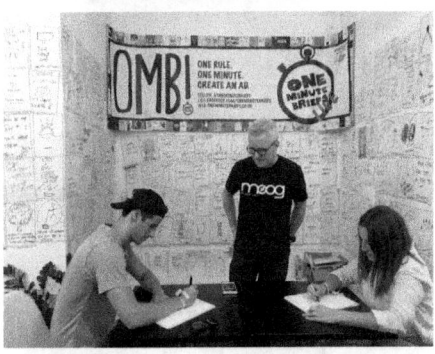
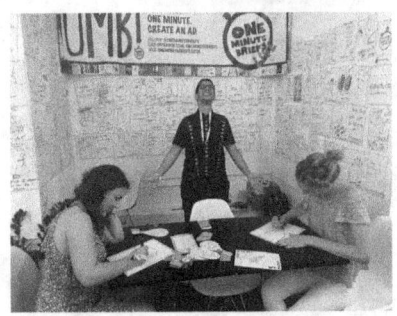
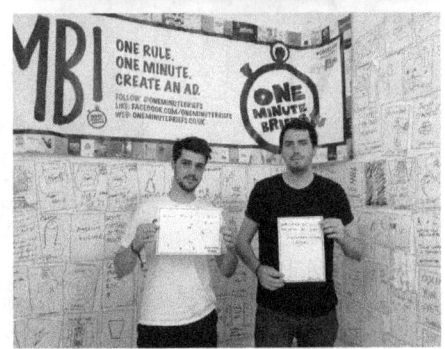

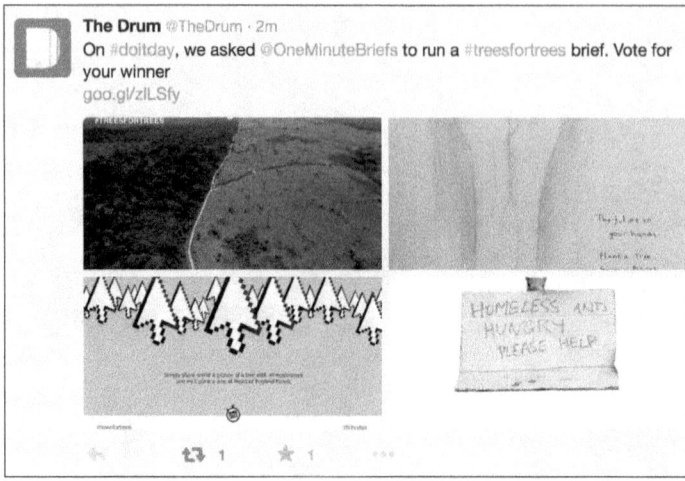

On #doitday we collaborated with The Drum to spread the message of good causes & feature on the screens in Piccadilly Circus.

Looking to collab with Glug more and more after doing a talk with them in Manchester.

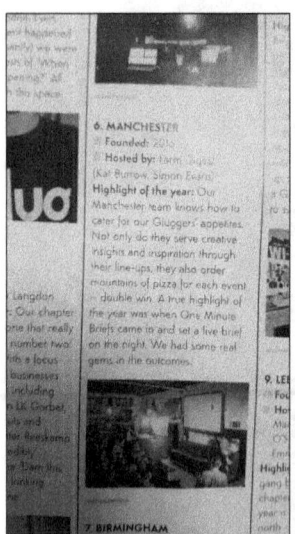

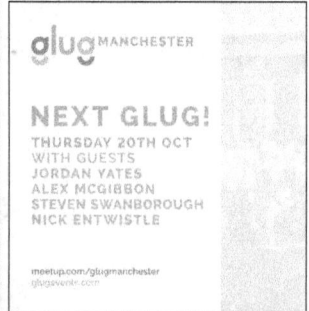

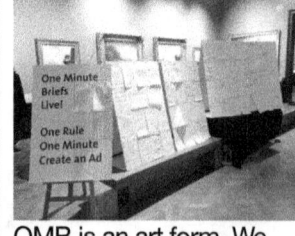

OMB is an art form. We hit the V&A museum to show them how it's done!

So much creativity around one table. After giving a talk at the Havas AGM, I met the D&AD President to talk all things OMB!

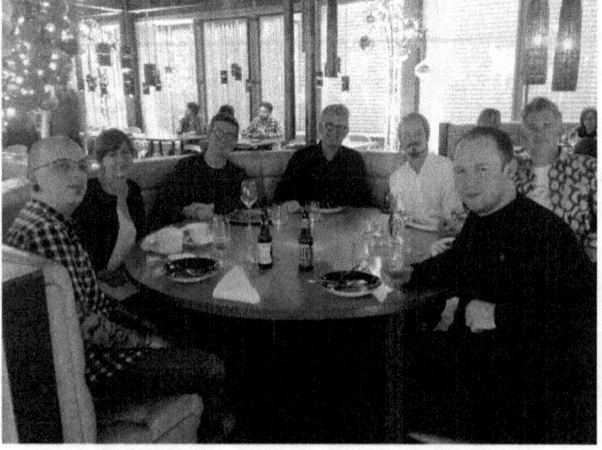

Collaborated with my favourite car magazine for an amazing brief which featured in their magazine and website.

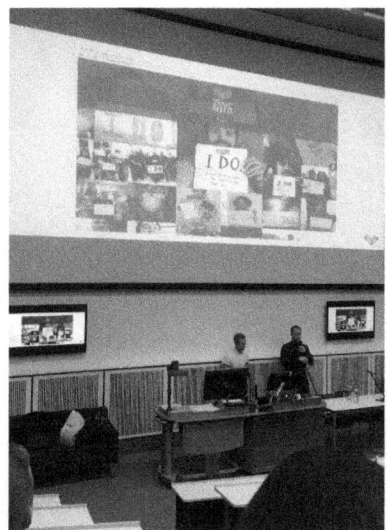

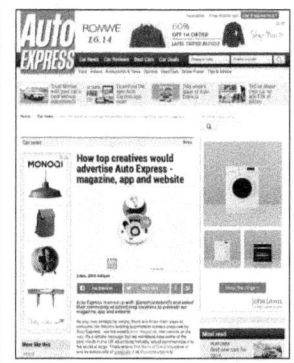

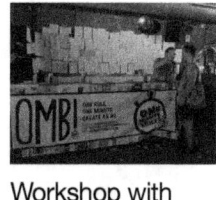

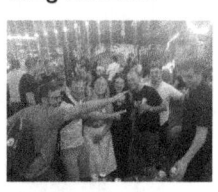

Workshop with Glug London.

Went back to Stockport College where OMB all began for a creative talk to the students.

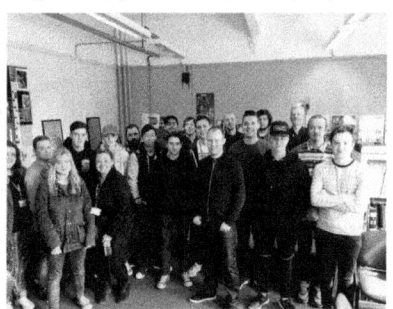

Great to talk at SASCon about how we used social media to power the campaign to get the NHS to Xmas. No.1.

We collaborated with Trunk to create a film featuring lots of celebrities and set a brief on #StopCyberBullyingDay

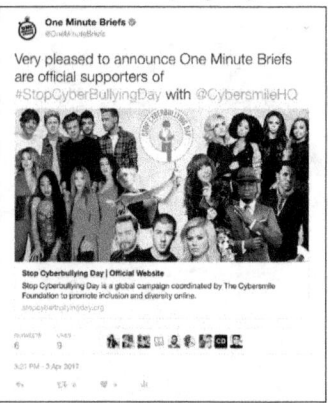

One of the best ever OMB moments. Challenging Bez from the Happy Mondays to an 'OMB off' to advertise Maracas!

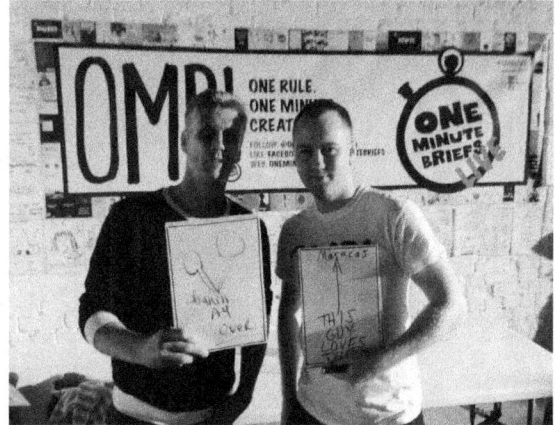

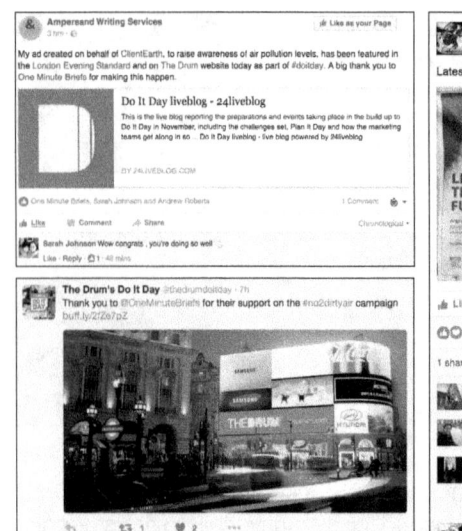

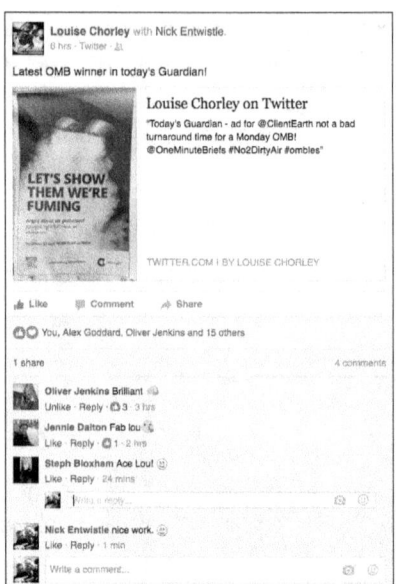

#NO2DIRTYAIR

@Chorles and @ClareWords had their work published in national press for their amazing One Minute Brief entries on #DoItDay

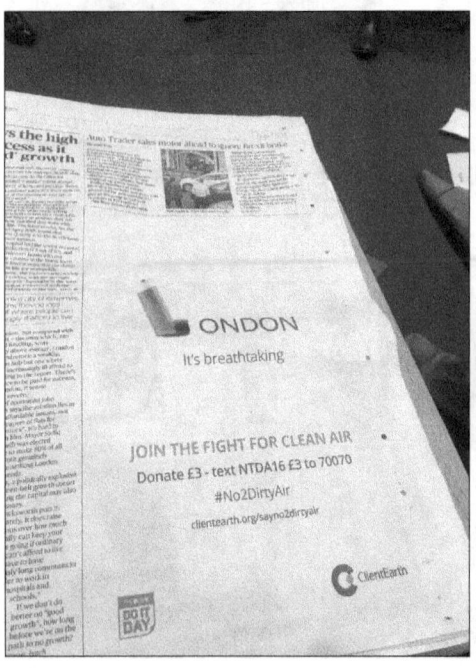

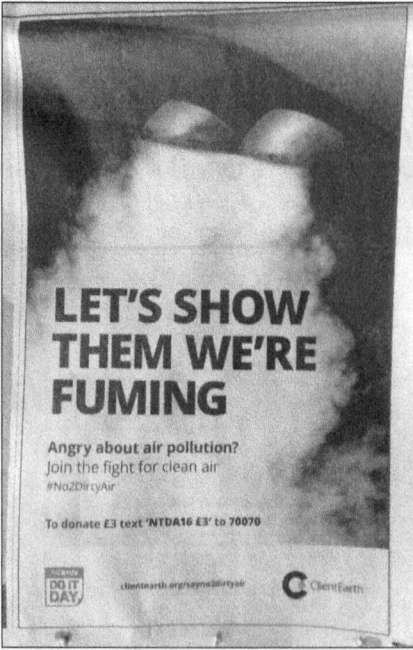

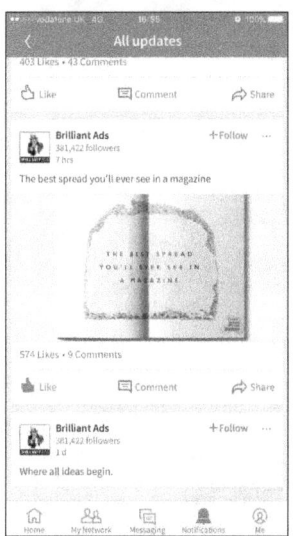

Matt Dunn had his OMB featured in Campaign Mag!

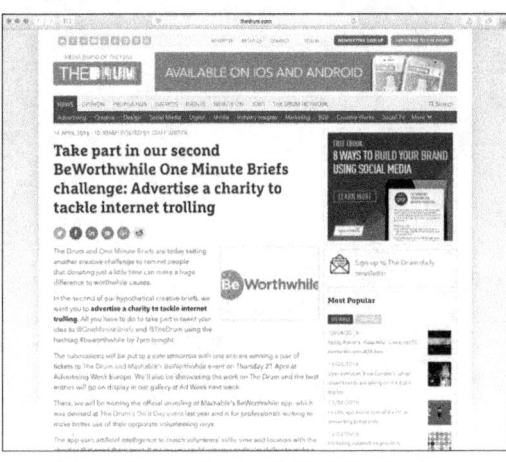

We collaborated with Be Worthwhile on a hard-hitting brief which linked with our anti-cyberbullying brief below.

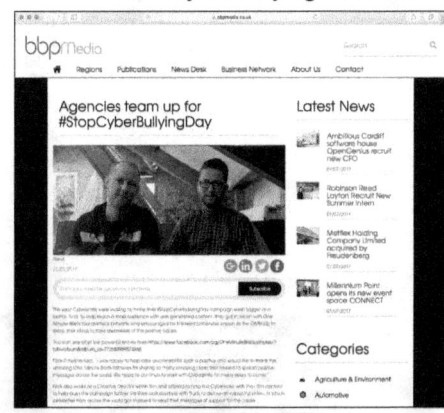

@ElevenBlackUK had his work featured on Brilliant Ads. Shame they don't credit work though!

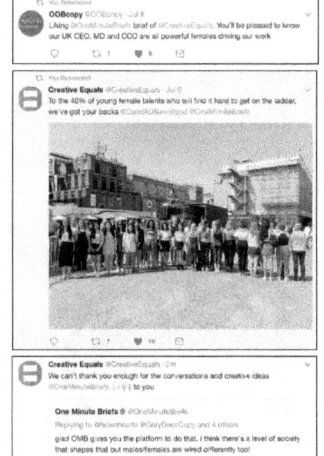

We partnered with Creative Equals to help promote equality in the creative industry.

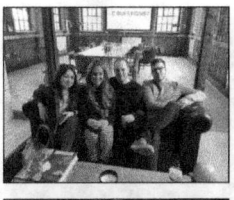
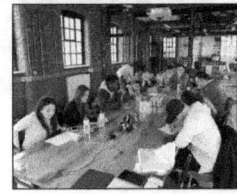
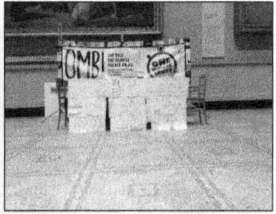

We have hosted talks and workshops at various universities and educational events with more planned this year.

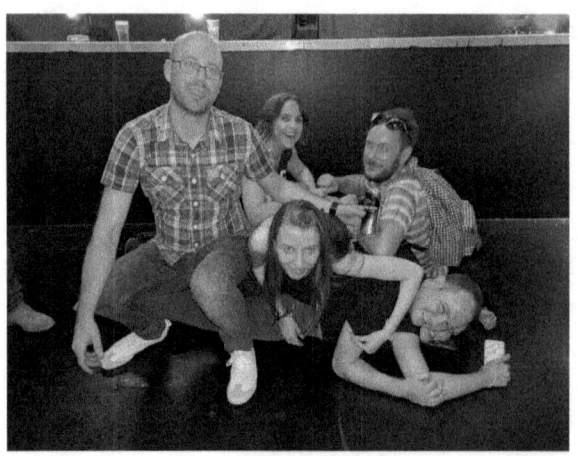

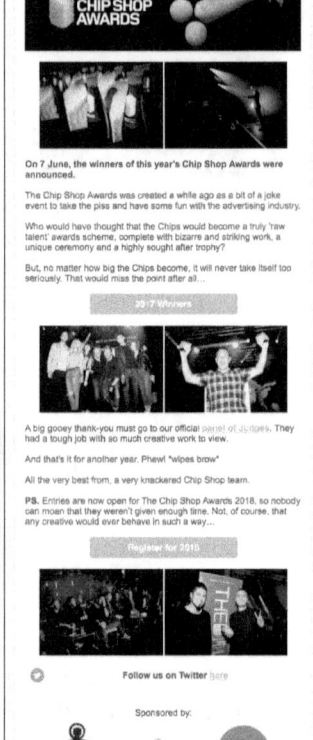

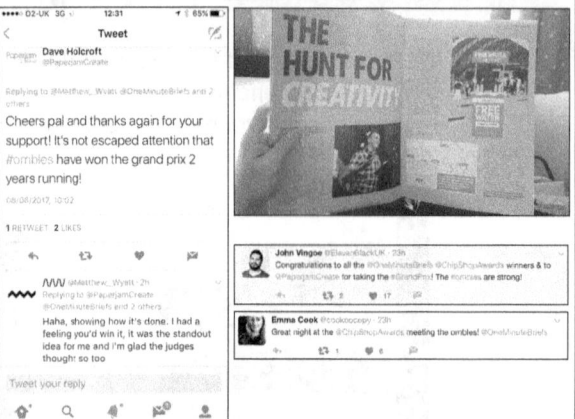

Dave Holcroft
Papejam @PapejamCreate

Replying to @Matthew_Wyatt @OneMinuteBriefs and 2 others

Cheers pal and thanks again for your support! It's not escaped attention that #ombles have won the grand prix 2 years running!

08/08/2017, 10:02

1 RETWEET 2 LIKES

@Matthew_Wyatt · 2h
Replying to @PapejamCreate @OneMinuteBriefs and 2 others
Haha, showing how it's done. I had a feeling you'd win it, it was the standout idea for me and I'm glad the judges though so too

John Vingoe @ElevenBlackUK · 23h
Congratulations to all the @OneMinuteBriefs @ChipShopAwards winners & to @PapejamCreate for taking the #Grandprix! The #ombles are strong!

Emma Cook @cookdoccopy · 23h
Great night at the @ChipShopAwards meeting the ombles! @OneMinuteBriefs

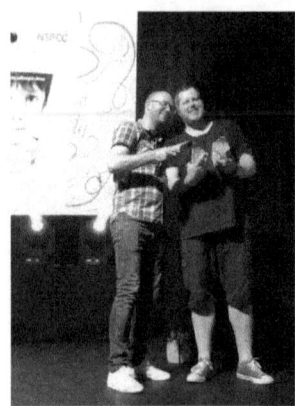

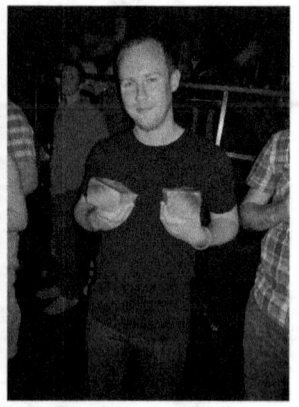

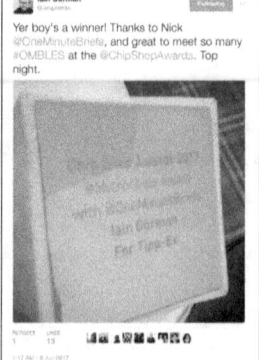

Iain Gorman
@Langomain

Yer boy's a winner! Thanks to Nick @OneMinuteBriefs, and great to meet so many #OMBLES at the @ChipShopAwards. Top night.

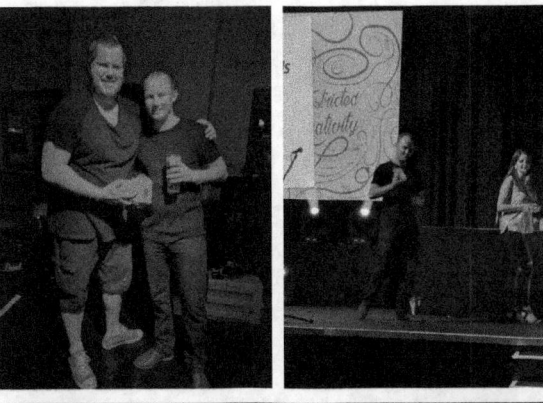

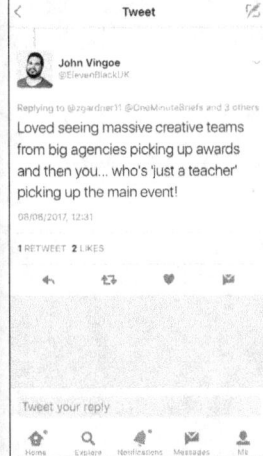

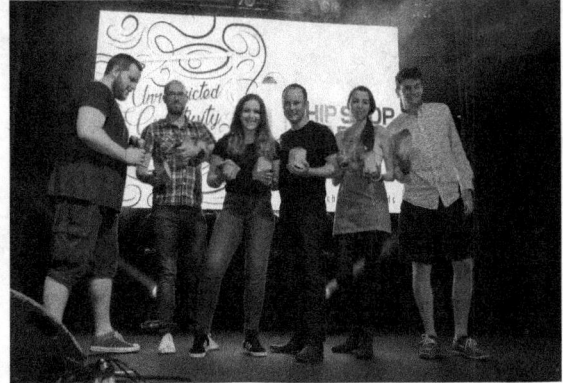

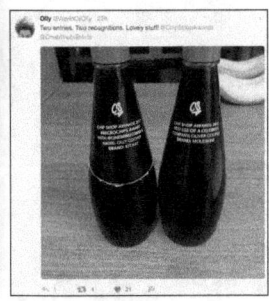

CHIP SHOP AWARDS

After the OMBLES taking over 2016's Chip Shop Awards, including a Chip of my own and Grand Prix for @Matthew__Wyatt and @PW_Bond, it was great to see more OMBLES win this year and ANOTHER Grand Prix for @PaperJamCreate. An amazing story. Very proud of everyone who entered!

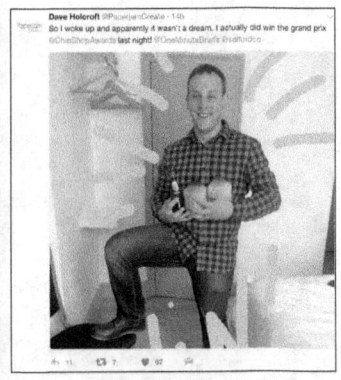

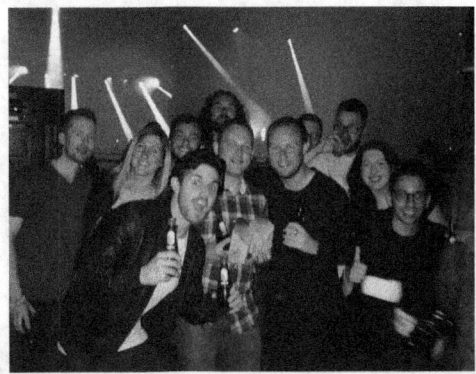

#OMBLIVE3

Our third event was better than ever with some great creative talks, competitions and JagerOMB consumption.
Very much looking forward to the next event as we make it even bigger!

Here's a few pics.
Which OMBLES can you spot?

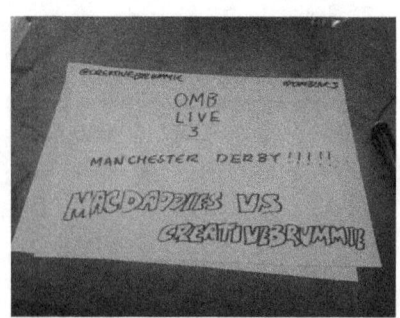

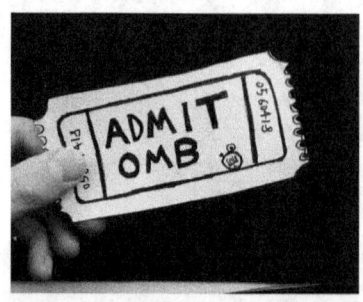

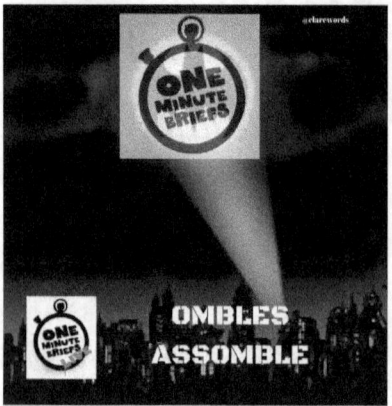

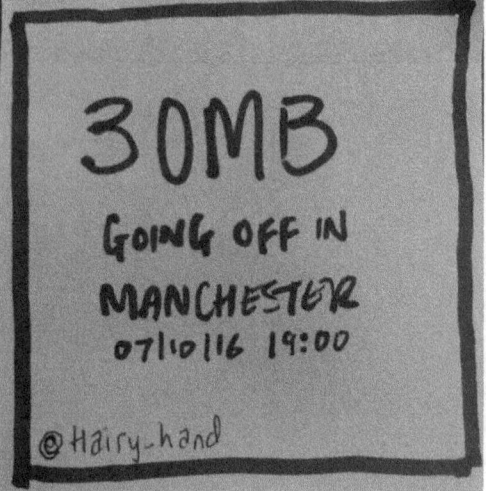

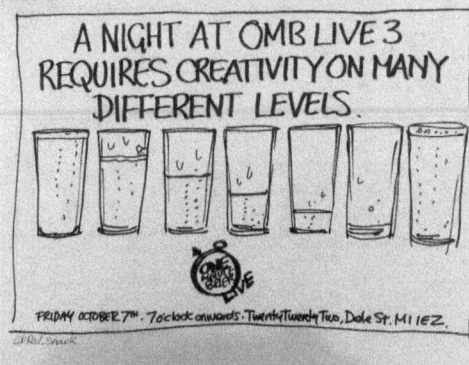

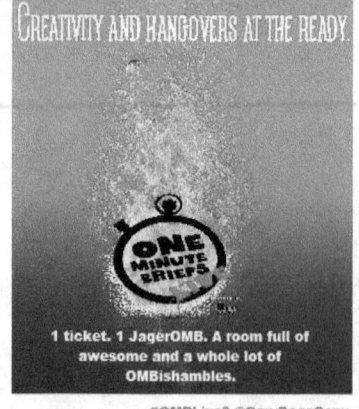

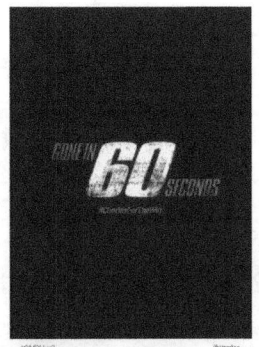

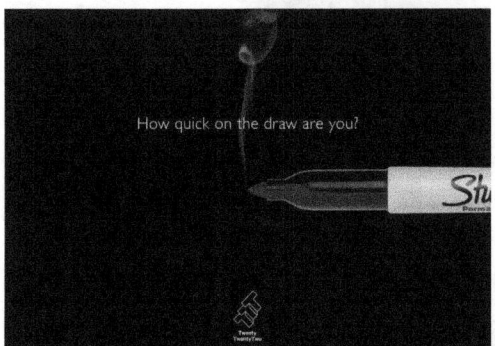

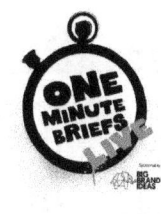

THREE'S
COMPANY

TWENTY TWENTY TWO
20 DALE ST, MANCHESTER, M1 1EZ

7 OCTOBER 2016 7PM
FREE JAGERBOMB WITH EVERY TICKET

@ONEMINUTEBRIEFS   #**OMB**LIVE3   @STEVESINYARD

Mortal
COMBat
comes to
Manchester

7.10.16
TWENTY TWENTY TWO
DALE STREET

@REDLETTERTWEET   #OMBLIVE3

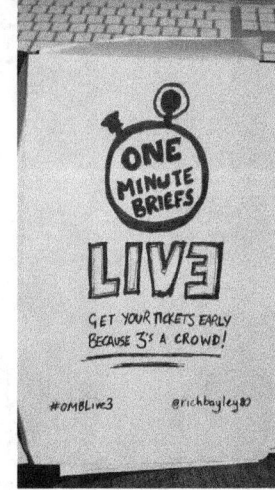

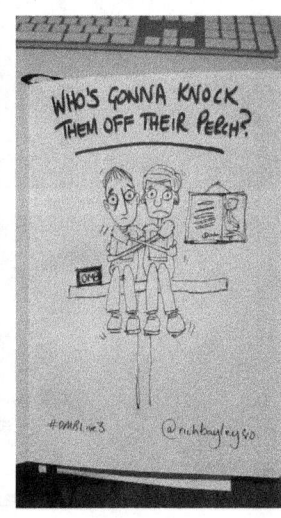

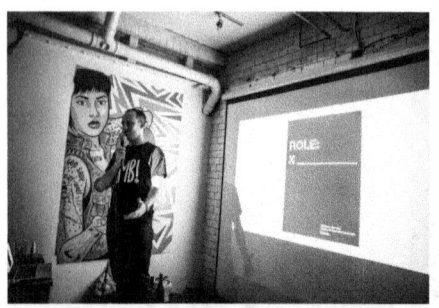

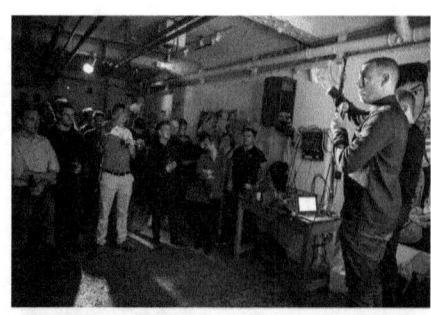

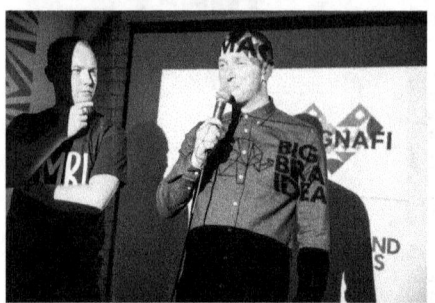

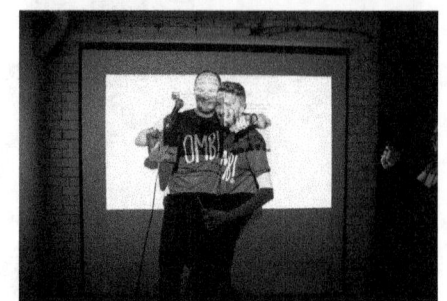

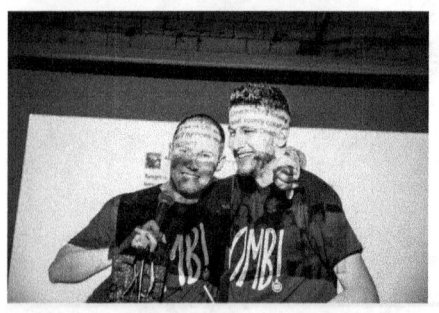

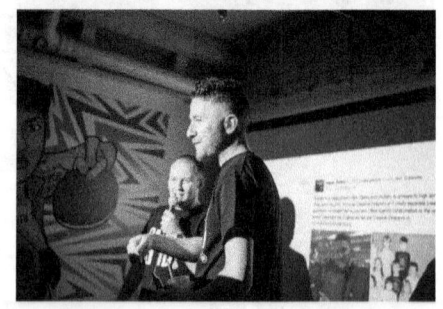

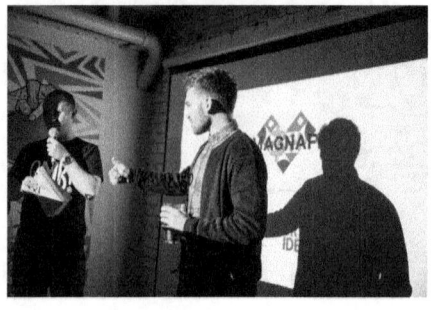

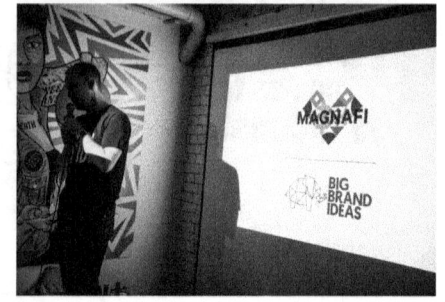

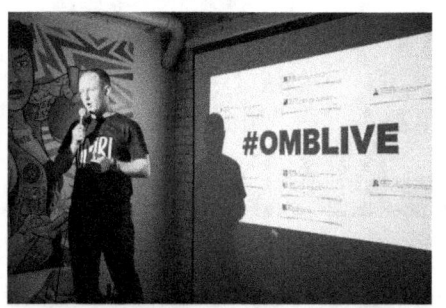 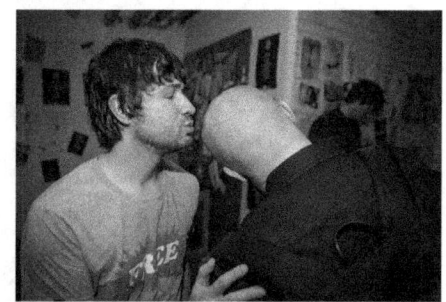

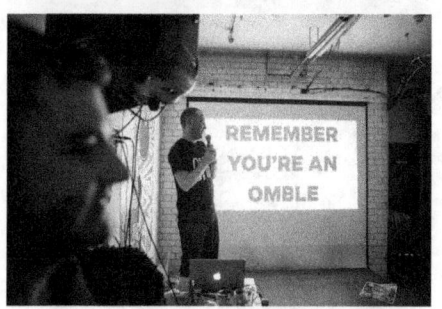 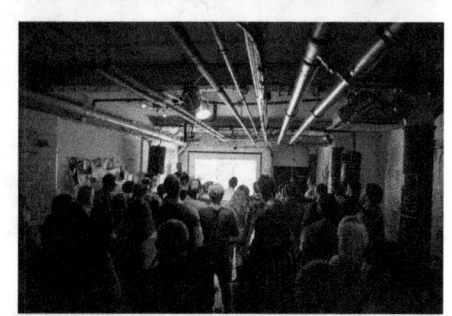

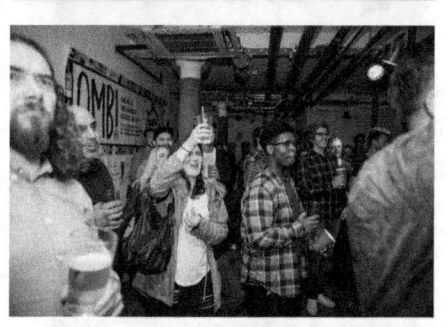 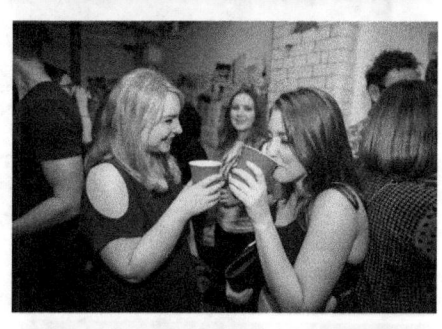

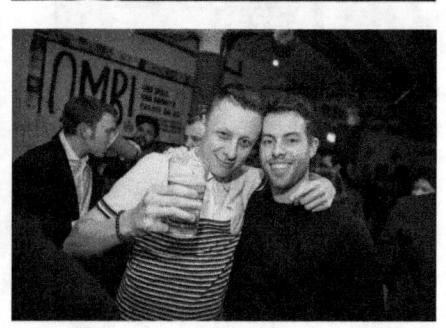 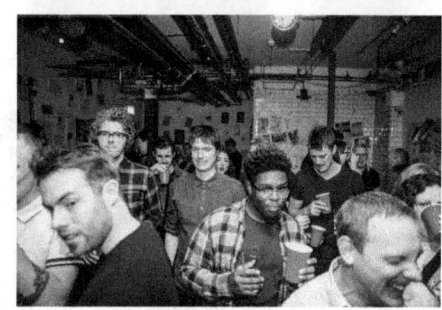

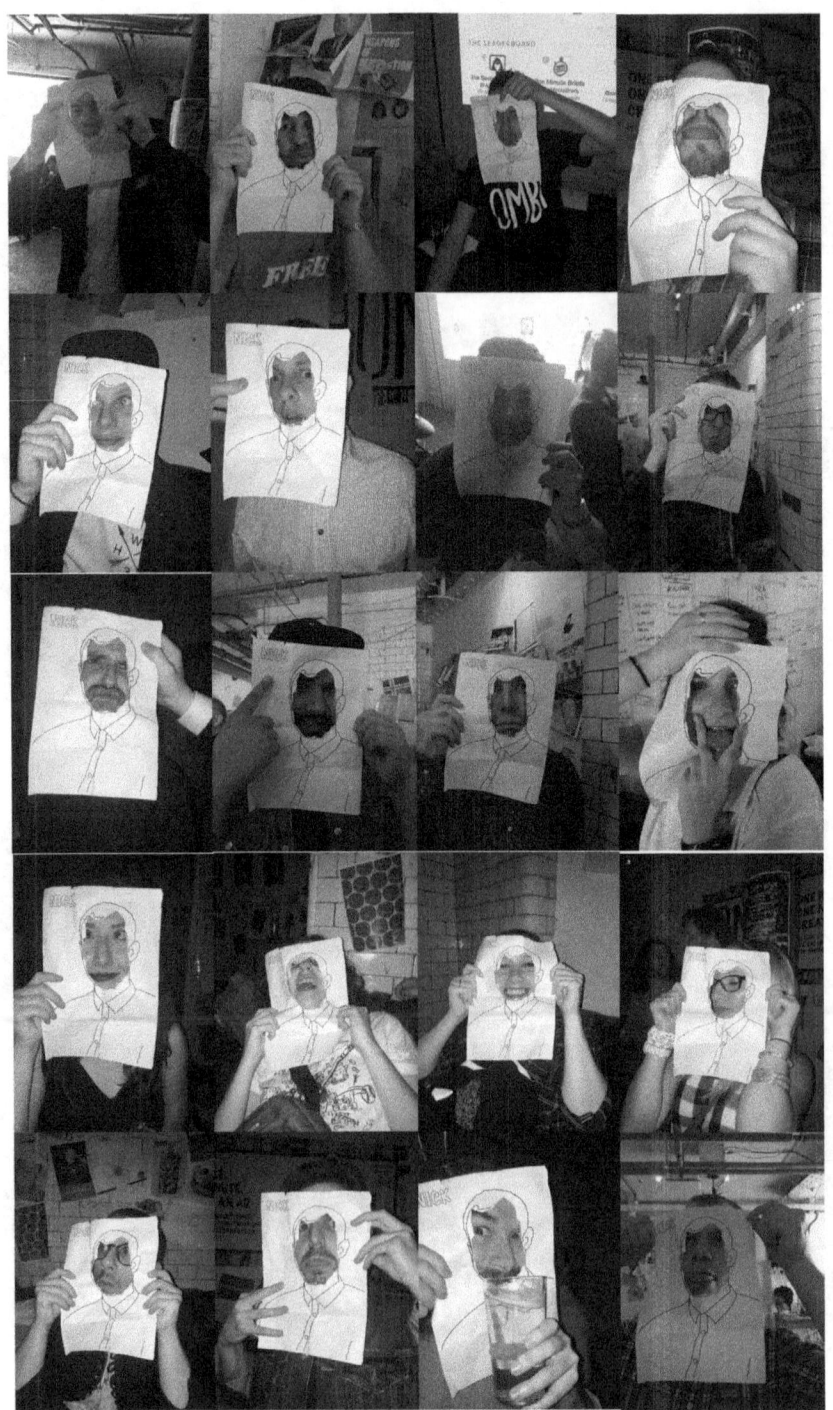

146.

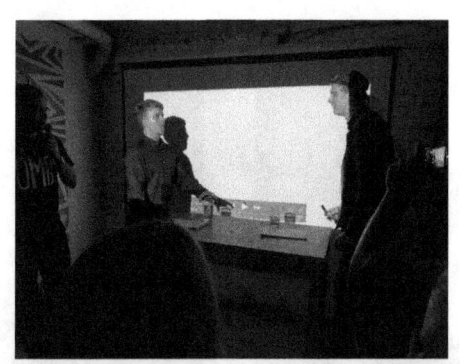

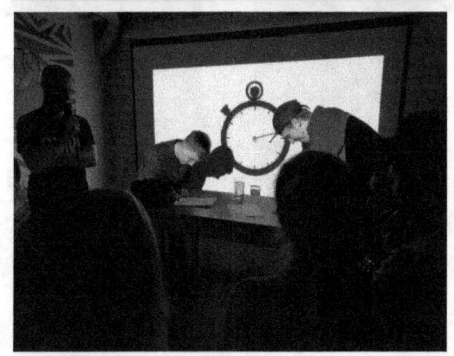

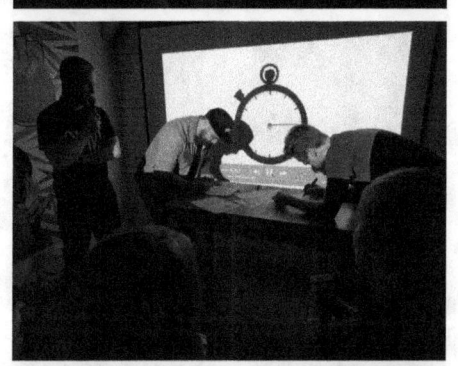

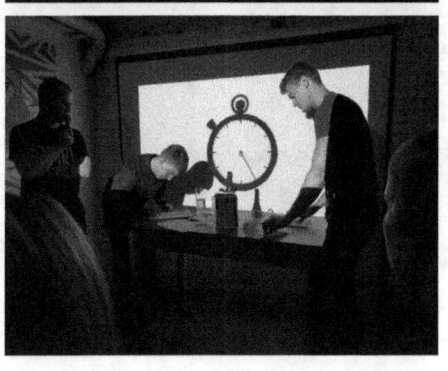

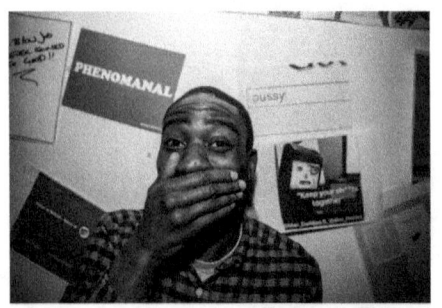
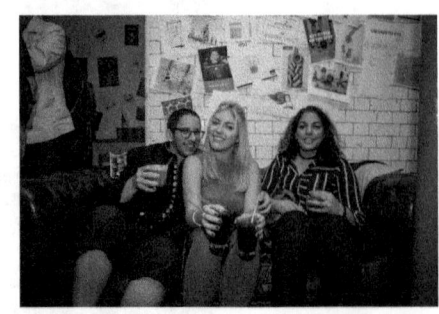
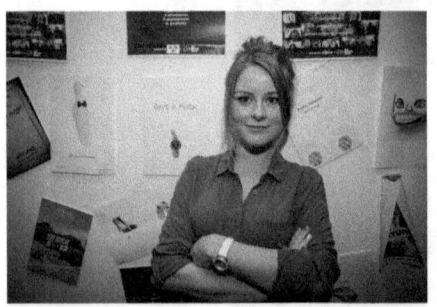
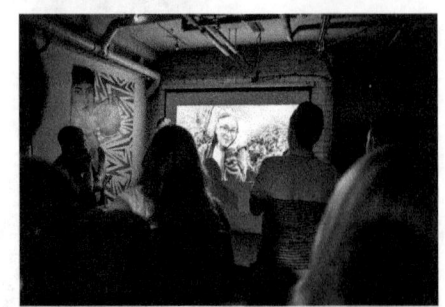
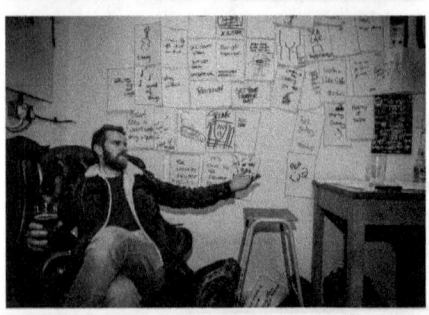
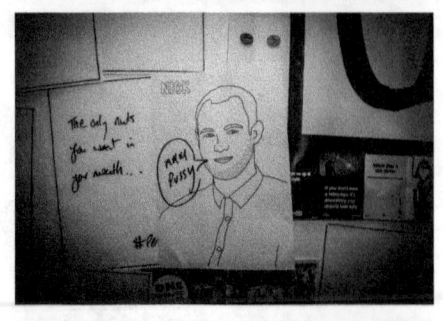
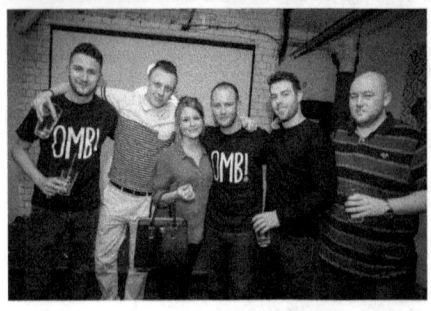
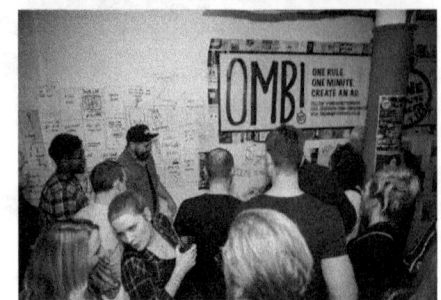

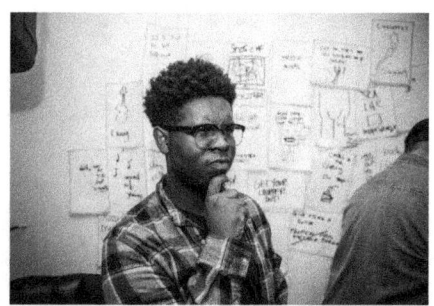
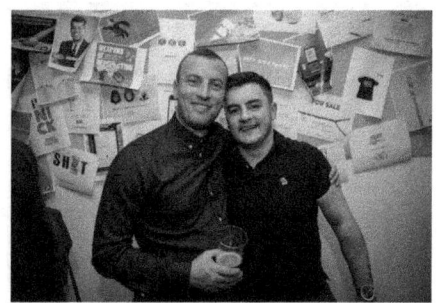
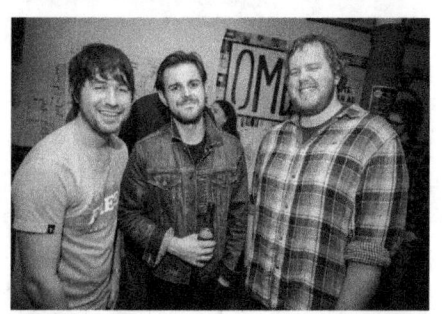
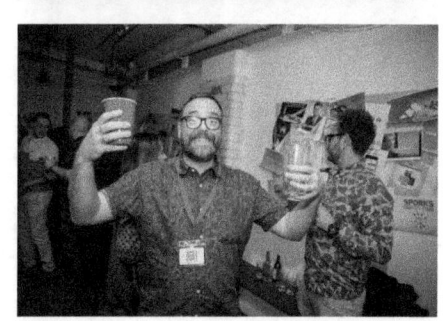
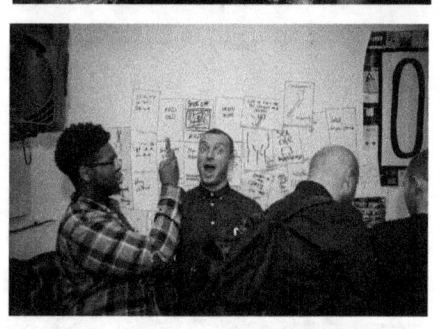
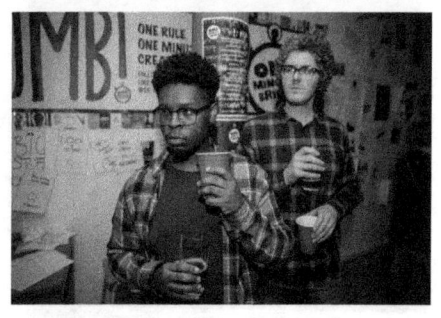
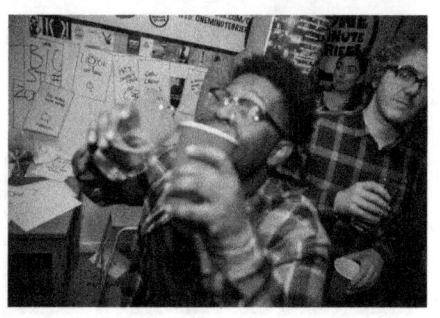
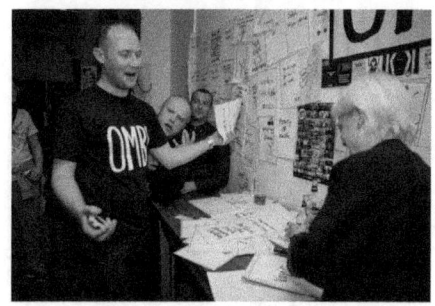

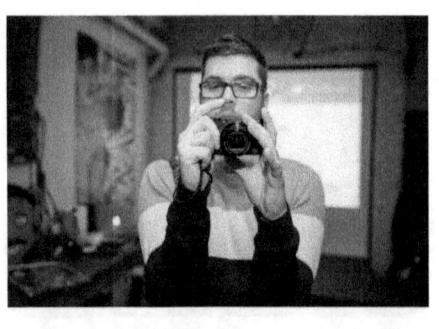
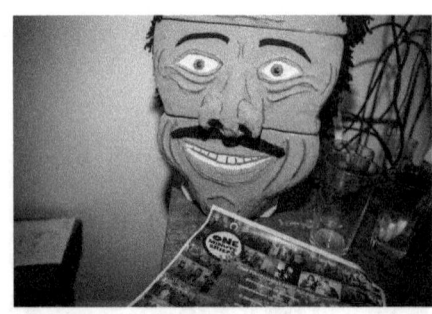
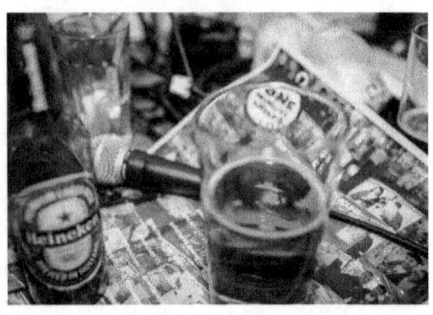
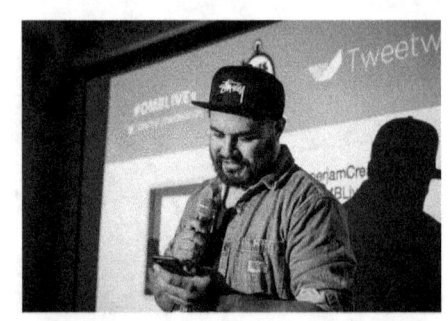
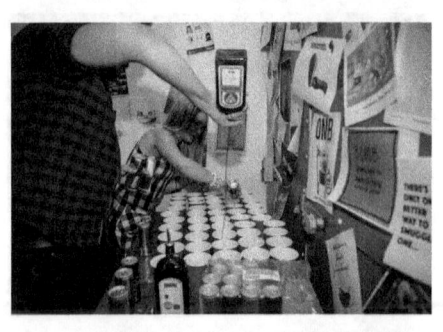
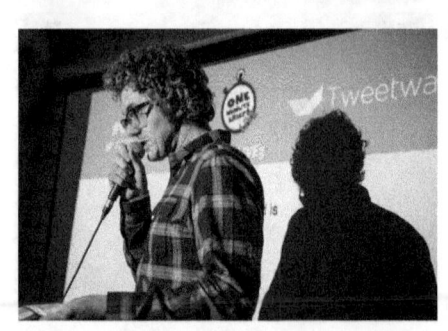
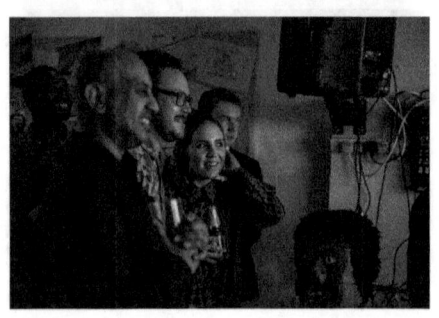
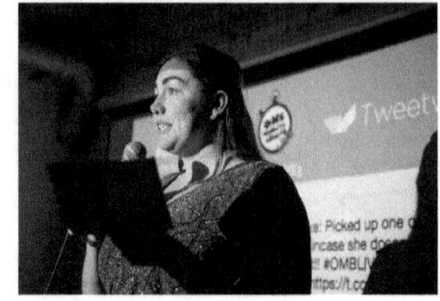

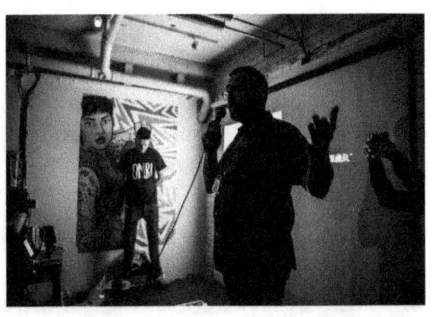
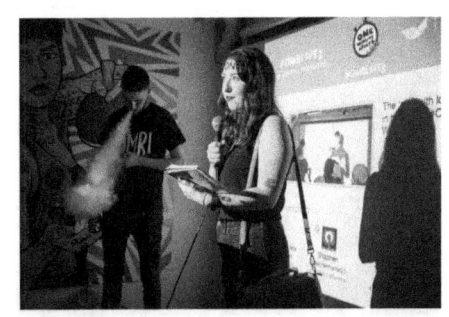
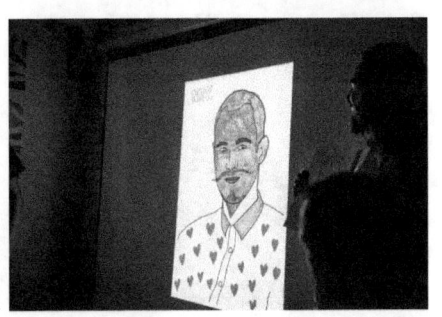
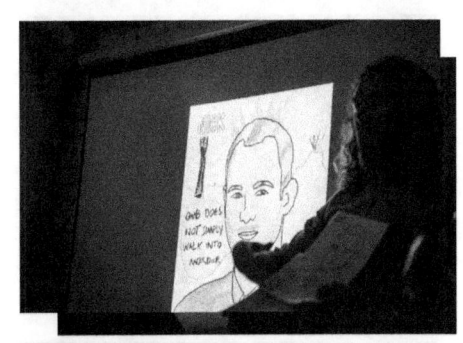
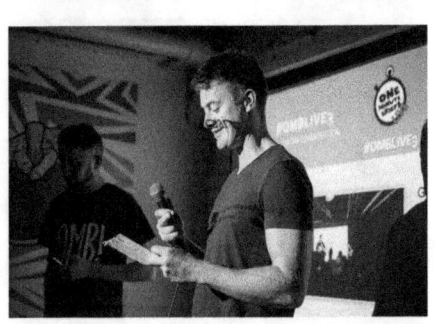
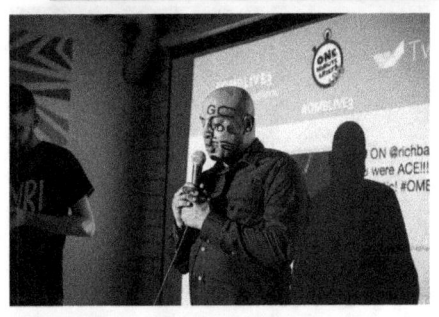
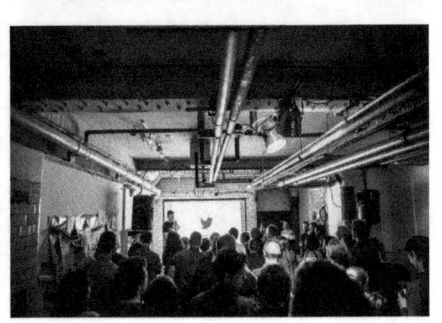
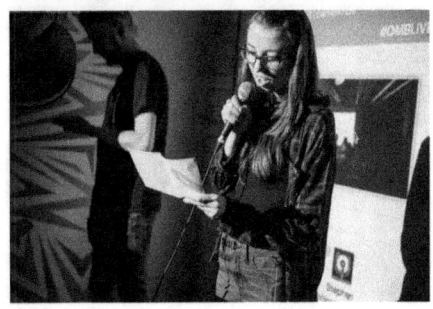

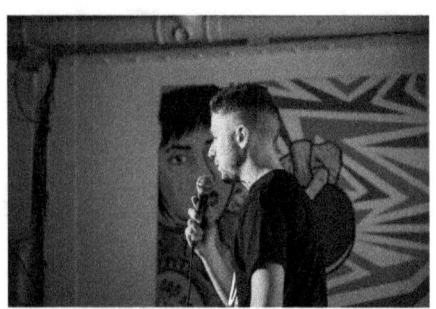 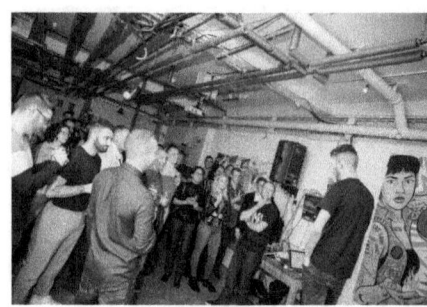

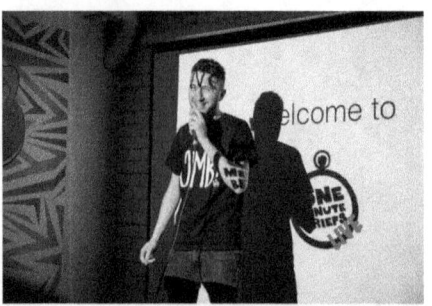 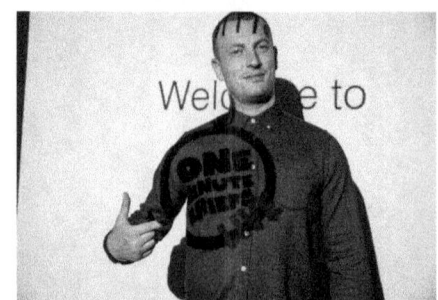

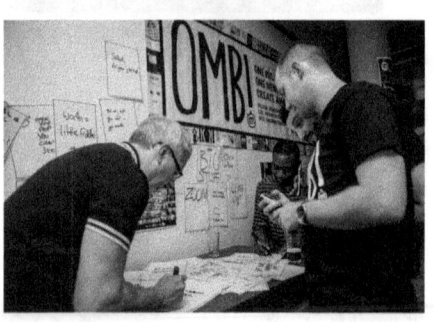 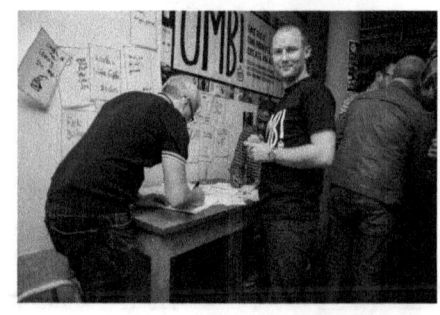

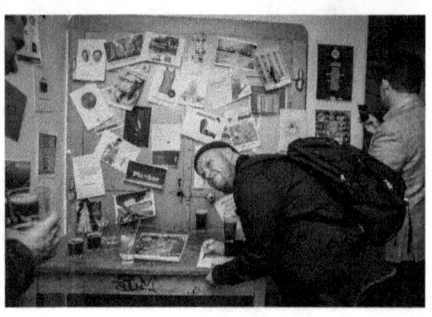 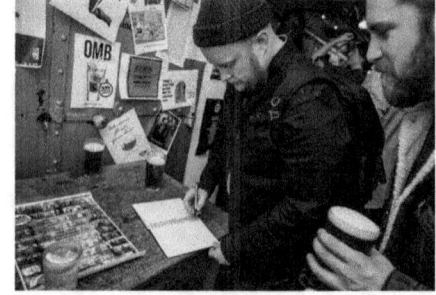

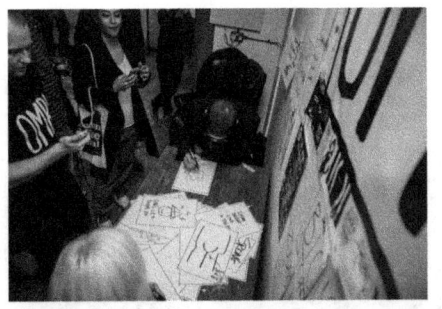 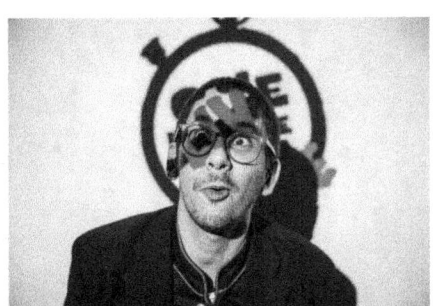

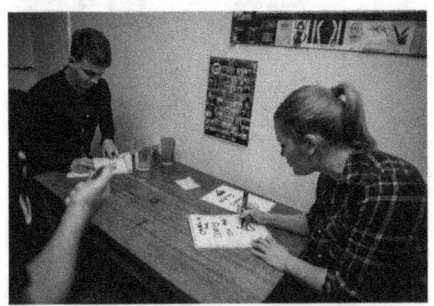 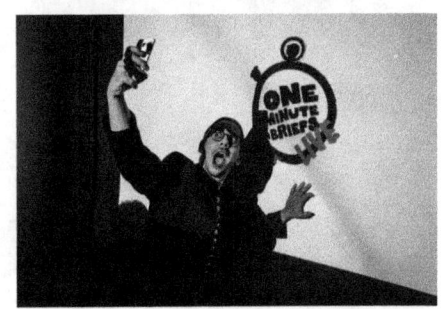

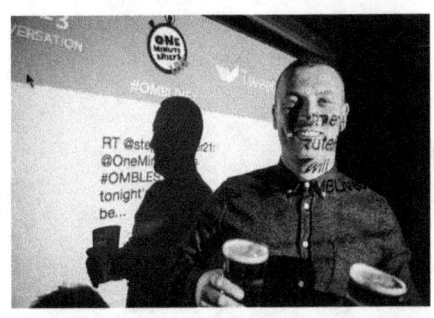 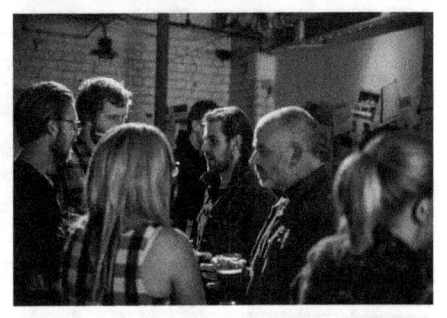

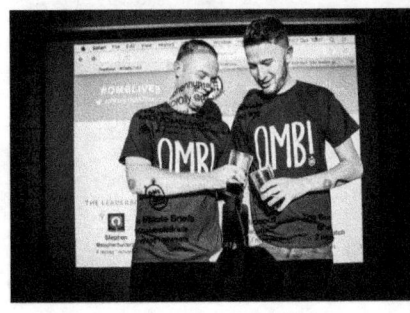 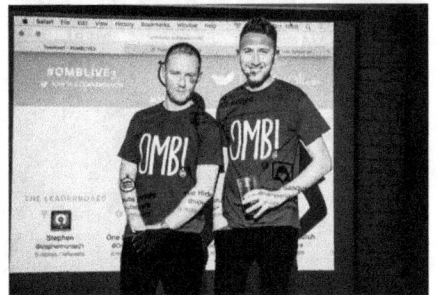

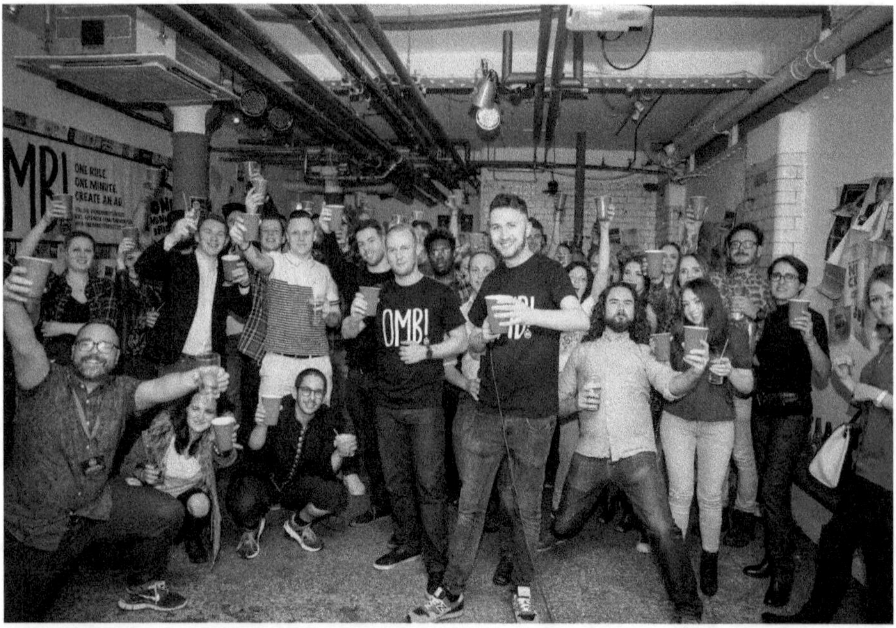

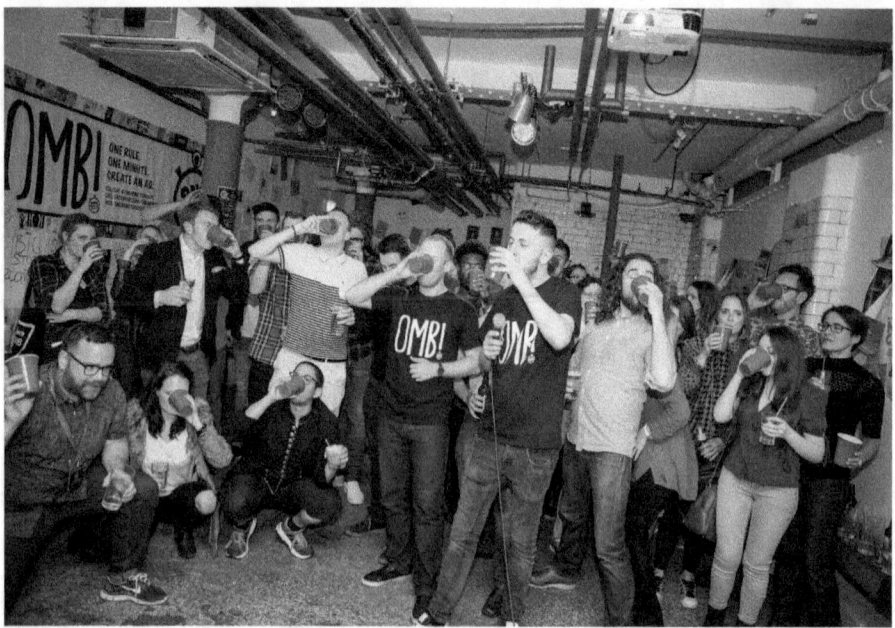

154.

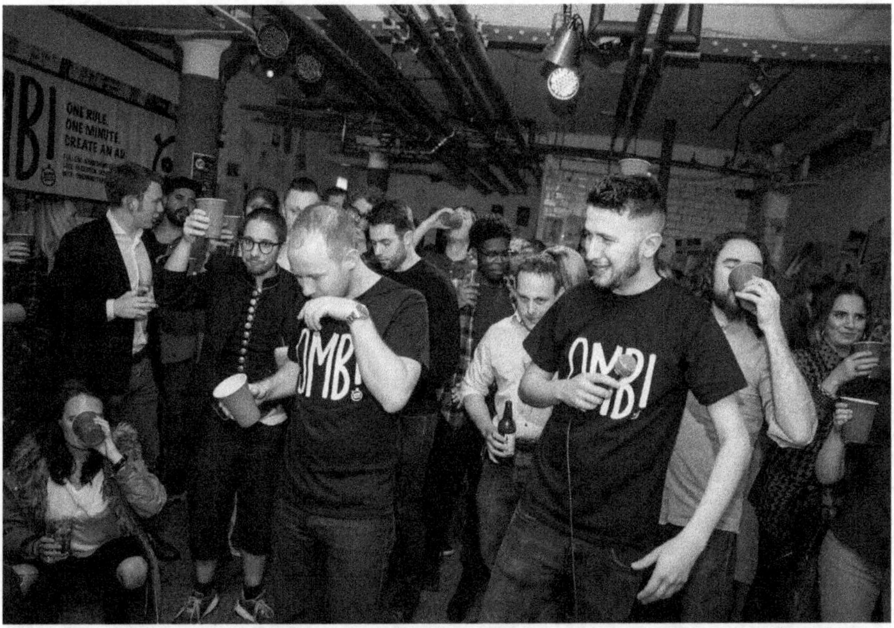

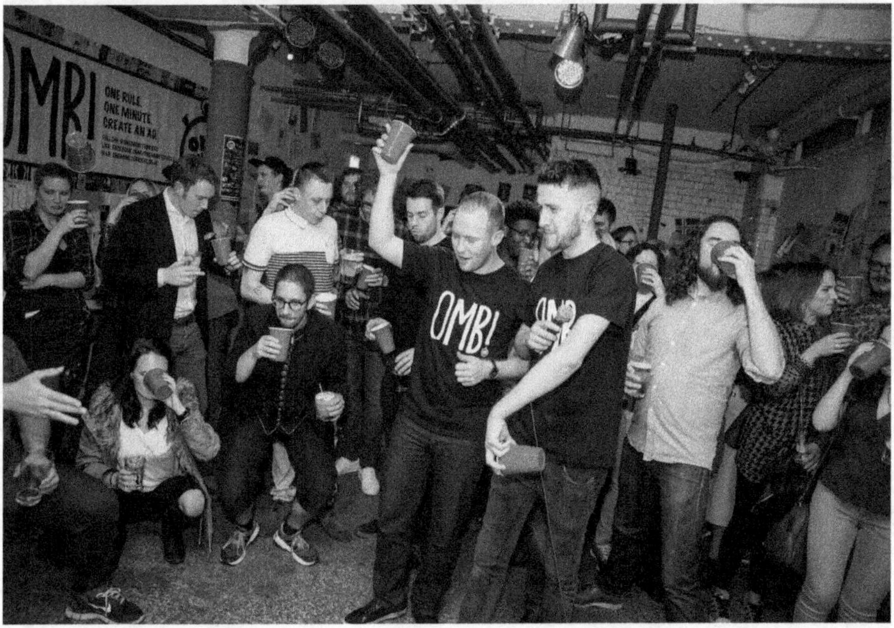

WHAT NEXT?

OMB PLANS

We will be creating an OMBoard so that the OMBLES can have more of a say and benefit even more from the future of OMB.
We will have an all-new website soon and are looking to create an app/game.
We might even release some One Minute Briefs briefs!
We will also be heading to London for our next event. The OMBLES have spoken!

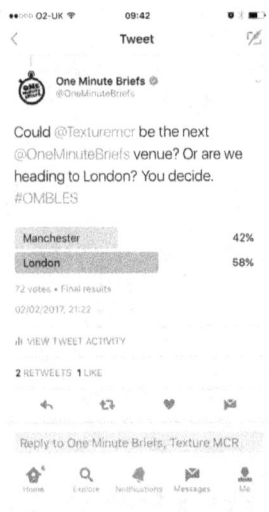

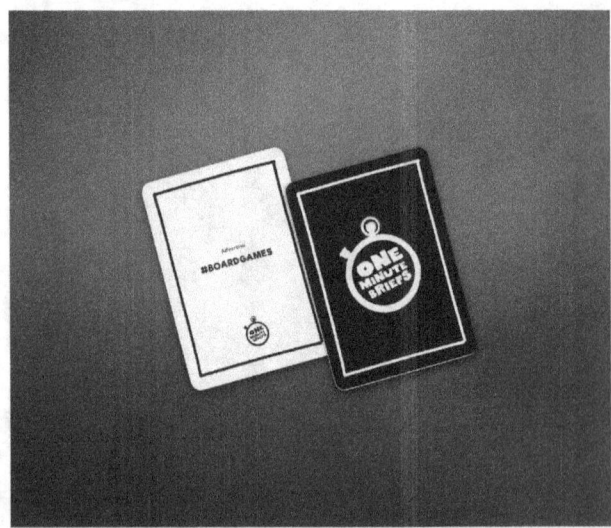

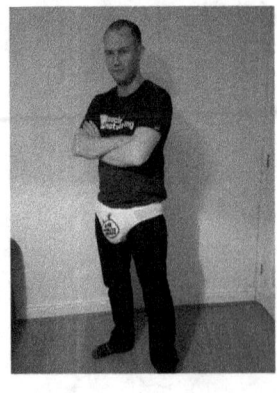

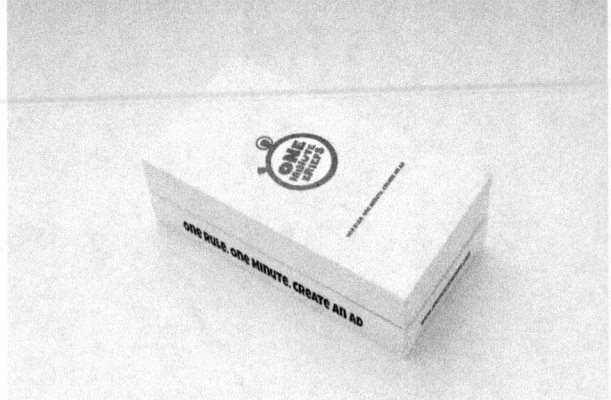

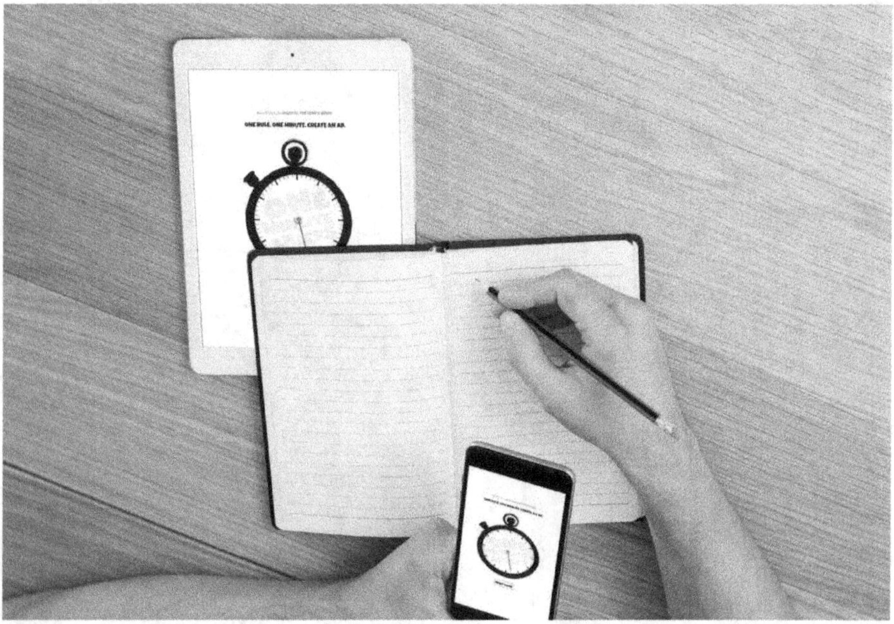
ONE RULE. ONE MINUTE. CREATE AN AD.

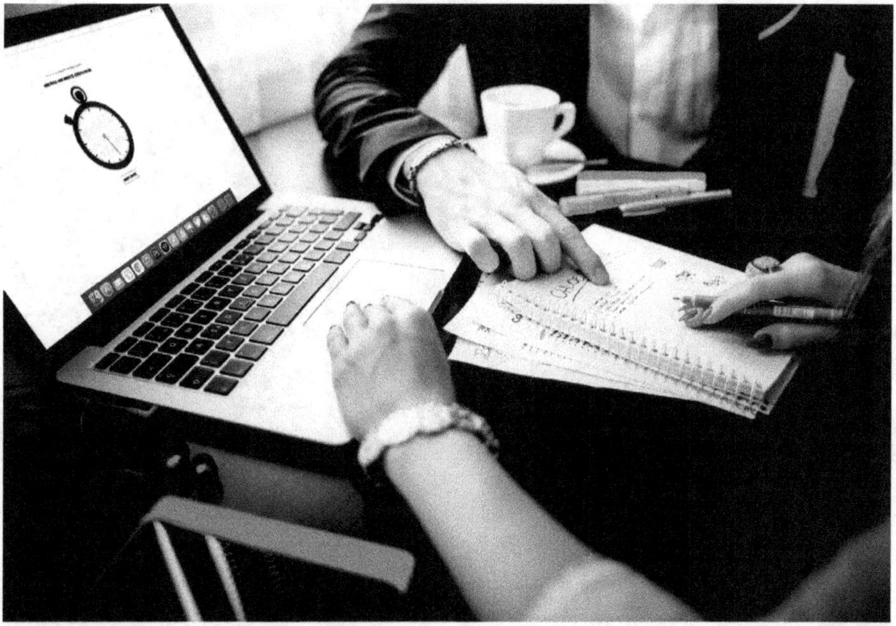

GOT A MINUTE?

That's all you'll need to enter our briefs every weekday and the following pages are there to help you get started.

Head to @OneMinuteBriefs on Twitter.
Find out what the brief is.
Scribble down your idea.
Take a pic of it.
Tweet it.
Easy isn't it?

Look forward to seeing them!

Your Twitter Name/E-mail: _____

Tweet your ad to @OneMinuteBriefs

Your Twitter Name/E-mail: _____

Tweet your ad to @OneMinuteBriefs

Your Twitter Name/E-mail: _____

Tweet your ad to @OneMinuteBriefs

Your Twitter Name/E-mail: _____

Tweet your ad to @OneMinuteBriefs

Your Twitter Name/E-mail: _____

Tweet your ad to @OneMinuteBriefs

THANKS
FOR
READING.

REMEMBER YOU'RE AN OMBLE.

@OneMinuteBriefs
oneminutebriefs.co.uk
facebook.com/oneminutebriefs
interest@bankofcreativity.co.uk

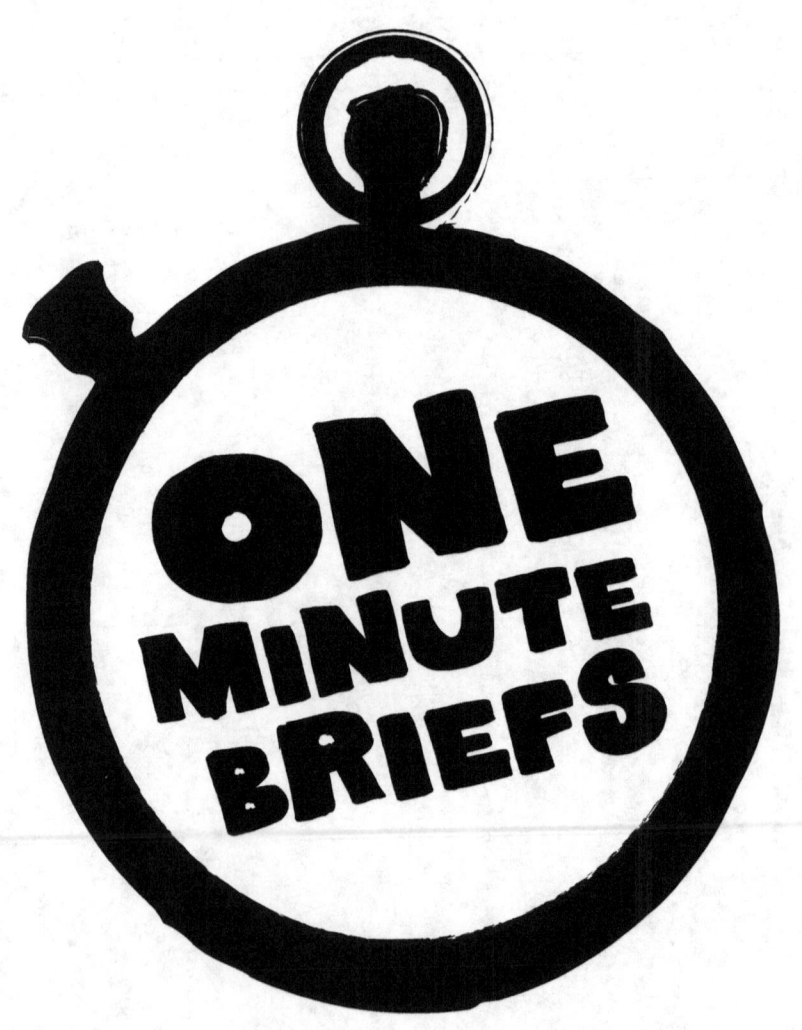

)